THE INTELLECTUAL ROOTS OF CONTEMPORARY BLACK THOUGHT

The Intellectual Roots of Contemporary Black Thought examines the ways in which the intellectual production of notable historical figures of African Diasporan Thought has shaped, and continues to shape, social and political discourses in relation to peoples of African descent.

With an internationalist approach, this volume places the philosophies of intellectuals and activists from different regions in cross-generational dialogues. The work studies seminal publications from the 1700s to the late 1800s, including monographs, manifestos, speeches, and letters, analyzing the subsequent influence of such publications on the works of later thinkers and scholars of the 1900s. Hinged in qualitative and critical analysis, it investigates the extent to which the intellectual works of the nineteenth and twentieth centuries have influenced education and institutions over time, scrutinizing the multifaceted contemporary outcomes of historical practices through the theories of historical knowledge. The excerpts and translations in the text engage readers in informed and meaningful interactions, with the philosophies of liberation, reparation, and rehabilitation.

This book contributes to the fields of intellectual historiography, human rights, political philosophy, social thought, and critical race theory and will be of interest to students and scholars of history, politics, and philosophy.

Kersuze Simeon-Jones is Associate Professor at the School of Interdisciplinary Global Studies, University of South Florida, USA.

THE INTELLECTUAL ROOTS OF CONTEMPORARY BLACK THOUGHT

Nascent Political Philosophies

Kersuze Simeon-Jones

Routledge
Taylor & Francis Group
NEW YORK AND LONDON

First published 2021
by Routledge
52 Vanderbilt Avenue, New York, NY 10017

and by Routledge
2 Park Square, Milton Park, Abingdon, Oxon, OX14 4RN

Routledge is an imprint of the Taylor & Francis Group, an informa business

Library of Congress Cataloging-in-Publication Data
Names: Simeon-Jones, Kersuze, 1974- author.
Title: The intellectual roots of contemporary black thought : nascent political philosophies / Kersuze Simeon-Jones.
Description: New York, NY : Routledge, 2021. | Includes bibliographical references and index.
Identifiers: LCCN 2020017044 (print) | LCCN 2020017045 (ebook) | ISBN 9780367485573 (hbk) | ISBN 9780367473013 (pbk) | ISBN 9781003041634 (ebk)
Subjects: LCSH: Blacks—Intellectual life. | Pan-Africanism—Philosophy. | African diaspora in literature.
Classification: LCC CB235 .S55 2021 (print) | LCC CB235 (ebook) | DDC 305.896/073—dc23
LC record available at https://lccn.loc.gov/2020017044
LC ebook record available at https://lccn.loc.gov/2020017045

ISBN: 978-0-367-48557-3 (hbk)
ISBN: 978-0-367-47301-3 (pbk)
ISBN: 978-1-003-04163-4 (ebk)

Typeset in Bembo
by Apex CoVantage, LLC

For My Daughter, With Eternal Love

CONTENTS

ACKNOWLEDGMENTS

All praise to the Creator, the Supreme Being. All reverence to the ancestors for their foundational work and sacrifices. Gratitude for my daughter, whose presence on this earth has helped me decipher life more insightfully.

INTRODUCTION

Intellectual Production and the Condition, Elevation, and Destiny of African Descendants of the World

The Intellectual Roots of Contemporary Black Thought: Nascent Political Philosophies examines not only the ways in which the intellectual production of notable historical figures of African Diasporan Thought has shaped—and continues to shape—social and political discourses in relation to peoples of African descent but also the extent to which intellectual production has influenced the process and progress of social transformation. Though specific figures and writings are examined, the analytical method of the work is conceptual and theoretical, and the structural approach is thematic; thus, it moves across regions and languages of the African Diaspora. With its international and diasporic framework, the present work will expand the fields of intellectual historiography, human rights, and social theory, particularly within the disciplines of Africana studies, African Diaspora studies or Black Diaspora studies (depending on the disciplinary nomenclature of a given college or university), world history, philosophy, and political science. The work contributes to African descendants' concepts of history, critical race theory, social thought, and their overarching epistemological framework; in so doing, it probes the effects of representation and misrepresentation as well as the social processes and politics of cultural inventions, that is, the link between power and cultural designations. The contents developed in the various intellectual productions of critical Black thinkers are vital for community psychological rehabilitation and structural/systemic adjustments. To that end, the present work is written with the objective of accessibility not only to scholars, graduate students, and advanced undergraduate students but also to informed lay readers. Methodologically, the text studies seminal publications from the late 1700s to the late 1800s, in the genres of monographs, manifestos, speeches, and letters; it analyzes the subsequent influence of these publications on the works of later thinkers and scholars of the 1900s; lastly, hinged in qualitative and critical analysis, it investigates the extent to which the intellectual works of the nineteenth and twentieth centuries have influenced contemporary institutions, particularly educational structures from K–12 to the university level. The mode of analysis is interdisciplinary—namely, history, political philosophy, and existential philosophy. Within the interdisciplinary analytical framework, the book scrutinizes the multifaceted contemporary outcomes of historical practices, through the theories of historical knowledge, as well as the philosophies and theories of liberation and advancement. In an *avant la lettre* Black Internationalist and African Diaspora approach, in 1829 David Walker addressed an *Appeal to the Coloured Citizens of the World*, in which he entreated them to read, "or get some one to read it to them," the religious, political, and social history of African descendants, from Ancient Africa to the Americas. The objective was for African descendants to thoroughly understand the reasons behind the enslavement of Africans, to grasp the history of Africa from antiquity to their current era, and to examine the lasting interconnection between politics, military and economic power, and social and cultural manipulations. Walker emphasized the words "or get some one to read it to them," as he was aware of the inability of African descendants to read the language of their respective enslavers; learning to read was, as a matter of fact, violently prohibited. Moreover, Walker was aware of the different languages that further divided and rendered it quasi-impossible for revolutionary thoughts to reach African descendants as a collective, in their tragic historical circumstances and in their rehabilitation processes; thus, he recognized that a process of transmission, translation, or interpretation would be necessary. In spite of the barriers, Walker insisted that

> all coloured men, women and children [who are not too deceitful, abject, and servile to resist the cruelties and murders inflicted upon us by the white slave holders, our enemies by nature] *of every nation, language and tongue under heaven, will try to procure a copy of this Appeal and read it, or get some one to read it to them*, for it is designed more particularly for them.[1]

Unveiling the lessons of history, he earnestly beseeched to remember that it will be, to a considerable extent, their work and level of enduring commitment that will lead them out of the "low, mean and abject condition" within which their enslavers have interred them.[2]

The growing research in the history of the Black Diaspora or history of the African Diaspora focuses on further unveiling the complex history of African descendants in order to help transform and remedy the various contemporary communities within the global world. The importance of this present work is precisely its international and diasporic scope, encompassing not only the academic subfield of intellectual history but also the subfield of human rights studies. For example, it probes the philosophies of the African revolutionaries of the late 1700s and early 1800s Saint-Domingue (present-day Haiti), from the direct writings of King Christophe and Baron De Vastey and the speeches of Jean-Jacques Dessalines, in relation to the revolutionary philosophies of such figures as David Walker and the revolutionary sacrifices of such harbingers of liberation as Nat Turner. Dessalines, Christophe, Vastey, Turner, and Walker are pioneer Pan-Africanists, Black Internationalists, and true humanist leaders, in their interrelated battles and philosophies for the complete liberation of African descendants—physical, psychological, and economic. The scrutiny of the observations and philosophies of such pioneers of human rights are essential for the thorough study and understanding of contemporary societies. One of the key merits of this work is that through translation it gives scholars, students, and the general public first-hand and substantial access to foundational texts. To that extent, it creates the opportunity for scholars, students, and lay readers to critically decipher and examine sociopolitical discourses and practices through the writings of influential figures, from different regions and eras of the Diaspora. With the inclusion of both original and unaltered excerpts and their translations, the book facilitates vital entry to seminal works from the eighteenth and nineteenth centuries that are not readily accessible. The author employs historical and cultural knowledge in order to transmit the most accurate translation of the pioneer texts included. Moreover, with direct interactions with the original and translated excerpts, readers have the resources necessary to further explore interpretations and expand analyses beyond the writer's own scrutiny. In so doing, readers will be able to contextualize fundamental philosophies and theories within their own contemporary and regional frameworks.

The Intellectual Roots of Contemporary Black Thought complements publications on the Black Diaspora that focus on cultural aspects such as religion, music, and literary works. It is a scholarly addition to the diasporic publications that focus on the social and political writings of the twentieth and twenty-first centuries, as it further elucidates their intellectual contents and trajectories. Among such works is my own book *Literary and Sociopolitical Writings of the Black Diaspora in the Nineteenth and Twentieth Centuries*. Moreover, *The Intellectual Roots of Contemporary Black Thought* is a research contribution to the contemporary publications on Black radical thought; it meticulously studies the specific political theories and philosophical principles of liberation and rehabilitation that undergird the revolutionary thought and practices manifested from the late eighteenth century onward. Grounded in Frantz Fanon's concept of *déviation existentielle* (existential diversion or deviation), Chapter 1, titled "Philosophies of Freedom, Existence, and Humanity," examines the philosophies of existence, self-knowledge, fortitude, and economic liberation, which are further studied in subsequent chapters. The chapter highlights the effects of an ill-defined notion of "inferiority" in connection to the impoverishing practices that were structured against Africans and African descendants. Stated differently, enslavement, colonialism, and subsequent methods of economic oppression enclosed Africans and their descendants in inferior economic and social positions. Chapter 2, "The Colonial System Unveiled:

From Baron De Vastey to Aimé Césaire," places Baron De Vastey's *Le Système Colonial Dévoilé*, 1814 (The Colonial System Unveiled), and *Réflexions Sur Une Lettre de Mazères, Ex-Colon Français*, 1816 (Reflections on a Letter from Mazères, Former French-Colonist), in philosophical and theoretical dialogue with Aimé Césaire's *Discours Sur Le Colonialisme*, 1950 (*Discourse on Colonialism*). With the dialogical method, the chapter efficaciously examines the degree of evolution in sociopolitical thought, from Vastey's era to Césaire's era, within the framework of African character defamation and economic ruination. Chapter 3, "The Words of J.J. Dessalines and H. Christophe: An Appeal to the Nations and Citizens of the World," studies the deeds as well as the political and existential concepts of Henry Christophe and Jean-Jacques Dessalines, the generals of the revolution of enslaved Africans in Saint-Domingue and founders of the Republic of Haiti. Their unaltered words and perspectives, in speeches and writings, are seminal theories of human rights—physical liberation, human well-being, and economic justice. Chapter 4, "Africa's Legacy of Ingenuity and Beauty in the Writings of Martin Delany, Anténor Firmin, and Cheikh Anta Diop," analyzes the fundamentals of Africa's social contributions and aesthetic legacy within a global context. The writings of Delany and Firmin helped establish the scholarship that Marcus Garvey would later use in his efforts to reclaim the value of Africa's aesthetics and to psychologically uplift his contemporaries. The Black and Beautiful Movement of the 1960s, which expanded from the United States to the African Diaspora of the world, also inherited the research and assertions of Martin Delany, Anténor Firmin, and Cheikh Anta Diop. All the preceding efforts from the nineteenth century and early twentieth century encouraged and paved the way for Cheikh Anta Diop's sociohistorical studies and scientific methods of the second half of the twentieth century. Diop further investigated ancient and modern Africa's achievements and philosophies—accomplished and expounded before the transatlantic slavery system—in order to "define the image of a modern Africa reconciled with its past and preparing for its future."[3] Chapter 5, "The Philosophies of Psychological and Structural Liberation: From M.M. Garvey and C.G. Woodson to M.L. King," draws attention to the philosophies of psychological and economic liberation, in the writings of Carter Godwin Woodson and Marcus Mosiah Garvey Jr., in correlation to the later principles of Martin Luther King, Jr. To that extent, Chapter 4 conceptually connects to Chapter 1 in the decipherment of the myriad impacts of social systems on both social and individual psychology. Chapter 6, "The Existential Rerouting: The Intellectual Formation of the Youth," is the twenty-first-century dialogue with the principles, prescriptions, and solutions advanced in the publications of the last three centuries (eighteenth, nineteenth, and twentieth) that not only remain unaddressed and unresolved but are further complicated with time and the multifaceted global changes. Additionally, the chapter examines the importance of cultural reevaluation in the preparation processes of the youth. Building on the analysis on culture and cultural performances, the epilogue, titled "Epilogue in Lieu of Conclusion: Toward the Twenty-First-Century Renaissance of the Black World," ponders one of the most fundamental dimensions of race regeneration and advancement. Through the observations and analyses of such scholars as Hubert H. Harrison, Harold W. Cruse, Amilcar Cabral, John Henrik Clarke, William M. Banks, Théophile Obenga, Molefi Kete Asante, Joy DeGruy, Bell Hooks, Manning Marable, and Lewis Gordon (among others), the chapters collectively ponder the multifarious and complex obstacles to *true* sociopolitical and psychological liberation, transformative education, and economic progress for African descendants.

With the objective to contribute to the historiography of intellectual thought and human rights, advanced by African descendant writers, the author's goal is to unveil the epistemological foundation of contemporary Black Thought, for the benefit of current and succeeding generations. *The Intellectual Roots* will help disseminate the direct reflections and examinations of seminal writers, thus far limited, disregarded, distorted, and/or concealed. From that approach, the work lays bare not only the contents of the philosophies of liberation, self-assertion, and fortitude but also the theories and prescriptions for rehabilitation, for the individual, the community, and the race. Within the context of rehabilitation, the work examines the principles of psychological recalibration, after centuries of brutal and demoralizing quotidian experiences. The irrefutable relevance of educational reform and the social, political, and economic enfranchisement of African descendants are salient aspects of consideration. Thus, the seminal and formative publications of the eighteenth, nineteenth, and twentieth centuries remain pertinent in the twenty-first century; for, the intellectual acuity, the psychological preparedness, and the consequential fortitude of the descendants of Africa will aid in their long-standing struggle for viable economic readjustment and social advancement.

Triumphs and Impediments to Elevation

Lamentably, the dire plight of the youth either within prejudiced education systems or without access to a functional education system remains one of the major thwarting factors hampering African descendants across the globe. It is an undeniable fact that appropriate education is connected not only to economic advancement but also to psychological and emotional well-being. It is against such quotidian impediments that Garvey, Woodson, and, later, Malcolm X cautioned. The physical violence against African descendants is well known and documented, whether or not there is a systemic good will for change. Visceral angst looms over African descendant communities because of the persistent physical violence destroying children: blatant famine, excessive imprisonment, and murder. Less actively conscious of, perhaps desensitized or resigned to, is the perennial slow and soft destruction of the mind and future of the African descendant youth—a destruction that has been taking place since the slavery era and continues, covertly and/or overtly, within and without the classrooms. In the introduction to the edited volume *Malcolm X: The Man and His Times*, John Henrik Clarke references Malcolm X's successful self-education process as "an indictment of the American educational system and a tribute to [Malcolm's] own perseverance."[4] Dr. Clarke underlined the educational aspect of Malcolm X's success as an essential element of Malcolm X's life and legacy. His self-education and his ability to regenerate group esteem among African Americans and other African descendants point to the nocuous effects of the global disregard and educational sabotage restricting the African descendants' intellect. Malcolm X's accomplishment of self-education, while incarcerated, "calls attention to the tremendous reservoirs of talent, and even genius, locked up among the masses in the black ghettos. It also indicates what can be accomplished when the talent of this oppressed group is respected and given hope and a purpose."[5]

To sabotage a student's instruction and designedly compromise or obstruct his or her success is the worst kind of slow depredation; "it kills one's aspiration"[6] and leads him or her to a life of economic, psychological, and emotional struggles. As Woodson discerningly underlines in *The Mis-Education of the Negro*, "to handicap a student by teaching him that his black face is a curse and that his struggle to change his condition is hopeless is the worst sort of lynching. It kills one's aspirations and dooms him to vagabondage and crime."[7] While in contemporary times most students are not directly taught "[his or her] black face is a curse," the blatant bias they encounter in the classrooms conveys a demoralizing message of helplessness and frustration. It is a mode of incarceration that imprisons the individual and, by extension, the community into a life of poverty, within which succeeding generations are hemmed. "It is strange, then, that the friends of truth and the promoters of freedom have not risen up against the present propaganda in the schools and crushed it. This crusade is more important than the antilynching movement."[8]

Without reformed education systems that equitably allocate resources and prioritize unbiased schooling for African descendant youth, the relentless depredation of confidence, the dismantlement of self-esteem, and the extinguishment of inspiration will persist; for, the youth will internalize the fatalistic mindset, so to speak, of their world as socially and politically predetermined to their detriment. The perpetuation of poverty, due to unemployment, underemployment, imprisonment, or resignation from discouragement, will all persist as conventional conditions. The muffled political voices of the adults prolong the victimization of the African descendant youth within education systems that continue to operate with prejudiced texts and where too many teachers, who are biased and/or incompetent, are daily failing and derailing millions of the youth. This problem of the race's full freedom and well-being controlled by discriminatory foreign entities is at the core of the principles of existence examined in the works of foundational thinkers such as De Vastey and Malcolm X. In his chapter "African-American Existential Philosophy," Lewis Gordon provides an accurate framework of existential philosophy, or philosophy of existence, which connects the conceptual preoccupations of the eighteenth century to the realities of the twenty-first century. "Existential philosophy," Gordon remarks, "addresses problems of freedom, anguish, dread, responsibility, embodied agency, sociality, and liberation. It addresses these problems through a focus on the human condition. . . . At the heart of existential thought are two questions: 'What we are?' and 'What shall we do?'"[9]

In the preface of the 2005 edition of *The Mis-Education of the Negro*, V.P. Franklin articulated an observation that deserves in-depth consideration. He wrote: "with the advances in communications technology and the levels of schooling, the likelihood of African Americans being 'mis-educated' has increased."[10] The inquiry that will be further examined in Chapter 6 of this present study is: the factors contributing to the perpetuation of miseducation or limited-education present even with advances in technology? Within the context of the United States, Franklin underscores "[t]he 'mis-education of the have nots' [as] doubly dangerous for African Americans because many have come to believe the negative stereotypes perpetrated by the media, and this prevents them from participating in and supporting organizations and movements for collective advancement."[11] With a K–12 system that is indifferent to or that disregards the extensive intellectual history embedded in the philosophies of liberation and advancement for African descendants—beyond a few words from Dr. King's "I Have A Dream" speech—individuals in general, and African descendants in particular, are confined within intellectual and social disequilibrium. It must be acknowledged, however, that the teachers and schools that have contributed to the full development of all youth, including African descendants, deserve due recognition. For, without intellectual, psychological, and emotional grounding, continuing social conflicts are inevitable. It is apropos to bring to mind a brief statement from W.E.B. Du Bois, quoted in more detail in *Literary and Sociopolitical Writings of the Black Diaspora*.[12] Du Bois remarked:

> Manifestly the civilized people of the world have got to be characterized by certain things, they must know this world, its history and the laws of its development. They must also be able to reason carefully and accurately. Attention must be paid to human feelings and emotions which determine and guide this knowledge, and reason.[13]

As contribution to the solution, in *The Mis-Education*, Dr. Woodson unprecedentedly unveiled the schemes and processes behind the centuries of systemic miseducation. Dr. Woodson's goal was to encourage posterity to learn and think, "so the future generations of educated African Americans would not become their own worst enemy."[14] In 1920 Marcus Garvey advocated for the study of African descendants' historical trajectories in all levels of education: "We demand that instructions given to Negro children in schools include the subject of 'Negro History,' to their own benefit."[15] Furthermore, he insisted: "we protest against the system of education in any country where Negroes are denied the same privileges and advantages as other races. . . . We demand the right of unlimited and unprejudiced education for ourselves and our posterity forever."[16] A body of incisive works published by African descendant thinkers, in the form of letters, speeches, and monographs, delineates each writer's contemporary conditions as well as their prescriptions for *attainable* and sustainable achievements. The philosophical and diplomatic writings of Toussaint Louverture, Jean-Jacques Dessalines, and Henry Christophe, as well as the pivotal and instructive publications of Baron De Vastey, reasserted the humanity of Africa and its descendants: a humanity that was violently defiled through the transatlantic slave trade, the slavery system, and beyond. The writings of their successors, from the early nineteenth century onward, not only unveiled the historical ills endured, and their continuing pernicious effects, but also pondered and proposed solutions for the purpose of a constructive future. For, in addition to purposively malevolent systemic sabotage—particularly within the education system—and the spurious misconceptions of blackness from outside of the race, also detrimental to Black advancement *are* the internalized misconceptions and low expectations of self from within the race. Anténor Firmin cautioned against such pitfall in his 1885 publication *De L'Égalité des Races Humaines: Anthropologie Positive* (*On the Equality of the Human Races: Positivist Anthropology*), Carter G. Woodson examined the impacts of self-disparagement in his 1933 work *The Mis-Education of the Negro*, Frantz Fanon psychoanalyzed the roots of the complexes of inferiority and superiority in his 1952 theoretical work *Peau Noire Masques Blancs* (*Black Skin White Masks*), and Cheikh Anta Diop substantiated the importance of accurate historical reference for individual and group esteem, in his seminal texts *Antériorité des Civilisations Nègres: Mythe ou Vérité Historique?*, published in 1954, (*Anteriority of Negro Civilizations: Myth or Historical Truth?*) and *Nations Nègres et Culture*, published in 1967, (*Negro Nations and Culture*).

In *The Philosophy and Opinions*, Marcus Garvey admonished against the mindset of self-underestimation and the deleterious behaviors it fosters and feeds. If one does not have confidence in self, he cautioned, he or she is "twice defeated in the race of life."[17] The confidence to which Garvey referred is one that goes beyond the individual to include confidence in the communities predominantly inhabited by African descendants. Confidence in self and the community consequentially influences one's level of responsible work. For, "the ends you serve that are selfish," he emphasized, "will take you no further than yourself; but the ends you serve that are for all, in common, will take you even into eternity."[18] The earthly *eternity* (so to speak) is the continuing and generational progressive effects of one's words and one's deeds. In 1919, in his compilation of articles published as *When Africa Awakes*, Hubert H. Harrison explains that the great duty of those who have knowledge is "to simplify and make clear, to light the lamps of knowledge that the eyes of the race may see; that the feet of their people may not stumble. This is the task of the Talented Tenth. To the masses of our people we say:

Read! Get the reading habit."[19] In the preface of *De L'Égalité des Races Humaines: Anthropologie Positive*, Anténor Firmin unassumingly but genuinely articulates the purpose of his work, the works of contemporaneous African descendants, as well as the work of the generations that will succeed him. He expresses:

> À la vérité que j'essaye de défendre, je n'apporte que mon dévouement et ma bonne volonté. Mais à quel point ne serais-je particulièrement fier, si tous les hommes noirs et ceux qui en descendent *se pénétraient*, par la lecture de cet ouvrage, qu'ils ont pour devoir de travailler, *de s'améliorer sans cesse afin de laver leur race de l'injuste imputation qui pèse sur elle depuis si longtemps*![20]
>
> (To the truth I endeavor to defend, I only bring my devotion and my good will. The level of my satisfaction and pride would be immeasurable if all Blacks and their descendants *would self-examine* through the reading of this work that they have the responsibility to decipher and understand, *to incessantly better oneself in order to wash the race from the unjust imputation that weighs on her for so long*![21])
>
> Digne et fière, intelligente et laborieuse, qu'elle grandisse donc, prospère et monte sans cesse, de progrès en progrès, cette race noire si pleine de sève et de généreuse vitalité! *Pour l'aider dans son ascension, il n'y aura jamais trop d'ouvriers, ni trop de dévouement.* Aussi est-ce religieusement que je lui apporte mon offrande humble et respectueuse. D'autres feront mieux que moi, un jour, mais nul ne sera plus désireux de son relèvement et de sa gloire.[22]
>
> (Dignified and proud, intelligent and hard-working, may it rise, prosper and incessantly climb from progress to progress, this Black race so full of life force and abundant vitality! *To help [the race] in its ascension, there will never be too many workers, or too much devotion.* Thus, it is religiously that I bring my humble and respectful offering. One day, others will do better work than I have done, but no one will be more desirous of its salvation and its glory.[23])

Moreover, Firmin expressly dedicated his intellectual production as a resource to inspire African descendants from passive acceptance or resignation, and to accelerate their work toward revitalization.

> Puisse ce livre être médité et concourir à accélérer le mouvement de régénération que ma race accomplit sur le soleil bleu et clair des Antilles! Puisse-t-il inspirer à tous les enfants de la race noire, répandus sur l'orbe immense de la terre, l'amour du progrès, de la justice et de la liberté! Car, en le dédiant à Haïti, c'est encore à eux tous que je l'adresse, les déshérités du présent et les géants de l'avenir.
>
> La soif de la vérité et le besoin de la lumière m'ont seuls soutenu dans le cours de mon travail . . . Il m'est agréable de penser qu'en réfléchissant

sur tous les points que soulève ma controverse, [les membres de la Société d'Anthropologie de Paris] inclineront à réformer ces opinions, en ce qui concerne les aptitudes de ma race.[24]

(May this book be pondered over and take part in accelerating the movement of regeneration that my race accomplishes under the sunny, clear and blue sky of the Caribbean! May it inspire all the children of the Black race, dispersed on this immense globe, the love of progress, of justice and liberty! For, in dedicating it to Haiti, it is also to all of them that I address it, the disinherited of the present and the giants of the future.

The thirst for the truth and the need for knowledge and understanding were the only factors that sustained me during the course of my work. . . . It is pleasant to think that in pondering all the points I advance in my argumentation [the members of the Society of Anthropology of Paris] will be inclined to reform [their] opinions, regarding the aptitudes of my race.[25])

Throughout the centuries, many critical observers and thinkers have brought their intellectual offerings to educate, fill the void of historical consciousness, and embolden African descendants to assert their natural, human, civil, and political rights. William Wells Brown's *The Black Man: His Antecedents, His Genius, and His Achievements* stands as another significant work that presents the record of the "genius, capacity, and intellectual development"[26] of African descendants who triumphed in spite of the unimaginable hindrances of enslavement and subsequent socioeconomic oppression. Addressed "To the Advocates and Friends of Negro Freedom and Equality, Wherever Found," Brown wrote: "If this work shall aid in vindicating the Negro's character, and show that he is endowed with those intellectual and amiable qualities which adorn and dignify human nature, it will meet the most sanguine hopes of the writer."[27]

All factors considered, including the relentless work the forefathers and foremothers accomplished against all odds, it is indisputable that the race—as a collective—has faced and continues to face tremendous and cumulative pressures. In the documentary "Marcus Garvey: A Giant of Black Politics," Ruth Prescott underlines the lasting detriments of economic destitution and psychological torment for African descendants of the twentieth and twenty-first centuries. Prescott submits that economic tyranny led to the adverse choices and behaviors of some members of the African Diaspora.

There is a lot of economic pressures . . . and the people of the capitalistic world find it to their benefit to make things so sticky for the black man and black woman that at times the black people really lose faith in themselves. The greatest reason for the behavior of some of the black people is the pressures which are brought to bear on them, literally to say well, if you don't come along with me then I am going to have you backed in the corner . . . all the traps are still being set to keep the black man underfoot.[28]

While, in the 2008 documentary, Prescott befittingly highlights the global realities African descendants currently endure, Garvey would have encouraged a greater level of commitment and character on the part of those with influential voices and agency to actively participate in the rehabilitation of the collective. It is precisely within the context of nuanced generational and regional viewpoints that *The Intellectual Roots of Contemporary Black Thought* studies the work of contemporary thinkers in dialogue with their intellectual and activist predecessors. The research and publications of foundational philosophies of liberation and theories of rehabilitation are imperative not only so "we may not wrongly be deprived of the spiritual nourishment of our cultural past, but also that the full story of human collaboration and interdependence maybe told and realized."[29] Pedagogically, the one statement that summarizes my own intellectual practice and guides my framework as an academic writer is Césaire's recommendation that we must "speak clearly and concisely to convey the message"[30] of restoration and to record the intellectual and political trajectories of the Black world. "[Il] faut parler clair, parler net, pour faire passer le message."[31] Moreover, for those who do not have access to the original language, I endeavored to provide the closest interaction possible with the chosen texts, by giving consideration to the era, the original author's historical and cultural contexts. For, ultimately—and to cite the outspoken wisdom of our honored and remarkable Malcolm X—"[education] is an important element in the struggle for human rights. It is the means to help our children and our people rediscover their identity and thereby increase their self-respect. Education is our passport to the future, for tomorrow belongs only to the people who prepare for it today."[32]

Notes

1. David Walker, *Appeal to the Coloured Citizens of the World, But in Particular, and Very Expressly, to Those of the United States of America* (Boston: Revised and Published by David Walker, 1830), 2. Emphasis added.
2. Ibid., 2.
3. Cheikh Anta Diop, *The African Origin of Civilization: Myth or Reality* (Chicago: Lawrence Hill & Co., 1974), xvi.
4. John Henrik Clarke, *Malcolm X: The Man and His Times*, assisted by Peter Bailey, Earl Grant, and Betty Shabazz (New York: The Macmillan Company, 1969), xv.
5. Ibid., xvi.
6. Carter G. Woodson, *The Mis-Education of the Negro* (Washington, DC: The ASALH Press, 2005), 4.
7. Ibid., 4.
8. Ibid., 4.
9. Lewis R. Gordon, "African-American Existential Philosophy," *A Companion to African-American Philosophy*, edited by Tommy L. Lott and John P. Pittman (Oxford: Blackwell Publishing Ltd., 2003), 34.
10. Ibid., viii.
11. Ibid., viii.
12. Kersuze Simeon-Jones, *Literary and Sociopolitical Writings of the Black Diaspora, in the Nineteenth and Twentieth Centuries* (Boulder: Lexington Books, 2010).

13. W.E.B. Du Bois, *Against Racism: Unpublished Essays, Papers, Addresses, 1887–1961* (Amherst: The University of Massachusetts Press, 1985), 252.
14. Woodson, *The Mis-Education*, viii.
15. Marcus Garvey, *The Philosophy and Opinions of Marcus Garvey* (Dover: The Majority Press, 1986), 142.
16. Ibid., 139.
17. Ibid., 11.
18. Ibid., 2.
19. Hubert H. Harrison, *When Africa Awakes: The "Inside Story" of the Stirrings and Strivings of the New Negro in the Western World* (New York: The Porro Press, 1920), 128.
20. Anténor Firmin, *De L'Égalité des Races Humaines: Anthropologie Positive* (Paris: Librairie Cotillon, 1885), xvi. Emphasis added.
21. Author's translation. Emphasis added.
22. Firmin, *De L'Égalité*, xviii–xix.
23. Author's translation.
24. Firmin, *De L'Égalité*, Dedication, x–xi.
25. Author's translation.
26. William Wells Brown, *The Black Man: His Antecedents, His Genius, and His Achievements* (Boston: James Redpath Publisher, 1863), 6.
27. Ibid., 6.
28. Howard Johnson, *Marcus Garvey: A Giant of Black Politics* (New York, N.Y.: Films Media Group, 2008, 2013), @44:44 minutes, DVD.
29. Arthur A. Schomburg, "The Negro Digs Up His Past," *The New Negro* (New York: Touchstone Book, 1997), 237.
30. Author's translation.
31. Aimé Césaire, *Aimé Césaire: A Voice for History* (San Francisco: Newsreel, 1994).
32. Malcolm X, *By Any Means Necessary: Speeches, Interviews, and a Letter by Malcolm X*, edited by George Breitman (New York: Pathfinder Press, 1970). Speech delivered at the Audubon Ballroom on June 28, 1954, to publicly announce the founding of the Organization of Afro-American Unity.

1

PHILOSOPHIES OF FREEDOM, EXISTENCE, AND HUMANITY

In his essay titled "Man Know Thyself," expounded in *The Philosophy and Opinions of Marcus Garvey*, Garvey advances for "knowledge of self," for the consequential awakening in confidence, character, purpose, and deeds, on the part of African descendants.[1] It is those components in conjunction with systemic political reforms, substantive economic readjustments, and social restructuring that will (in unison) rehabilitate contemporary Africans and their descendants from their perennial historical circumstances. Confidence and knowledge of self are vital conditionings that must be developed as constitutive elements of the general human formation; such characteristics must be further deepened with a comprehensive education in one's particular collective history (histories). Knowledge of self and confidence relate reciprocally; thus, each component continually reinforces the other and synchronically build the individual's character, in a progressive process. Significantly, the development of confidence in self and confidence in one's community cultivates the necessary level of courage and integrity vital to further seeking comprehensive and profound knowledge. Knowledge, in turn, not only helps to continually elevate one's confidence, thus bolstering one's determination to achieve beyond misconceptions and stereotypical expectations, it also serves as the impetus that encourages and leads the individual to contribute to the rehabilitation of the community. In his essay "Man Know Thyself," Garvey conveyed what he understood as one of the primary truths of humanity; that is, "[f]or man to know himself is for him to feel that for him there is *no human* master."[2] Written between 1920 and 1925, Garvey's message not only honed into the indispensable substantive politico-economic restructuring, for the purpose of economic opportunities, self-sufficiency, and freedom, it concurrently advocated the process of unfettering the psychology and spirit of African descendants. That message awakened African descendants to the fact that after physical liberation great work remained to be accomplished in order to reach psychological liberation. The awakening to the impacts of mental slavery was Garvey's foremost caution to the Africans and their descendants; later, Bob Marley would reiterate the same message of mental freedom and fortitude in his "Redemption Song."[3] In Garvey's era of the early twentieth century to Marley's era of the late twentieth century, as it remains true in the twenty-first century thus far, the descendants of Africa have had to face two fundamental impeding factors, one circularly affecting the other; they are economic and psychological: economic to psychological ↔ psychological to economic.

It is evident that the dis-alienation or de-marginalization of Africans and their descendants around the globe can only be meaningful when the economic labyrinth—an ultimate cul-de-sac for the majority—with its resultant psychological, educational, and intellectual impacts, is addressed and redressed. One of the rudimentary factors perpetuating the adverse psychological effects and the material destitution of the majority of African descendants *is* centuries of the inadequate, inappropriate, and misleading education of the world community in their regard. With global miseducation, that is the distortion of historical truths, came centuries of normalized social denigration and socioeconomic disenfranchisement. Carter G. Woodson's 1933 publication, *The Mis-Education of the Negro*, unveiled more thoroughly than previously accomplished the factual miseducation of the world. Though the text is titled *The Mis-Education of the Negro*, its historical and analytical contents proved beyond any doubt (if there were any) the global miseducation system. Employing the United States of America as the region of focus, Woodson laid bare the sources of the world's unresolved psychological chaos as well as its mass economic imbalance and sociopolitical conflicts. In his pivotal examinations, Woodson argued that the education system not only cruelly failed Blacks but also did "not hit the mark" for Whites and others. However, while the education system did "not hit the mark" intellectually/academically and morally/ethically for Whites and others, it has not affected their economic and sociopolitical standing within the material world. In consequential contrast, the miseducation of the African descendant was and remains a mode of manacles, impeding access to basic human survival and well-being as well as obstructing access to economic, political, and social opportunities. To levels that are irreparable, the general miseducation of the world, along with the resultant ill-will toward Africans and their descendants, indeed effectuated centuries of disparaging perceptions of and pernicious interactions with African descendants throughout the globe. Thus, the falsifications and misrepresentations embedded in the education systems in Europe and the Americas have exerted dreadful impacts on the fundamental existence of Blacks not only materially but psychologically. Woodson explained:

> [The] so-called modern education, with all its defects, however, does others so much more good than it does the Negro, because it has been

> worked out in conformity to the needs of those who have enslaved and oppressed weaker peoples. For example, the philosophy and ethics resulting from our educational system have justified slavery, peonage, segregation, and lynching. The oppressor has the right to exploit, to handicap, and to kill the oppressed. Negroes daily educated in the tenets of such a religion of the strong have accepted the status of the weak as divinely ordained . . . their pouting and resolutions indulged in by a few of the race have been of little avail.[4]

On Economics: The Social Complex of Inferiority and the Illusion of Superiority

There is sufficient scholarship on the intents and outcomes of the slave trade, whereby the constructed socioeconomic hierarchies and the sociopsychological race relations have over time morphed into structural and normalized racism. In fact, in numerous countries of the Americas the practices of racism are so inherently ingrained in the educational, social, political, and economic fabric—as a normalized way of life—that the term was not used or acknowledged as part of respective national realities until the late twentieth century. To frame the significant effects of epistemic formation, within the context of history and historical trajectories as well as the lasting acceptance of historical distortions, it is crucial to examine from the outset two elemental concepts at the base of historical and social deformation: the complex of inferiority and the complex of superiority. We are examining these concepts within the framework of *groups* rather than individuals. Both concepts and subsequent praxes are manifested in the slave trade, the slavery system, and the long-standing structural impoverishment of African descendants. Primarily, it is vital to recollect two foundational facts from the established scholarship on the study of the slave trade and slavery. One, the objective of the slave trade was economic, with the purpose of unending accumulation of profit. Thus, the slave trade was the appropriation of human flesh through fiendish means, for forced human labor, for free human labor. Second, as part of the politics of economy, emergent racist discourses were concocted as pseudo-justifications for an iniquitous act—the slave trade and slavery. To levels that are preponderantly conscious, but at time simultaneously subconscious and unconscious, racist ideologies, discourses, and practices reciprocally reinforced and normalized what *was* and what *is* inherently unjustifiable and indefensible—that is, the centuries of physical and psychological terror employed as relentless efforts to dehumanize and disenfranchise Africans and their descendants. The perennial discursive strategies—with tactical phenomenological deformation—would continue to justify or simply ignore the lasting distressing economic and psychological impacts on African descendants, for centuries thereafter. The relentless and terrorizing actions of the enslavers, upheld with the combination of conscious as well as subconscious and unconscious discriminatory ideologies, have culminated into the current psycho-social chaos and neuroses to which Aimé Césaire and Frantz Fanon, respectively, refer in *Discours sur le Colonialisme* (*Discourse on Colonialism*) and *Peau Noire Masques Blancs* (*Black Skin White Masks*). Essentially, the social complex of superiority and the social complex of inferiority were born out of and sustained by two realities: one, the wicked reality of the new world's chattel slavery system, with its physical violence for extortionate profit; two, the mechanisms of psychological terror that were exerted on the Africans through various forms of tortures and torments. The tangible situation of armed European enslavers tyrannizing the chained and displaced Africans, the unmitigated physical and psychological horrors, the inhumane lasting extortions that left the enslaved Africans and their descendants economically destitute, *all* made possible the creation of entrenched systems of oppression. Consequently, all set the stage for the socially established complex of superiority and the imposed complex of inferiority. Within contemporary contexts, the ensuing complex of superiority that elevates some and the complex of inferiority that cripples others can only be addressed at the source: the mind. It is, undoubtedly, from the scrutiny of the roots of imposed and implanted complexes, through the study and the unveiling of historical trajectories, can the aftereffects be grasped and remedied. It is significant to recall that the term *complex* in psychology underlines the psychological exercise of conceiving reality based on self-conscious emotions and feelings, bolstered by social conditioning and expectations. Such emotions and conditioning lead to pathological behaviors, particularly when fundamental facts are purposefully hidden, and truths are manipulated.

Equally important to our discussion is an overall consideration of Alfred Adler's work on the human mind, human nature, and the impact or influence of society on human development. In *Understanding Human Nature*, published in 1927, Alfred Adler psychoanalyzed the connection between the complex of inferiority and the complex of superiority within the context of the individual—from childhood to adulthood—and in relation to his or her sociality.[5] Adler maintained that every child is born with a certain level of inferiority complex (or a subconscious sense of insufficiency) in the midst of a world established by adults. Within this generalization, those who were born with a greater inclination to or, based on their environment, have developed excessive feeling of inferiority, insecurity, and insufficiency are more likely—from childhood to adulthood—to aim for power over others, to assert himself or herself aggressively, and to rule over others. In other words, deep-seated complex of inferiority and insufficiency generates an aggressive complex of superiority. Adler's research on the individual provides a framework that is consistent with the psychoanalysis of groups of individuals, particularly groups of individuals within a system that is constructed to reach and maintain a common objective; the common objective creates a group identity—the identity of an entity. Within the context of European enslavers, such group objective was the appropriation of Africa's natural resources and inhabitants, to be used as tools of production in the Americas. It was the lack of resources and inadequate economic potential that propelled European enslavers to head to the Americas, and subsequently to Africa, in order to create a certain level of material and existential power. The scholarship on the weak economic state of Europe before the enslavers—initially from Portugal, Spain, France, and Britain—headed to the continents of America and Africa is established. From the obsession with procuring resources and securing wealth grew a mindset of entitlement by any means. With the unrestrained greed to seize the other's resources in order to establish lasting economic and social power, European enslavers and colonists conceived themselves as superior. The conceived and constructed superiority was inevitable; it was a psychological requisite, so to speak, to self-arrogate and justify the unjustifiable. Stated differently, material insecurity and insufficiency in the conceptualization of self led to the desire to seize the other's resources, to control and dominate the other. In order to enslave the unsuspecting Africans, take possession of their resources, and thereby control their livelihood, one must first conceive himself as superior, thus titled.

The examination of the concept of inferiority and the illusion of superiority is crucial for a thorough understanding of the lasting structural realities they have created, as well as the normalized practices that have been established. In *Discours sur le Colonialisme* Aimé Césaire cites Psichari-soldat-d'Afrique, a French soldier in Africa also known as Ernest Psichari. In a self-persuasion mental exercise, Psichari affirms:

> Je sais que je dois me croire supérieur aux pauvre Bayas de Mambéré. *Je sais que je dois avoir l'orgueil de mon sang.* Lorsqu'un homme supérieur cesse de se croire supérieur, il cesse effectivement d'être supérieur. . . *Lorsqu'une race supérieure cesse de se croire une race élue, elle cesse effectivement d'être une race élue.*[6]
>
> (I know that I have to believe that I am superior to the wretched Bayas de Mambéré. *I know that I have to have* the pride of my blood line. When a man ceases to believe that he is superior he, in fact, ceases to be superior. . . . *When a race ceases to believe to be a chosen race, it indeed ceases to be a chosen race.*[7])

One would note two simultaneous processes that lead to the complex of superiority: conviction and illusion. Part of the complex is conscious=conviction. (*I have to* believe that I am superior. . . . *I know* that I have to have the pride of my blood.) Thus, the individual must constantly remember and make repeated conscious efforts to believe that he or she is "superior." In time, with repetitive mental conditioning and social reinforcement, the other part of the complex lodges in the subconscious/unconscious=illusion. (When a [being] ceases *to believe* [himself or herself] superior, [he or she] ceases to be superior.) The use of the reflexive verb tense in the deliberate thought process is remarkable—"*de se croire.*" It unveils the *creation of oneself*: that is, the process of self-creation, of self-formation, through an acknowledged illusion. Simultaneously, it is the process of self-formation *through* the conceptual deformation and the eventual existential deformation of the other. Yet, the process could not be successful or complete without the physical and material coercion of the other to accept or, at least, endure the outcomes of the illusion. For, a social being—as society has come to grasp—is not only who he or she constructs and sees but also who others construct or perceive him or her to be. To be sure, the emphasis here is on the social being and not the authentic self. Enslaved and transported into a foreign system of terror, the Africans were violently coerced into an imposed *structured* reality where the construction of "superiority" and "inferiority" was maintained by unimaginable physical violence (with guns, chains, whips, ropes, rapes, fire, furnaces, drowning, dogs, guillotines, incarcerations, etc.). In addition, economic and political subjugation, through utter destitution, blatantly removed or muffled any significant agency for the protection and definition of self, as individuals and as a group. Without the relentless practices that reinforce the illusion of superiority and transform it into a generalized norm and a structural reality, the illusion would have subsided. It is unequivocally clear, thus, that the psycho-social normality of the complex of superiority was in fact nurtured by incessant conscious and subconscious affirmations, supported by unabated terrorizing violence. Deplorably, the processes of the intricate web of conviction and illusion continue to operate contemporarily. Some operate mainly from conviction, usually those aware of historical trajectories but are committed to maintaining unjust advantages; in order to preserve the state of affairs, they are engaged in self-serving and feigned blindness to the current pernicious impacts of the past on African descendants. Others operate mainly from illusion/delusion, generally, those who are unaware, miseducated, uneducated, or insufficiently educated. As generations grow temporally further from the realities of the slavery system and as the primary objective of enslavement and its ensuing and lasting socioeconomic structures are disregarded in the education system and general discussions, the superiority complex continues to manifest as an illusion that serves to maintain some levels of empty self-importance, solely based on skin complexion.

In *The Black Jacobins*, C.L.R. James evidences that the enslavers and the colonists of the slavery era as well as the neo-slavery era were "the type for whom race prejudice was more important than even the possession of slaves."[8] Those groups experienced first-hand the machinery of enslavement, the mechanization of the Africans, and the accruing economic profit. In his in-depth research and insightful analysis (more particularly in his chapter II titled "The Owners"), James discerns the various groups and classes of Whites with reference to their socioeconomic interests. For the enslavers in the colonies of the Americas, slavery was not only a barbarous and inhuman exploitation; it also became tantamount to reducing Africans to an existential inferiority. For those groups the feeling of superiority, based on the color of the skin, became an illusion of self-importance to guard at all costs, with or without the possession of enslaved Africans. The skin hierarchy, based on the legacy of race prejudice and hatred, remains a priority for ignoramuses of any era. Ultimately, it is the conceptualization of self-worth based on the illusory reconstruction of the self. Consequently, for such groups, concocting and maintaining race prejudice became a prime mission in their unyielding efforts to dehumanize the Africans—for profit—while disseminating follies about one race's inherent superiority over the other. "The distinction between a white and a man of colour was for them fundamental. It was their all. In defence of it they would bring down the whole of their world."[9] For, regardless of a White's low character or origin, in the New World's colonies he or she assumes a farcical level of social and self-importance. Initially, the Spaniards, the Portuguese, the French, and the British came from the world of petty criminality as well as organized crimes. It is in the Americas they sought abundant and extortionate capital as well as easy status. In the Americas "consideration was achieved at so cheap a price."[10] To be sure, "So cheap a price" refers to the mere color of one's skin. In his 1967 text *On Afro-American History*, Malcolm X educated his audience and readers on the history of British enslavers who, similar to other European enslavers, sought to mask low character with color. He emphasized:

> When America was discovered and colonized by England, England populated her American colonies not with people who were refined and cultured, but, if you read the history, she did the same thing here that she did in Australia. All the convicts were sent here to found this country. The prisons were emptied of prostitutes and thieves and murderers . . . they were such artful, skillful liars that they were able to take a criminal system and, with lies, project it to the world as a humanitarian system.[11]

In his chapter "The Seat of the Trouble" of *The Mis-Education*, Woodson scrutinizes the ways in which the indoctrination of a *manufactured perception* of African descendants' inferiority is taught and practiced at every level, particularly in the classrooms. In schools, instructors used texts that reiterate the propaganda of White superiority or supremacy. Schools "are places where [the students] must be *convinced* of their inferiority. The thought of the inferiority of the Negro is drilled into him in almost every class he enters and in almost every book he studies."[12] Thus, the sequelae of the education system and the myriad economic hindrances *sustained* the socioeconomic inferiority of some and the illusory superiority of others. Some would argue that this last sentence can be written in the present tense and maintain its accuracy of analysis (i.e., the sequelae of the education system and the myriad economic hindrances *sustain* the socioeconomic inferiority of some and the illusory superiority of others). It is crucial, then, that adults and schoolchildren are educated in comprehensive historical trajectories so they may be able to discern and decipher the two major complexes that continue to shape social, political, and economic realities. For, profound understanding and viable social transformation require constant work of: observation→ knowledge→ analysis→ observation→ praxis→ knowledge→ praxis. The study of corrective and transformative published works is vital in the reevaluation of quotidian behaviors, policies, and laws. As a case in point, the seminal writings of the fore-thinkers of contemporary Black Thought[13]—particularly Baron De Vastey's *Le Système Colonial Dévoilé* and *Réflexions sur une Lettre de Mazères, Ex-Colon Français*, and King Christophe's *Manifeste du Roi*—challenge the European publications that purposefully vilify the Africans in order to justify their practices of continuous exploitation and profit. Cognizant of the influence of disseminated written words, King Christophe reminds his readers of the detrimental impacts of European published words on the basic existence of Africans and that of their descendants. He explains: "[the enslavers/colonists] have taught us enough, *more so in their writings* than with the tortures that we have endured, that the only and solid guarantee to our political rights, to our very existence, is through the conservation of our independence."[14] (" ils nous ont assez *enseignés par leurs écrits*, plus que les tortures mêmes que nous avons endurées, que la seule et solide garantie de nos droits politiques, de notre existence même, tient à la conservation de notre indépendance.")[15] That King Christophe placed more weight on the effects of defamatory European writings than on the physical tortures that crippled and killed millions of Africans evidences the king's insight into the inveterate psychological, political, and economic damages of such writings on the African's well-being.

Given that educational and psychological enslavement facilitate economic enslavement, the inverse of Psichari's psychological exercise would be: *When a being ceases to see himself or herself as inferior, he or she ceases to be inferior. When a race ceases to see or to accept itself as a condemned race, it ceases to be a condemned race*. Conscious work of belief and reconditioning of the mind must be part of an insistent process. As Marcus Garvey posits in *The Philosophy*, "action, self-reliance, *the vision of self and the future* have been the only means by which the oppressed have seen and realized the light of their own freedom."[16] In his *De L'Égalité des Races Humaines: Anthropologie Positive*, Anténor Firmin reminds his readers of François Rabelais' timeless observation on human nature, "Autant vaut l'homme comme il s'estime," to assert that such disposition is true for the individual, a nation, or a race. In Firmin's words, "[this] high esteem that one has of self is perhaps the best resource for maintaining an awakened character: *in principle it augments one's confidence in his/her own strengths*; that is the secret to mastery."[17] ("Cette haute estime qu'on a de soi est peut-être le meilleur ressort pour tenir le caractère en éveil: *elle érige en principe la confiance en ses propres forces* qui est le secret de la domination.")[18] Here, the French word "domination" refers to exercising control over oneself (*soi-même*); it is the assertive control that one assumes over her or his own life while respecting others' humanity and rights. The esteem of one's self is, by extension, the source for meaningful accomplishments. To recognize, understand, and assume one's strengths as well as one's weaknesses (not the illusory "weaknesses" assigned by the other) is the key to the psychological mastery of one self; it is the secret to navigating one's own multifaceted condition—the human condition, the race condition, and individual condition. Such maxim is applicable through time; it can manifest in the individual, the nation, and the race. It is worth re-emphasizing, however, that while psychological tenacity is indispensable to progress, it is imperative that one bears in mind and acknowledges that the so-called black inferiority complex is firmly entrenched in established economic and social disadvantages. It is the result of *inferior access* to material resources, inferior education, lack of agency, and muted political voice. That acknowledgment is fundamental. Fanon's perspicacious examination remains relevant; that is, if there is an inferiority complex, it is first economic, followed by internalization. Such complex (for some) or resignation (for others) emerged out of economic destitution and drastic social injustices that are at times fatal: murders with impunity, famine, untreated illnesses due to dire poverty, and so on. Ultimately, the *very real* inferior economic condition is the outcome of quasi-insurmountable socioeconomic and political barriers. As Fanon notes in *Peau Noire Masques Blancs*, "There will not be authentic disalienation until, in the most material context, things are repositioned in their proper order."[19] ("Il n'y aura d'authentique désaliénation que dans la mesure où les choses, au sens le plus matérialiste, auront repris leur place.")[20] With similar understanding this present work seeks to demonstrate the correlation between the root of material inferiority and its impact on group psychology, and the connection of group and individual psychological *state* to normative social practices and established institutions. Without an international restructuring of economic order, the majority of African descendants will remain marginalized. In the final analysis, the psycho-existential complex is derived from the socio-existential reality. In *The Philosophy*, Garvey examines that "[so] long as Negroes occupy an inferior position among the races and nations of the world, just so long will others be prejudiced against them, because it will be *profitable* for them to keep up their system of superiority."[21] Because of the circular complexity of the African descendants' predicament, it is clear that the essential solution *is* reparation, in tandem with fair access to resources, not only to material resources but also to appropriate education and historical truths through the social, political, and economic writings of foundational thinkers, who prescribed rudimentary solutions as early as the eighteenth century. The precepts of unfettered existence and economic autonomy became key elements in the publications of nineteenth-century and twentieth-century figures. Such texts will continue to serve, in the twenty-first century, as guide to self-knowledge as well as guide to navigate respective communities, nations, and the global world more efficaciously. The lessons of strengths, failures, persistence, resilience, resistance, service to the family and the community, service to the nation and the world are crucial.

In *Discours*, Aimé Césaire calls attention to the common practice of character defamation of Black leaders. Marcus Garvey also addressed the cunning tactic throughout his political career and articulated it in *The Philosophy and Opinions of Marcus Garvey*, and Malcolm X discussed it in *Malcolm X Speaks: Selected Speeches and Statements*. The discrediting stratagem wily depicts progressive Black intellectuals and leaders as disturbing the peace—the status quo—and as enemies of society. When Césaire straightforwardly avowed that certain circles *feigned* to have found in him an "enemy of Europe," he revealed that the pretense is foremost tactical.[22] He wrote:

> il paraît que, dans certains milieux, *l'on a feint* de découvrir en moi un "ennemi de l'Europe" et un prophète du retour au passé *anté*-européen. Pour ma part, je cherche vainement où j'ai pu tenir de pareils discours. . . . La vérité est que j'ai dit tout autre chose: savoir que le grand drame historique de l'Afrique a moins été sa mise en contact trop tardive avec le reste du monde, que la manière dont ce contact a été opéré; que *c'est au moment où l'Europe est tombée entre les mains des financiers et des capitaines d'industrie les plus dénués de scrupules que l'Europe s'est "propagée"*[23]
>
> (It seems that in certain circles *they feigned* to find in me an "enemy of Europe" and a prophet of the return to the *pre*-European past. As for me, I search in vain where I could have held such discourses. . . . The truth is I have said something completely different: that is, the great historical tragedy of Africa has been not so much because it was too late in making contact with the rest of the world but rather the manner such contact was operated; *it was at the moment when Europe had fallen into the hands of the most unscrupulous financiers and captains of industry that Europe "propagated" itself.*)[24]

To *pretend* or *concoct* so-called enemies out of well-intentioned thinkers is to knowingly and resolutely incite venom against their works of historicity. Such detractors calculatedly peddled the idea of enmity in order to hinder, or curb (at the very least), the dissemination of influential works with the potential to remedy and transform the ills of Black communities. Césaire continues his precision to emphasize that he is not an "enemy" of Europe but a progressive and committed proponent of Africa's future, Africa's socioeconomic and political recovery. The acknowledgment and the study of Africa's complete history, and the histories of African descendants dispersed throughout the globe, are essential for rehabilitation. To pretend and to frame such vital work of rebuilding as antagonistic to Europe and European descendants is a disingenuous scheme, however transparent at this juncture of world history. In *The Philosophy*, Garvey asserted that he is not opposed to Europeans and their descendants "as charged by [his] enemies"; the fact was that he sacrificed all his time "to the up-building and development of the Negro Race."[25] In similar reasoning Césaire's emphasis on *pretense* resonates with

Garvey's keen observation that "the whole world is run on bluff." In a didactic method, for individual and collective introspection, Garvey underscores a fundamental human principle in order to pose the ultimate question. "[No] race, no nation, no man has any divine right to take advantage of others," he noted. "Why allow the other fellow to bluff you?"[26] In this approach Garvey not only sought to address the character defamation against him but also sought to awaken his listeners to the wiles used to persuade African descendants into believing that the quest for true historical knowledge as well as fair material access and advancement is antagonistic to others. While Black leaders and thinkers such as Garvey, Césaire, and Malcolm X were vilified for encouraging the awakening of African descendants, the world continued "to run on bluff," through manipulation, duplicity, and self-serving subterfuge. Within the context of pretense, deceit, and masquerade, Woodson's thought on the "great theatre of events" also underlines the ploys used to fabricate the material world and the wretched conditions of the majority of African descendants within it. "The conditions of today have been determined by what has taken place in the past," Woodson further explained, "and in a careful study of this history we may see more clearly the great theatre of events in which the Negro has played a part. We may better understand what his role has been and how well he has functioned in it."[27]

On Existence: Redefining Humanity and the Concept of Civilization

In 1816 Pompée Valentin, Baron De Vastey was one of the first critical Black thinkers to unveil, in writing, the root and the reasons for the character defamation against a whole race of human beings. De Vastey demonstrated, with a level of analysis unprecedentedly accomplished, the degree of European arrogance that led to the invasion of Africa. Moreover, De Vastey was one of the first critical thinkers to question the humanness of European enslavers, given the ease of fiendish actions as a way of life.

1) Je me sens humilié, je suis homme, je le sens dans tout mon être, je possède des facultés, *j'ai la pensée, la raison, la force, j'ai tout le sentiment de ma sublime existence* et je me vois obligé de réfuter des puérilités, d'absurdes sophismes, pour prouver à des hommes comme moi, que je suis leur semblable! Mon âme indignée de cet excès de déraison et de méchanceté, me force de douter à mon tour, s'ils sont hommes, ceux qui ont osé mettre en discussion une question aussi impie, aussi immorale, qu'elle est absurde![28]
   (I feel humiliated, I Am [human], I feel [my humanness] in all my being, *I possess faculties, I have thought, I have reasoning, I have strength, I have the profound sentiment of my sublime existence*, and I find myself obliged to refute puerilities and absurd sophisms, to prove to men like me that I am their fellow man! My soul, filled with indignation from this excess of nonsense and

wickedness, forces me to doubt, in turn, if they are humans, those who dared to put for discussion a question so impious, so immoral that it is absurd!)[29]

2) Souvent je me suis fait cette question, quels droits les ex-colons avaient-ils donc de torturer ainsi leurs infortunés esclaves? Quoi? Y aurait-il dans ce monde comme dans l'autre une race de bourreaux destinée à tourmenter les humains? Les ex-colons sont-ils sur la terre, ce que sont les démons dans l'enfer? mais il n'y a, me disais-je, que les criminels qui soient condamnés aux flammes éternelles, et les innocents sont ici-bas condamnés pendant leurs vies entières, aux plus horribles supplices; non, me disais-je encore, c'est calomnier un Dieu juste, bon et bienfaisant; *c'est une impiété que d'attribuer à l'auteur universel nos cruels infortunes; l'esclavage est l'ouvrage des hommes corrompus et méchants; c'est la plaie la plus affreuse qui ait jamais désolé l'humanité; c'est le droit que s'est arrogé le plus fort sur le plus faible, du plus rusé sur le plus ignorant.*[30] (I have often asked myself this question, what rights had the former-colonists to so torture their unfortunate slaves? What? Could there be in this world, as in the other, a race of beasts destined to torment humans? Are the former-colonists on earth what demons are in hell? Only criminals, I told myself, are condemned to eternal flames, but innocents are here condemned during their entire lives to the most horrific sufferings; no, I reminded myself, it is slandering a just God, good and magnanimous; *it is a sacrilege to attribute our cruel misfortunes to the creator of the universe; slavery is the work of corrupted and cruel men; it is the most horrific scourge that has ever devastated humanity; it is the right that the stronger self-arrogated on the weaker, the more deceitful on the more ignorant.*)[31]

In his reasoning that "it is a sacrilege to attribute our cruel misfortunes to the creator of the universe," De Vastey frames the horrors of slavery within its wicked human dimension and rejects blasphemy. His framework antecedently negated the sacrilegious propaganda of colonists, ex-colonists, and apologists of enslavement who profanely connected the transatlantic slave trade and slavery to the Creator, with intentional misinterpretations of the Bible. Similarly, in *The Philosophy and Opinions*, Marcus Garvey reasoned that "the power that holds Africa is not Divine. The power that holds Africa is human, and it is recognized that whatsoever man has done, man can do."[32] In his emphasis of a good and just God, De Vastey—and later Garvey—set the theoretical and theological foundation for James Cone's pivotal work, *A Black Theology of Liberation*. In his work, Cone advances the primary thought that God is the God of the oppressed, "liberating them from bondage . . . making right what men have made wrong. . . . [T]he resurrection-event means that God's liberating work is not only for the house of Israel but for all who are *enslaved by principalities or powers*."[33] The writings and speeches of the founders of Black liberation in the Americas—Toussaint Louverture, Jean-Jacques Dessalines, and Henry Christophe—also express gratitude to God for protection during all the battles fought for liberation and for their freedom from enslavement. For that reason, it is also significant to reprove the misguided and/or racist pastors and missionaries who have chosen to link Haiti's long-lasting poverty to the *Cérémonie du Bois-Caïman*, where a pig was killed as a sacrifice to God.[34] Given that Haiti's cumulative dire poverty grew from and remains from a myriad of verifiable historical politico-economic reasons as well as ensuing ecological disasters, to the rational mind, the immediate sensible question is: how can a caste of men—enslavers and colonists—who murdered millions of Africans in Africa, in the belly of the slave pit, the bottom of the Atlantic Ocean, and throughout the Americas be "blessed" and Haiti, which stood for the liberation and dignity of humankind, be "cursed" for the revolution to end the enslaving terrors against human beings: adults, children, and babies? How can Haiti be "cursed" for the blood of *one* pig, while others are stained with the blood of millions of human beings? Such asinine claim *is* the quintessential practice of the sacrilegious writings and attacks to which De Vastey referred in his 1816 publication. The Hebrews (Hebrews 9: 13, 9: 19) verse that follows is crucial in our analysis. It presents a direct revelation and interpretation of the spiritual practices of the *Cérémonie du Bois-Caïman*. It reads:

> The blood of goats and bulls and the ashes of a heifer sprinkled on those who are ceremonially unclean sanctify them so that they are outwardly clean. . . . When Moses had proclaimed every commandment of the law to all the people, he took the blood of calves, together with water, scarlet wool and branches of hyssop, and sprinkled the scroll and all the people. He said "This is the blood of the covenant, which God has commanded you to keep . . ."[35]

The blood of the pig was used—during the *Cérémonie du Bois-Caïman*—as part of the communion that reconciled the enslaved Africans with their ancestors and the Creator. It was the symbolic ritual to expiate existing sins before continuing with the ceremony which called for protection and guidance. The blood of the pig served to seal the covenant between the enslaved Africans, their ancestors, and the Creator. Thus, during prayers, the African revolutionary Dutty Boukman professed his faith and reminded his followers of their collective belief[36]:

> The god who created the sun which gives us light, who roused the waves and rules the storm, though hidden in the clouds, he watches us. He sees all that the white man does. The god of the white man inspires him with crime, but our god calls upon us to do good work. Our god who is good to us orders us to revenge our wrongs. He will direct our arms and aid us. Throw away the symbol of the god of the whites who has so often caused us to weep, and listen to the voice of liberty, which speaks in the hearts of us all.[37]

For Boukman the idea of the soi-disant (so-called) god for the enslaver/oppressor cannot be the same conception of God for the enslaved/oppressed. During the 1791 ceremony the enslaved Africans prayed to God, the supreme liberator. To restate James Cone's assertion in *A Black Theology of Liberation*, "the resurrection-event means that God's liberating work is not only for the house of Israel but for all who are *enslaved by principalities or powers*." Slavery, and the lasting abject poverty it created, De Vastey underlines, was the work of the most corrupt, wicked, and guile men who cruelly desecrated the natural rights of human beings, the rights of those who were unsuspecting, and weak in armament. In De Vastey's mention of "*le plus fort sur le plus faible*" ("the strongest on the weakest"), "the strongest" refers to those with access to such means of dominance as guns and slave ships. In "*le plus rusé sur le plus ignorant*" ("the most deceitful on the most ignorant"), "ignorant" refers to those who were incognizant of the duplicitous schemes of their enslavers and who could not have imagined the macabre realities of the transatlantic slave trade.

Moreover, De Vastey's position that slavery is the most horrific scourge ever infected humankind precedes Aimé Césaire's most salient argument developed and published in 1950. In *Discours sur le Colonialisme*, Césaire avers that colonization, also known as "civilization," worked as a universal regression, a continuously spreading infection, a lodged gangrene, and a poison that will steadily afflict the world. European "civilization mission," as it has been worked out, was a misnomer; it was a euphemism that stood for "enslavement" and "colonization." With similar examinations, Dr. John Henrik Clarke addresses the concept of "civilization" in his writings and lectures, to explain that true civilization "is the art of being civil." "The word civil," he highlights, "means peaceful. There's nothing peaceful about aggression."[38] Transatlantic slavery and colonization were, in fact, beyond "aggression"; they were the apogee of inhumane destruction. Dr. Clarke's analysis is well taken, however. Equally important, he calls to mind another fundamental fact, which is that "no people ever brought civilization to another people at no time and at no place in history." The belief or the acceptance of a specious European civilizing mission is "one of the most protracted lies we ever listened to."[39] In *How Europe Underdeveloped Africa*, published in 1972, Walter Rodney minutiously studies the concepts of civilization and development in relation to the actual outcomes left in Africa, to prove the extent to which European presence in Africa immeasurably devastated the continent: the land and the lives of the people for generations to come.

Philosophies of Fortitude and Redemption

For the intellectuals of the African Diaspora, the call was and remains one for constructive, corrective, and sober-minded scholarship and activism, in order to counter long-standing deliberate defamation. The term "sober mind" in research and activism, in the face of blatant and violent racism, appears in many writings of the twentieth century. Such appeal permeates C.L.R. James' *The Black Jacobins*, particularly in his description of Toussaint Louverture's character and political method. In Aimé Césaire's play *La Tragédie du Roi Christophe*, King Christophe impressed upon the people that if they are to climb out of their social circumstances, the economic pit, and the overall effects of enslavement on the newly free nation, they must work hard and harder than others, must be self-reliant, and must think clearly and dispassionately. "[And] if we want to climb out, see how we overcome firm on our feet, with tense muscles, clenched teeth, *the mind, ah! clear and cool heads*!"[40] ("et si nous voulons remonter, voyez comme s'imposent à nous, le pied qui s'arcboute, le muscle qui se tend, les dents qui se serrent, *la tête, oh! la tête, large et froide*!")[41] In addition to the Human condition, King Christophe stresses the Black condition that was created from the transatlantic slave trade and the resultant structures. Such historical conditions formed the socio-genesis of African descendants, with the ensuing cultural, economic, educational, and political phenomena of the contemporary world. "Therein lies the inequality."[42] Hence, if they are to climb out, they need "clear and cool heads." In 1927, after his arrest on charges fabricated by J. Edgar Hoover, within the Federal Bureau of Investigation, Garvey wrote a poem of fortitude and sober mindedness to his international followers before his deportation. In his poem "Keep Cool," Garvey aimed to keep African descendants, and members of the Universal Negro Improvement Association (UNIA) in particular, focused on their agenda of economic and psychological liberation, in spite of the circumstances of his arrest, imprisonment, and deportation.

In *The Mis-Education*, Woodson refers to the ancient proverb "whom the gods would destroy they first make mad," to emphasize that the Association for the Study of Negro Life and History does not promote "fire-eating agitation," for nothing can be gained by "inflaming" the African descendant's mind against his or her oppressor.[43] Hotheadedness, which later Frantz Fanon would refer to as "fièvre" ("fire") and "enthousiasme" ("fervor") in *Peau Noire Masques Blancs*, is the reaction of those who have been immured within despair and powerlessness. For that reason Fanon cautions against outbursts that can destroy the foundations already built. He explains:

> Nous nous méfions de l'enthousiasme. Chaque fois qu'on l'a vu éclore quelque part, il annonçait le feu, la famine, la misère . . . Aussi, le mépris de l'homme. L'enthousiasme est par excellence l'arme des impuissants. Ceux qui chauffent le fer pour le battre immédiatement. Nous voudrions chauffer la carcasse de l'homme et partir. Peut-être arriverions-nous à ce résultat: l'Homme entretenant ce feu par auto-combustion.[44]
>
> (We do not trust fervor. Every time we've seen it explode somewhere, it has brought fire, famine, misery . . . [a]nd contempt for man. Fervor is, par excellence, the weapon of the impotent. Of those who heat the iron in order to shape it immediately. We prefer to warm man's carcass and leave him. Perhaps we might reach this result: mankind retaining this fire through self-combustion.)[45]

To "warm man's carcass" is to renew the fatigued body or human carcass and to revive the sleeping or frozen mind. It is to know the sources of one's condition and to devise a program of change. To that extent, education and continuous actions are the self-combustion that will tenaciously transform the mind as well as the existing rapacious social structures. In spite of the oppressive and violent realities, cool heads and sober minds remain essential for persistent strategic activism and sociopolitical adjustments.

The intellectual writings of African descendants elucidate the political and social stratagems devised to hinder advancement. Equally important, those writings address the intricate psychological recalibration the African descendant community owes to self, from centuries of physical, economic, emotional, and psychological trauma, endured from the late 1400s onward. Garvey noted that "[the] Negro race [is] suffering more than any other race in the world from propaganda—Propaganda to destroy our hopes, our ambition and our confidence in self."[46] Consequently, the ability to discern propagandas and schemes informs the methods by which they can persist forward: knowledgeable, calm, and resolved. In *The Mis-Education* Dr. C.G. Woodson observed and incisively articulated that the biased and inferior education of African descendants has been a perfect success in the failure of the majority. He states: "The lack of confidence of the Negro in himself and in his possibilities is what has kept him down. *His mis-education has been a perfect success in this respect.*"[47] Thus, notwithstanding disparaging propaganda and all-ensuing tangible historical and contemporary institutional factors, the sagacious consensus among critical thinkers has been that African descendants must continuously develop their consciousness and intellect, for knowledge of self and the preparation of the youth. That remains a primordial responsibility. Bob Marley's 1980's message, "emancipate yourselves from mental slavery. None but ourselves can free our minds,"[48] was spoken from the legacy that advocated knowledge, introspection, accountability, and fortitude. Those were the principles set forth in order to restore what has been destroyed, distorted, and defamed. Lastly, in "Man Know Thyself" Garvey questions, with consternation, the state of collective leadership within communities: "Where can we find in this race of ours real men. Men of character, men of purpose, men of confidence, men of faith, men who really know themselves?" With that inquiry Garvey raised awareness on the web within which African descendants are bound. It simultaneously raised issues of leadership not only within Black communities but also within unscrupulous global realities. In this context, I did not find it accurate to substitute his repetition of "men" by "humans" given that the world leadership, with its various loci of power, has been predominantly male. "I have come across so many weaklings who profess to be leaders, and in the test I have found them to be the slaves of a nobler class," Garvey continued,

> They perform the will of their masters without question. . . . If . . . Negroes can only get to know themselves, to know that in them is a sovereign power,

> is an authority that is absolute, then in the next twenty-four hours we would have a new race, we would have a nation, an empire,—resurrected, not from the will of others to see us rise,—but from our own determination to rise, irrespective of what the world thinks.[49]

Clearly, Garvey was unwavering in his belief, and articulated countless times, that no human being should ever accept or endure a human "master." His use of "masters" in the above reflection conveys his level of exasperation with the Black predicament. To find its way out of the web of disenfranchisement, exploitation, and misrepresentation, Garvey reasoned that the race needs "men of vision and ability. Men of character and above all men of honesty, *and that is so hard to find*."[50] Garvey's last point highlights the tragedy of the Black world: trying to climb out of its economic pit in a world that is overall unjustly materialistic—some would argue that it is a world that is overall materially *corrupted*. Since the 1400s the majority of African descendants have struggled to repossess their divine human gift, as well as the sociopolitical rights to operate as full human beings, with the strengths and weaknesses of all humans. After being enslaved and hemmed within a position of *subhuman*, in order to climb out and to operate as a *being* among all beings, they must transcend human realities and muster a level of *will*, strength, and consciousness that no other group is required to have; they must produce a level of hard work that no other group is required to perform. If the African descendants must advance as a race, without the reparation due to them, they would have to transform into *supra-humans*, and that is an impossible feat. Garvey affirms that in order for the race to advance, it needs "[m]en of character and above all men of honesty," but "that is so hard to find" in all humans. Therein lies part of the tragedy of the Black race. Essentially, if they are not given the economic and educational restitutions due to them, they are doubly economically fettered: within the world context of materialism and within the race context of long-standing destitution from unabated exploitation. If it is generally hard to find humans of character and honesty and—relatedly—if the economic interests of the world's top echelon dictate the direction of the world, can/will substantive reparation ever be implemented? To what extent, then, have systems of exploitation fundamentally and irreversibly derailed the very existence of African descendants?

Notes

1. Marcus Garvey, *The Philosophy and Opinions of Marcus Garvey* (Dover: The Majority Press, 1986), 38, Volume I.
2. Ibid., 38. Emphasis added.
3. Robert Nesta Marley, "Redemption Song," *Uprising* (Jamaica: Island Records, 1980).
4. Carter G. Woodson, *The Mis-Education of the Negro* (Washington, DC: The ASALH Press, 2005), xii–xiii.
5. Alfred Adler, *Connaissance de l'Homme: Étude de Caractérologie Individuelle* (Paris: Éditions Payot, 1927, 1949).
6. Aimé Césaire, *Discours sur le Colonialisme* (Paris: Présence Africaine, 1955), 33.

7. Author's translation.
8. C.L.R. James, *The Black Jacobins* (New York: Vintage Books, 1989), 34.
9. Ibid., 34.
10. Ibid., 33.
11. Malcolm X, *On Afro-American History* (New York: International Socialist Review Publishing Association, 1967), 30.
12. Woodson, *The Mis-Education*, 3. Emphasis added.
13. In this study (as in my other publications) my use of the term "Black" is synonymous to "African descendant" and "Africana." In other words, here "Black" does not hold the various stereotypes of the "construction of Blackness." "Black" or "Blackness" in this context is rooted in its comprehensive history; it is grounded in its African-ness while acknowledging the infusion of other "races" in the ethnic make-up of some of its members. That said, it first acknowledges Africa as the region of origin, with its history, philosophical, and socio-cultural rudiments.
14. Author's translation. Emphasis added.
15. King Henry Christophe (Roi Henry 1er), *Manifeste du Roi* (Cap-Henry: Chez P. Roux, Imprimeur du Roi, 1814), 15. Emphasis added.
16. Garvey, *The Philosophy*, 1. Emphasis added.
17. Author's translation.
18. Anténor Firmin, *De L'Égalité des Races Humaines: Anthropologie Positive* (Paris: Librairie Cotillon, 1885), 575. Emphasis added.
19. Author's translation.
20. Frantz Fanon, *Peau Noire Masques Blancs* (Paris: Editions du Seuil, 1952), 9.
21. Garvey, *The Philosophy*, 26.
22. Césaire, *Discours sur le Colonialisme*, 26.
23. Ibid., 26. Emphasis added.
24. Author's translation. Emphasis added.
25. Garvey, *The Philosophy*, 13.
26. Ibid., 8.
27. Woodson, *The Mis-Education*, 7.
28. Pompée Valentin Baron De Vastey, *Réflexions sur une lettre de Mazères, ex-colon français, adressée à M.J.C.L. Sismonde De Sismondi, sur les Noirs et les Blancs, la Civilisation de l'Afrique, le Royaume d'Hayti, etc.* (Cap-Henry: Chez P. Roux, imprimeur du Roi, 1816), 15. Emphasis added.
29. Author's translation. Emphasis added.
30. De Vastey, *Réflexions*, 92. Emphasis added.
31. Author's translation.
32. Garvey, *The Philosophy*, 7.
33. James H. Cones, *A Black Theology of Liberation* (Philadelphia and New York: J.B. Lippincott Company, 1970), 19–22. Emphasis added.
34. In 2010, following the massive earthquake in Haiti, a so-called pastor, Pat Robertson, dared to profess that Haiti is paying for its "pact with the devil." How can a caste of men—former enslavers and colonists, as well as current-day neo-enslavers and neo-colonists—who murdered millions of Africans in Africa, at the bottom of the slave pit and the Atlantic Ocean, and throughout the Americas profess that Haiti is "cursed," for a revolution to end the enslaving terrors and fiendishness against human beings: adults, children, and babies? How can Haiti be "cursed" for the blood of *one* pig, while others are stained with the blood of millions of human beings?
35. Hebrews, *The Holy Bible* (Grand Rapids, MI: Zondervan Corporation, 1996), 1014.
36. For further analysis of Boukman's distinction between the "God" of the enslaved and suffering Africans and the "god" of the European enslavers, within the context of Theology of Liberation, please see *Literary and Sociopolitical Writings of the Black Diaspora in the Nineteenth and Twentieth Centuries*, 65–66.

37. James, *The Black Jacobins*, 87.
38. John Henrik Clarke, *A Great and Mighty Walk*, distributed by Cinema Guild (New York: Black Dot Media, 1996), @53:49 minutes, DVD.
39. Ibid., 55 minutes.
40. Author's translation. Emphasis added.
41. Aimé Césaire, *La Tragédie du Roi Christophe* (Paris: Présence Africaine, 1963), 59.
42. Ibid., 59. Author's translation.
43. Woodson, *The Mis-Education*, 107–108.
44. Fanon, *Peau Noire*, 6–7.
45. Author's translation.
46. Garvey, *The Philosophy*, 15.
47. Woodson, *The Mis-Education*, 60. Emphasis added.
48. Marley, "Redemption Song."
49. Garvey, *The Philosophy*, 38–39.
50. Ibid., 49. Emphasis added.

2

THE COLONIAL SYSTEM UNVEILED

From Baron De Vastey to Aimé Césaire

The published works dating from the 1790s to the 1820s scrutinized, questioned, and challenged the theories and practices of economic, social, and political interests, in relation to the natural rights or human rights of African descendants, during the slavery and post-slavery eras of the Americas. The philosophies of Toussaint Louverture, Emperor Jean-Jacques Dessalines, King Henry Christophe, Pompée Valentin De Vastey (Baron De Vastey), Louis Boisrond-Tonnerre, and their contemporaries unmasked, as early as the 1700s, the roots of racist ideologies as well as the fiendish practices and brazen ideals that would impact the world's structure and human relations for centuries to come. The fore-thinkers of contemporary Black Thought contended with and sought to disprove the malign propaganda that, with unrestrained effrontery, justified the enslavement of Africans and the consequent debasement of an entire group of human beings. Equally important, their writings exposed the infamous scheme of the enslavers/colonists, which was, unequivocally, perpetual enslavement in all its forms: physical, spiritual, emotional, psychological, and intellectual. Chapter 1 of this present work introduced Baron De Vastey's seminal articulation, taken from *Réflexions sur une Lettre de Mazères, Ex-Colon Français, adressée à M.J.C.L. Sismonde De Sismondi Sur les Noirs et les Blancs, la Civilisation de l'Afrique, le Royaume d'Hayti, etc.* His logic—at once a sentiment and a fundamental reasoning—transcends time, from the enslavement era to the present. The following assertion of De Vastey was at the heart of the anti-slavery movements of the eighteenth and nineteenth centuries:

> I find myself obliged to refute puerilities and absurd sophisms, to prove to men like me that I am their fellow man! My soul, filled with indignation for this excess of nonsense and wickedness, *forces me* to doubt, in turn, if

> they are humans, those who dared to put for discussion a question so impious, so immoral that it is absurd."[1]

It resonates with the objectives of the Civil Rights Movement and the African liberation movements of the twentieth century; lastly, it undergirds the continuous sociopolitical efforts of the twenty-first century, among which stands the Black Lives Matter movement. It is for the in-depth understanding of the forced existential rerouting of African descendants that the first Black thinkers of the Americas sought—for the benefit of posterity—to record knowledge. Within the same objective of continuous teaching and awakening, this chapter aims to contribute to the process of repositioning the writings of leading and preeminent African descendant thinkers to their proper place in intellectual history. Consequently, the chapter lays bare their philosophies as well as their influential deeds for the accessibility of contemporary and future generations who are deprived of comprehensive historical contexts. From the scrutiny of their writings, the trajectory of modern-day injustices become, simultaneously, more comprehensible (in terms of economic and political interests) and incomprehensible (in terms of the defilement of human beings and the brutal violation of their natural and human rights).

In *Réflexions Sur une Lettre de Mazarès, ex-colon français*, Vastey straightforwardly avows that "the colonists will never convert fighters of human rights into adherents of the science of enslavement."[2] ("Les ex-colons ne feront jamais des adeptes parmi nous dans la science de l'esclavage!")[3] The discerning word choice "science" calls attention to the methodical and abominably successful systemic approach to slaveocracy and its entrenched social structures. In his analysis—marked by sharp sarcasm—Vastey continues,

> A qui persuaderont-ils que l'esclavage est un bien? Est-ce à nous qui en avons éprouvé toutes les horreurs? *Eh! Si leurs assertions étaient vraies*, que ne se mettent-ils à notre place, ils nous convaincraient bien mieux encore par des exemples, que des raisonnements absurdes.[4]
>
> (Whom would they persuade that enslavement is a benefit? Would it be us who have endured all its horrors? And! *If their assertions were true*, why would they not put themselves in our place, they would convince us much better by examples than by absurd arguments.)[5]

In his denouncement of the colonists' wiles, Vastey's message is categorical. He condemns the colonists' stratagem of a traumatic enslavement system and its aftermath, not only for the Africans but for all their descendants to be born. Baron De Vastey ultimately maintains that Mazères, along with other enslavers, colonists, and their descendants, will never succeed in persuading contemporaries and posterity that enslavement was in the benefits of the Africans. Writing from the twenty-first-century purview, and having studied numerous occurrences and ideologies from the last three centuries, I find it pertinent to modify Baron De Vastey's perspective, only to add that enslavers, colonists, and their descendants will never *fully* convince African descendants of the soi-disant "benefits" of enslavement. It is vital to draw attention to the precision *fully* because through the power of brainwash and miseducation, and also faced with anguish at the sight of the catastrophic ruination of Africa and predominantly Black nations, some Blacks tend to accept such absurdities that maintain slavery saved them from Africa's poverty. Such persons are disconcertingly ignorant of the fact that slavery, colonialism, and the continuous exploitation of Africa—sub-Saharan Africa in particular—are the joint fundamental reasons for the inhumane contemporary poverty of most Africans in Africa, and most of their descendants across the globe. One hundred thirty-four years after the publication of *Réflexions*, Aimé Césaire continued Baron De Vastey's arguments in his *Discours sur le Colonialisme* (*Discourse on Colonialism*), first published in 1950. Césaire particularly built on Vastey's categorical question: Whom would they persuade that enslavement is a benefit? Would it be us who have endured all its horrors? *Discours* details the cumulative nefarious impacts of slavery and colonialism, from the date of Vastey's publication to Césaire's era.[6] With perspicuity, Césaire enumerates the lasting ills of colonialism: from societies depleted of their resources to cultures denigrated, to religions demonized, to lands confiscated, and to institutions seized. "They talk to me about progress, about 'achievements'," he stresses, ". . . I am talking about millions of men torn from their gods, their land, their habits, their life, from life, from dance, from wisdom."[7] ("On me parle de progrès, de 'réalisations' . . . Je parle de millions d'hommes arrachés à leurs dieux, à leur terre, à leurs habitudes, à leur vie, à la vie, à la danse, à la sagesse.")[8]

Césaire's most salient examination in *Discours* is the concept and practice of Hitlerism. He reasoned that it was not the crime in itself, nor the crime against mankind, nor the humiliation of the human being that rendered Hitler contemptible; rather, it was the crime against fellow Whites that was concluded as unpardonable. Hitler is reprehensible because he applied terrorizing colonial procedures that hitherto had only been applied to Africans on manifold levels, and to Indians. Moreover, Césaire brought attention to the fact that Hitler's practices (Hitlerism) have been taking place for centuries before the birth of Adolf Hitler, the individual, in 1889; thus, the barbarity of Hitlerism was active in every enslaver and colonist and laid dormant in countless others. In Césaire's simplest terms, Hitlerism is barbarism; Hitlerism is inhumanness. To address the necessity to eradicate the long-standing sociality of inhumanity within contemporary contexts, Césaire called in 1950—in *Discours*—for detailed clinical studies that would investigate the psychological impacts of slavery and colonialism on both the enslaved/colonized and the enslaver/colonizer, from one generation to the next. Frantz Fanon would publish such study in his 1952 *Peau Noire Masques Blancs* (*Black Skin White Masks*), and Joy DeGruy would develop such study in her 2005 *Post Traumatic Slave Syndrome: America's Legacy of Enduring Injury and*

Healing. In *Discours*, Césaire challenged everyone to sincere introspections that would reveal the extent to which too many harbor the ideals of Hitlerism within, and the extent to which too many have been victimized by active/direct or indirect Hitlerism. "Hitler is his *demon*; if he reviles him, it is by lack of logic," he remarks.[9]

> Oui, il vaudrait la peine d'étudier, cliniquement, dans le détail, les démarches d'Hitler et de l'hitlérisme et de révéler au très distingué, très humaniste, très chrétien bourgeois du XXe siècle qu'il porte en lui un Hitler qui s'ignore, qu'Hitler *l'habite*, qu'Hitler est son *démon*, que s'il le vitupère, c'est par manque de logique.[10]
>
> (Indeed, it is worth studying, clinically, in details, the maneuvers of Hitler and Hitlerism, and reveal to the very distinguished, very humanist, very Christian bourgeois of the 20th century that he subconsciously harbors a Hitler within, that Hitler *lives in him*, that Hitler is his *demon*, that if he vituperates him, it is by a lack of logic.)[11]

Césaire's sarcastic "very distinguished, very humanist, very Christian bourgeois" points to the hypocrisy and dissimulation in those self-acclaimed characteristics. In essence, one should speak of *pseudo*-distinction, *pseudo*-humanist, and *pseudo*-Christian. *Discours sur le Colonialisme* is, par excellence, the observational and analytical continuation of *Le Système Colonial Dévoilé* and *Réflexions*. As such, *Discours* connects the historical and intellectual trajectory of the eighteenth and nineteenth centuries to the publications and sociopolitical occurrences of the twentieth century. Such seamless example of intellectual trajectory underlines the fact that without access to, and the study of the foundational writings of Africa's first published thinkers of the Americas, of the late 1700s and early 1800s, there will remain historical and intellectual lacunae in the study of contemporary thought, particularly of contemporary Black Thought.

The Social Deviation of the Africans: What History Must Restore!

In the introduction to *Peau Noire Masques Blancs* (*Black Skin White Masks*), Frantz Fanon advances his concepts of existential void and existential deviation within the context of Black *beingness*.[12] He examines the extent to which the feigned White "civilization," which in actuality equates to the European transatlantic slave trade, slavery, and colonialism, has imposed an *existential deviation* or *diversion* on African descendants.[13] Fanon's analytical framework employs Alioune Diop's study of twentieth-century Black intellectualism. In so doing, he builds on one of Diop's fundamental arguments: that is, the questioning of the positionality of the "Black genius" in the chorus of the universal.[14] From his examination of Alioune Diop's philosophy, Fanon resultantly expanded the inquiry to argue that one cannot speak of the "Black genius" until Blacks reclaim their authentic being and are repositioned in their proper place within the world's economic, political, and social structures. Furthermore, Fanon argues—throughout his chapter "Le Nègre et la Psychopathologie" ("The Negro and Psychopathology")—that an authentic self cannot come into being in an atmosphere of relentless systemic prejudices and quotidian life-altering and fatal racism. In such environments, the manifestation and acceptance of the African descendants' true genius have been covertly, when not overtly, obstructed; equally consequential, the perception of their intellectual abilities and genius has been tainted for centuries. While the concepts of the Black genius and the manifestation of the authentic being are complex theories to fully decipher, it is an undeniable fact that enslavement and the various forms of exploitations and oppressions that followed—through actions, social structures and institutions, policies, and various genres of published writings—have rerouted and fundamentally diverted the African from his or her natural human conditions. Moreover, they have been derailed from socioeconomic opportunities and individual capabilities, because of the lack of proper and meaningful education. The contemporary relevant question remains: The extent to which African descendants have had the opportune landscape to explore all of their potentials, unfettered—excepting, perhaps, music and sports? All factors considered, one could unhesitatingly argue that the intellectual opportunities of Blacks have been socially curtailed on one level or another; their intellectualism and intellectual production are shaped and affected on various degrees.

While most are aware of the fallacies that perception inheres, it continues to undergird educational methods and sociopolitical policies. Blaise Pascal's philosophical thought on perception made a memorable impression on me many years ago as an undergraduate student and is pertinent to our analysis: "Imagination [perception] prompts everything; it makes [constructs] beauty, justice, and happiness, which are the basis for everything in the world. . . . *Opinion [perception] rules the world.*"[15] ("L'imagination dispose de tout; elle fait la beauté, la justice, et le bonheur, qui est le tout du monde. . . . *Della opinione regina del mondo.*")[16] Given that perceptions construct the world, and objectives reign over the world, Fanon's concept of a "déviation existentielle" remains pivotal in the development of this chapter, within the contexts of physical and psychological enslavement, as well as the resultant material destitution and intellectual confinement. Moreover, the scrutiny of the concept of an existential diversion or redirection is essential to the continuous intellectual and social efforts toward contemporary awareness and readjustment. It is through intellectual production and the access to the works produced can the Africans and their descendants reclaim their positions and frame their own destiny, free of ignoble prejudicial contingencies.

> L'on voit déjà Alioune Diop se demander quelle sera la position du génie noir dans le chœur universel. Or, nous disons qu'une véritable culture ne

> peut naître dans les conditions actuelles. On parlera de génie noir quand l'homme aura retrouvé sa véritable place.[17]
>
> (We already see Alioune Diop questioning the position of the Black genius in the chorus of the universal. Yet, we say that a real culture cannot be born in these present conditions. We will speak of the Black genius when [humans] would have reclaimed their true place.)[18]

In the steady efforts to bequeath a body of historical accounts, for the purpose of recovery from the long-standing historical vacuum, the study of Baron De Vastey's works remains central. His publications reveal and address the principal causes of the historical and existential void, as well as the sources for the purposeful rerouting of the African individual. Baron De Vastey, secretary to King Christophe and loyal supporter of his kingdom, was a politician and writer committed not only to the freedom and prosperity of Haiti but also to the liberation of African descendants in the Americas. From 1814 to 1819—he died in 1820—De Vastey penned and legated a body of work on the history of Saint-Domingue and the onerous course to the making of Haiti. His body of work unveils the impacts of the practice of slavery in Saint-Domingue as well as its effects on early 1800s Haiti. De Vastey wrote for the benefit of historical record in the struggle to complete and true freedom. The focus on *record*, for substantive advancement, was fundamental not only for De Vastey's generation but remained such for succeeding generations. Significantly, in his 1925 essay titled "The Negro Digs Up His Past"—published in Alain Locke's anthology *The New Negro*—the historian Arthur A. Schomburg reasserts the necessity for record and one's legacy. As a historian and an influential figure of the Harlem Renaissance and the broader New Negro Renaissance, Schomburg worked to preserve the historical and intellectual writings of the Black world. In "The Negro Digs Up His Past," Schomburg affirms that:

> History must restore what slavery took away, for it is the social damage of slavery that the present generations must repair and offset. . . . [T]here is *a definite desire and determination to have a history, well documented, widely known at least within race circles*, and administered as a stimulating and inspiring tradition for the coming generations. . . . The bigotry of civilization which is the taproot of intellectual prejudice begins far back and must be corrected at its source.[19]

"[At] least within race circles" is certainly limited, but, at the minimum, the group that is the most affected by miseducation would have in-depth access to its history. Descendants of Africa must know their own national and diasporic histories. Descendants of other continents must also know the true history and contributions of Africa, within the inter-relational contexts of world history. In an essay published in 1992, as homage to Schomburg's commitment to the preservation of African history and the history of Africa's descendants, John Henrik Clarke underlines Schomburg's lasting intellectual impact. In "The Influence of Arthur A. Schomburg on My Concept of Africana Studies," Dr. Clarke reasons that it is not sufficient to know the history and the contribution of pre-enslavement Africans; "it is necessary to understand their relationship to all people in the world throughout history and the influence of non-African people on African people."[20] Stated differently, it is crucial to understand the effects of the actions of non-Africans on African descendants, within "the great theater of events."[21] It is weighty to comprehend and gauge the extent to which distorted interactions and malicious actions have established entrenched sociopolitical dynamics, thus far ineradicable. Hence, the published words of the 1700s and 1800s are the written legacies to spearhead the corrective process, given that the first step to the corrective process is knowledge, awareness, and responsibility. The words of the fore-thinkers of the Diaspora aim to unmask the continued bigotry of civilization, to which Schomburg referred in "The Negro Digs Up His Past." Their words, simply put, are the reclamation of the African humanity and dignity. Their intellectual production—in spite of momentous obstacles to dissemination and access—contextualized and recorded the political as well as the social practices of their era, which are the roots of contemporary discriminatory ideals, racist structures, and prejudiced behaviors. In *Le Système Colonial Dévoilé*, published in 1814 (which preceded his 1816 *Réflexions sur une Lettre . . .*), Baron De Vastey asserts his responsibility in documenting the intents and executions of the colonial system. He wrote:

> *Qu'ami de mes semblables, de mon roi et de mon pays*, je sens le besoin, la nécessité de dévoiler le barbare *système colonial* qui a pesé sur nous pendant des siècles. Heureux si mes faibles écrits peuvent être utiles à mes semblables et contribuer au bonheur de mes compatriotes.
>
> . . . Mon but en écrivant, n'est pas d'aspirer à la gloire d'être homme de lettres, mais bien d'être utile à mes compatriotes, de les éclairer et de dévoiler la vérité aux européens.[22]
>
> (*Friend of my kind [kinfolk], of my king and of my country*, I feel the need, the necessity to disclose the barbarous *colonial system* that weighed on us for centuries. Fortunate would I be if my poor writings can be useful to my kind and contribute to the good fortune of my compatriots.
>
> . . . My goal in writing is not to aspire to the glory of being a man of letters, but to be useful to my compatriots, to enlighten them, and to reveal the truth to the Europeans.)[23]

De Vastey's emphatic statement on his commitment "to enlighten [his compatriots], and to reveal the truth to the Europeans" is vital. In order to reach meaningful resolutions for suffering communities, all groups must learn the various historical facts and occurrences, particularly the groups directly affected disadvantageously and the groups directly affected advantageously: Africans and African descendants, Europeans and European descendants. His statement unprecedentedly acknowledges the fact that miseducation—*avant la lettre*, as coined by C.G. Woodson—not only undermines African descendants but also conditions European descendants and other groups. For, "no one can be thoroughly educated until [he or she] learns as much about the Negro as he knows about other people."[24] The illusory teaching of superiority-cum-entitled privileges and the illusory teaching of inferiority-cum-inevitable destitution create infinite exploitation and subjugation, which lead to grave and incessant conflicts within society. For De Vastey, Europeans and European descendants must be aware of the factual reasons for African disparagement and global oppression; they must be educated in comprehensive and relational world history. As analyzed in Chapter 1, for approximately six centuries to date, the illusory belief of superiority and the perpetuation of the propaganda of inferiority have globally hemmed African descendants into *real* economic destitution, thus into real and tangible economic inferiority. Recollecting and highlighting the reasons for enslavement and its lasting outcomes, De Vastey submits the following:

1) Tourmentés par la soif intarissable des richesses, suscités par un esprit de malédiction, que d'absurdités, de divagations, de calomnies et d'assertions mensongères, ces apôtres de satan n'ont pas inventées pour légitimer la traite et les horreurs de l'esclavage! *Que de blasphèmes! Que d'infamies n'ont-ils pas osé imprimer pour ravaler et dégrader l'espèce humaine! . . .*[25]
   (Consumed by the inexhaustible thirst for riches, aroused by a spirit of malediction, what absurdities, divagations, calumnies, and mendacious assertions that these apostles of Satan have not invented in order to legitimize the slave trade and the horrors of enslavement! *What blasphemies! What infamies have they not dared to print in order to humiliate and degrade the humankind!* . . .)[26]
2) Un Mazères, un ex-colon, encore tout souillé de notre sang, ose insulter au vertueux et généreux Sismonde de Sismondi! Parce qu'il a une certaine facilité de coucher sur le papier ses idées extravagantes et superficielles, ce pédant de Mazères s'est permis de vociférer des injures et des calomnies les plus atroces contre les africains et les haytiens leurs descendans.[27]
   (A Mazères, an ex-colonist, still stained with our blood, dares to insult the virtuous and generous Sismonde de Sismondi! This arrogant Mazères, because he has a certain ease to lay outlandish and superficial ideas down on paper, gave himself the right to vociferate the most atrocious insults and calumnies against the Africans and the Haitians, their descendants.)[28]

In defense of the work of the European historian M. Sismonde de Sismondi, who contributed to the reclamation of the Africans' humanity, De Vastey asserts:

> La plume savant de M. Sismonde de Sismondi n'a certainement pas besoin du secours de la mienne pour réfuter les absurdités de Mazères, mais étant partie intéressée, *je ne dois pas rester spectateur tranquille de la discussion*; je dois

> faire tous mes efforts pour aider nos défenseurs dans la grande cause qu'ils ont embrassée. . . . *j'espère qu'Hayti sera le point d'appui où les philanthropes pourront poser le levier puissant qui doit soulever le monde morale, contre les ennemis du genre humain.*[29]
>
> (M. Sismonde de Sismondi's erudite pen did certainly not need my help to refute Mazères' absurdities. But, being an invested party I must not remain a quiet spectator; I must put forth all my efforts to help our defenders in this grand cause they have embraced. . . . *I hope that Haiti will be the pillar where all philanthropists can rest the powerful lever that must elevate the moral world against the enemies of humankind.*)[30]

De Vastey regarded the Black republic as "*the pillar where all philanthropists can rest the powerful lever that must elevate the moral world against the enemies of humankind*" because of its commitment to human dignity and its sacrifices for human freedom. His work lays bare the historical significance of the nation for the global world. Thus, the historical record Baron De Vastey offers, and the intellectual contribution he envisioned, would be of service not only to his king and to his nation but also to mankind. His trenchant *Réflexions sur une Lettre* confronts and deconstructs F. Mazères' vitriol. In a preceding published letter written to esteemed historian Jean Charles Léonard de Sismondi, Mazères—the odious French colonist—criticizes the historian and political economist M.J.C.L de Sismondi for his nonracist and positive presentation of the Africans' aesthetics, intelligence, and achievements. In an effort to undermine de Sismondi's 1814 publications, which consistently condemned the enslavement of Africans and sought to help reestablish the Africans in their proper global framework, the colonist Mazères disseminated his virulent arguments of utter denigration against the Africans and their descendants of the Black republic: the Haitians. Mazères' publication set the path for later racist writers, such as the infamous Arthur de Gobineau. Lastly, it is in seething anger and hatred against the African descendants who established a free Black Republic that in 1815, 11 years after Dessalines' formal proclamation of Haiti's independence, Mazères found it necessary to denigrate—in print—the Africans and their descendants. In an extensive response, De Vastey reflects on Mazères' letter. In *Réflexions*, Baron De Vastey methodically addresses and deplores Mazères' venom. He wrote:

> A mesure que Mazères contemple de nos progrès dans la civilisation, sa rage s'augmente; dans l'impuissance où il est de ne pouvoir se venger, se baigner encore dans notre sang, il exhale toutes ses fureurs par des injures les plus ignobles; les expressions les plus viles, les plus dégoûtantes, échappent de la plume de cet homme qui se dit *si poli*. . . . Ne voilà-t-il pas, que ces grands enfans s'avisent de construire des citadelles, d'édifier des palais, de rédiger des almanachs, d'avoir des écrivains, des poëtes, des ministres et des hommes d'état noirs, quels malheurs! Quels désappointemens pour un

> ex-colon! Violà les véritables causes des fureurs de cet énergumène, et qui ont valu tant d'injures et de sottises à MM de Sismondi et de Limonade.[31]
>
> (As Mazères contemplates our progress in civilization, his rage augments; in his impuissance whereby he is unable to take revenge, to bathe again in our blood, he breathes all of his furies through the most ignoble insults; the most vile and the most revolting expressions come from the pen of this man who claims to be *so polite*. . . . Today these "big children" are making plans to build citadels, to erect palaces, to write almanacs, to have Black writers, poets, ministers and statesmen, what a shame! What disappointments for the ex-colonist! Here are the true sources of this maniac's fury that prompted so many insults and nonsense against MM de Sismondi and Limonade.)[32]

While De Vastey specifically addresses Mazères' publication, along with the deeds of all enslavers and colonists—in both *Réflexions* and *Le Système Colonial Dévoilé*—, Césaire's *Discours sur le Colonialisme* addresses the deeds of such colonists as Lucien de Montagnac and Armand-Jacques de Saint Arnaud (officers to Africa) and the words of Ernest Renan, Jules Romains, and Dominique-Octave Mannoni (French writers). Similar to King Christophe's attention to both practices, Césaire's unveiling of the deplorable actions as well as the written vilifying words of the colonists underlines the weighty adverse effects of their defamatory writings against the Africans. Césaire's primary points of analysis, in a continuum relation to De Vastey's publications, are as follow. One, that the enslavers' civilization = colonialization = objectification ("*chosification*") of the Africans; in other words, the pretended civilization dehumanized the African into objects and nothingness. Two, "Hitlerism" precedes/predates and survives the actual man; Hitlerism is the manifestation of the same mindset that initiated the enslavement of Africans. Three, that enslavement and colonialism turned a caste of men into beasts. "They prove that civilization, I repeat, dehumanize the most civilized man," Césaire asserts. More specifically,

> que le colonisateur, qui, pour se donner bonne conscience, s'habitue à voir dans l'autre *la bête*, tend objectivement à se transformer lui-même *en bête*. C'est cette action, ce choc en retour de la colonisation qu'il importait de signaler.[33]
>
> (that the colonizer who, in order to ease his conscience, accustoms himself to see *the animal* in the other, trains himself to treat him like an animal, tend objectively to *transform himself* into *an animal*. It is this action, this adverse rebound of colonization that had to be indicated.)[34]

Vexed with the systemic defamation and torture against the Africans, De Vastey reminds his readers that it is on a people who have given abundant proofs of wisdom, vertu, energy, and courage that Mazères dared to print the crassest nonsense. "C'est sur des hommes qui ont donné tant de preuves de sagesse, de vertu, d'énergie et de courage, que Mazères a osé imprimer les plus plates inepties; c'est lui qui n'a pas honte d'affirmer."[35] De Vastey procedes to quote Mazères directly. In this study I refrain from reprinting racist absurdities of the past centuries; however, for analytical context and for the simple fact that these verminous thoughts linger in the minds of too many contemporaries of the twenty-first century, it is worth briefly gauging Mazères' language—published in 1815. In his *Réflexions*, De Vastey quotes the following from Mazères:

> Le nègre est un grand enfant borné, léger, mobile, inconsidéré, ne sentant avec force ni le plaisir ni la douleur; sans prévoyance, sans ressort dans l'esprit ni dans l'âme . . . insouciant comme tous les êtres paresseux; le repos, le chant, les femmes et la parure composent le cercle étroit de ses goûts; je ne dis pas de ses affections, car les affections proprement dites, son trop fortes pour une âme aussi molle, aussi peu réactive que la sienne.[36]
>
> (The Negro is a big narrow-minded child, happy, mobile, thoughtless, does not feel neither pleasure nor pain strongly; without foresight or forethought, without spirit in the mind or the soul . . . carefree, as all who are lazy; rest, music, women, and adornments compose the small circle of their likes; I don't say affections, because actual affections are too strong for such a weak and barely reactive soul.)[37]

Similar acrimonious, moronic and disrespectful language of denigration was frequently found in the writings of enslavers and colonists during the slave trade, during the slavery era, and beyond. Their aim was self-satisfaction and arrogated permission to carry out the most villainous acts. Following the same vein of psychoanalysis employed in Fanon's *Peau Noire Masques Blancs* and Césaire's historical and psychology approach in *Discours sur le Colonialisme*, Dr. Joy DeGruy's focus on cognitive dissonance—developed in *Post Traumatic Slave Syndrome*—exposes the psychological disposition and behaviors of countless enslavers and colonists. Building on works of history and psychoanalysis, DeGruy's clinical approach complements the scholarship that studies the magnitude of the impacts of the past on contemporary realities. To justify inexpiable acts, the enslavers/colonists had to convince themselves and everyone else that the Africans were incapable of feeling strong pain or pleasure. The dismantling of families, the mutilation of bodies, the mutilation of the female genitalia, the mutilation and murder of babies and kids, the exertion from incessant toil, the lynchings, and so on were all justified as acceptable and normal. Moreover, Mazères' sentence "carefree, as all who are lazy; rest, music, women and adornment . . ." describes, in actuality, aristocratic and bourgeois French behavior not only in the colonies but also in France. For, how can a group of people who work from dawn to dusk, in the most inhuman conditions, be lazy? Such claim is utterly unreasonable to the sensible mind, yet it was propagated for centuries. Moreover, it is evident that Mazères uses psychological manipulation to attribute to the Africans the French behaviors that are considered disreputable. Numerous French writers from Medieval to the Renaissance era, from the seventeenth to the twentieth century, have criticized aristocratic and bourgeois way of life, centered within gossips, theater, music, entangled sexual relationships, excessive use of alcohol, and mere appearance. Among such writers one would note: Michel de Montaigne, Jean de La Fontaine, Blaise Pascal, François de La Rochefoucauld, and Albert Camus. Within the context of Saint-Domingue, in *The Black Jacobins*, C.L.R. James highlights the lifestyle of enslavers and colonists in Saint-Domingue in comparison to the life of toil and discipline of the Negroes and the Mulattoes. Describing the colonists' ways of life in Saint-Domingue, James points out:

> The chief reading of the population consisted of lascivious novels. For amusement there were theatres, not only in Le Cap and Port-au-Prince, but in such small towns as Léogâne and St. Marc. . . . What the towns lacked in intellectual fare they made up for in opportunities of debauchery—gambling dens, dance-halls, and private brothels. . . . The regular clergy of San Domingo instead of being a moderating influence were notorious for their irreverence and degeneracy.[38]

James also reminds his readers that descendants of aristocrats and famous Marshals of France (Maréchaux de France) would spend their time "between a bowl of rum and a Negro concubine."[39] Thus, taking into consideration the fact that erroneous notions of the Africans and their descendants pervade published Europeans' and European descendants' propaganda, from the 1400s onward, it is crucial to transmit excerpts from De Vastey's response in extenso so readers may independently analyze and evaluate historical contexts. He explains:

1) Mazères défend la cause des ex-colons, de cette caste d'hommes, dont le système affreux et les crimes inouïs font frémir la nature; et moi la cause que je défends est celle de l'humanité entière. Blancs, jaunes et noirs, nous sommes tous frères, tous enfans du père éternel, tous intéressés dans cette cause: Ô homme, quel que soit la couleur de ton épiderme! Quels que soient la nation et la religion que tu professes! Tu es intéressé au triomphe des haytiens, à moins que tu n'ait étouffé tous les sentimens de justice et d'équité que Dieu a gravés dans tous les cœurs; tu ne peux mettre dans la balance les intérêts d'une caste d'hommes flétris par les crimes, avec les intérêts du genre humain![40]
   (Mazères defends the cause of the ex-colonists, this caste of men whose atrocious system and inconceivable crimes make nature shudder; and I, the cause that I defend is the cause of humanity in its entirety. Whites, Yellows and Blacks, we are all brothers, all children of the Eternal Father, all interested in this cause: Oh humankind, whatever the color of your skin! Whatever the

nation or the religion that you profess! You are interested in the triumph of the Haitians, unless you have stifled all the sentiments of justice and equity that God engraved in all hearts; you cannot weigh the interests of a caste of men debased by crimes with the interest of humankind!)[41]

2) Le système de nos détracteurs, étant de vouloir matérialiser l'homme noir, par la diversité primitive des races humaines, démentir le récit de la création, et dans l'infériorité supposée de notre espèce, se faire un titre pour nous traiter comme les plus vils animaux; je ne répondrai donc pas seulement à Mazères, mais à toute la caste des ex-colons français; je vais commencer par débarrasser mon champ des ordures que nos ennemis y jettent pour obscurcir la vérité; je vais remonter à la source des choses, rétablir les faits, les appuyer par les autorités les plus respectables; je vais combattre toutes leurs objections; j'espère que je ne manquerai pas de preuves et d'argumens victorieux pour renverser leurs sophismes et leurs absurdités.[42]
(The system of our detractors denies the account of creation, with the goal to materialize the Blacks through their primitive diversity of the human races, and the supposed inferiority of our kind. They give themselves the right to treat us as the most vile of animals; I will not solely respond to Mazères, but to the entire caste of French ex-colonists; I am going to start to rid the field of the filth that our enemies dump to obscure the truth; I am going to go back to the sources, re-establish the facts, and support them with the most respectable authorities; I'm going to challenge all of their objections; I hope I will not miss any of the proofs and victorious arguments to topple their sophisms and absurdities.)[43]

Réflexions and *Le Système Colonial Dévoilé* are not only works of record but also works of defense, of defense through record. They simultaneously engage in a twofold process. First, the works stand against physical enslavement in the Americas and against attempts at the re-enslavement of African descendants in Haiti. Second, the works stand as defense against racist ideological claims of intellectual and racial inferiority. In his cogent analyses, De Vastey's remark on the materialization of the Africans (*matérialiser* l'homme noir) preface Césaire's concept of "chosification," expounded in *Discours*. In *Réfléxions* De Vastey refutes Mazères' notion of the "primitive diversity of the human races" to demonstrate the "primitive" *unity* of the human race, as Anténor Firmin would further develop in his *De L'Égalité des Races Humaines; Anthropologie Positive*, published in 1885.[44] In De Vastey's examination of Mazères' *Lettre à M.J.-C.-L.* he underlines a distinction between the French and, by extension, the European citizens/consumers and those who were directly, actively, and viciously engaged in the sale of human flesh at all levels—specifically the enslavers/colonists. Moreover, in his account De Vastey lays bare the actions of the Europeans in juxtaposition to the attributes of "savage" and "barbaric" they assigned to the Africans. His approach reveals, once again, the enslavers'/colonists' process of cognitive dissonance as well as the undertaking of imputing onto the Africans behaviors they (the Europeans) have themselves actualized (not the Africans). De Vastey's detailed account and examinations are to unveil, beyond any doubts, that such attributes, imposed on the Africans and their descendants, are the foremost misplaced qualifications in human history; the most protracted lies in modern human history.

In Defense of Humanity

In his 113-page *Réflexions* and defense of the Africans' humanity, De Vastey discloses:

1) Nous avons vu nos concitoyens, nos amis, nos parens, nos frères, hommes, femmes, enfans, vieillards, sans distinction d'âge ni de sexe, traînés aux derniers supplices par ces monstres: ceux-ci expiraient dans les flammes des bûchers; ceux-là attachés aux gibets servaient de pâture aux oiseaux de proie; les uns étaient livrés aux chiens pour être dévorés, les autres plus heureux périssaient sous les coups de poignard et de bayonnette . . .[45]
(We have seen our fellow-citizens, our friends, our parents, our brothers, men, women, children and the elderly, without any distinction to age or gender, dragged to the worst tortures by these monsters: these perished in flames; those, attached to the gallows, served as pecking food for the birds; some were delivered to dogs to be devoured; others, more fortunate, perished under the blows of a knife/dagger and the bayonet . . .)[46]
2) . . . S'il fallait raconter toutes les injustices et toutes les cruautés que les français ont exercées sur nous, j'enflerais des volumes; il me suffit de signaler les principaux traits, mes lecteurs jugeront de la manière barbare dont nous avons été traités. Témoin oculaire et auriculaire des faits que je rapporte, on ne peut douter de leur véracité. Trois hommes devaient être brûlés vifs sur la place Royale (alors Cap-Français). . . . A trois heures de l'après-midi, le général français Claparède [Michel Marie Claparède], commandant la ville de Cap, se rend sur la place Royal accompagné d'un nombreux état-major.[47] Les trois victimes étaient placés dans le corps-de-garde voisin, en attendant l'heure de leurs supplices . . . l'infâme Collet, capitaine de la gendarmerie les précède, la joie et la férocité sont peintes sur son visage. . . . Claparède ordonne de mettre le feu au bûcher; à l'instant la flamme pétille, les pieds commencent à être embrasés . . . ils ne remuent pas même les pieds; ils restent immobiles, les regards fixes, ils bravent leurs bourreaux et le feu qui les dévore . . . un sentiment de haine et de vengeance s'élève dans le cœur de l'haytien consterné; les bourreaux seuls restent sur la place, et ne se retirent que lorsque leur victimes sont entièrement réduites en cendres![48]
(. . . If I had to recount all the injustices and cruelties that the French exerted on us, I would fill up volumes. It suffices to underline the principal traits; my readers will judge the barbarous manner we were treated. Ocular and

auricular witness to the facts that I report, one cannot doubt of their veracity. Three men were to be burnt alive at the Royal Square (then Cap-Français). At three o'clock in the afternoon, the French general Claparède, Commander of the town le Cap, arrived at the Royal Square accompanied by numerous officers. The three victims were left with a nearby regiment to wait for the hour of their torture. The infamous Collet, captain of the gendarmerie, ushered them in, with joy and ferocity painted on his face. . . . Claparède ordered to set fire to the logs; the flame crackles instantly. The feet of the long-sufferers were set aflame. They don't even move their feet around; they remain immobile, their gaze fixed, they brave their executioners and the fire that devours them . . . a sentiment of hatred and vengeance grows in the heart of each terrorized Haytien. Only the executioners remain on the Square and would only leave after their victims were completely reduced to ashes!)[49]

3) Plusieurs jours d'avance, ils avaient eu la précaution de faire jeûner les chiens, pour stimuler leur faim, de temps en temps on leur présentait une victime, que l'on retirait aussitôt que les chiens voulaient s'élancer dessus pour la dévorer; enfin, le moment fatal arrive où quelques hommes ou femmes vont leur être définitivement livrés; ces infortunés sont attachés à des poteaux, en présence des commissaires, pour les empêcher de pouvoir se sauver ni de se défendre. Les dogues sont lâchés; ils se précipitent sur leurs proies; dans un instant les victimes sont déchirées, leur chair palpitante est en lambeaux, leur sang ruisselle de toutes parts; on entend plus que les cris de la douleur d'une horrible agonie; les victimes aux abois implorent la pitié de ces monstres; en vain ils demandent la mort comme dernière faveur, prières superflues; rien ne peut émouvoir le cœur de ces tigres, *ils se sont dépouillé de tous sentimens humains: aux accens lamentables de leurs tristes victimes, ils ne répondent que par un ris sardonique et ils continuent à exciter les dogues à mieux dévorer leur proies.* Cependant, la voix des victimes s'est éteinte, l'on entend presque plus leurs gémissemens, et leurs cadavres décharnés palpitent encore; les dogues haletans, sont lassés; ils sont repus de chair et de sang humains: en vain les bourreaux les excitent encore, ils refusent de continuer leur terrible curée; on les retire pour les faire rentrer dans leurs repaires; *et les monstres à figures humaines achèvent d'ôter à coup de poignard le reste de vie des infortunées victimes.* D'un bout de l'île à l'autre les mêmes cruautés se commettaient par les français.[50]

(Many days in advance they followed the precaution to have the dogs fast, in order to stimulate their hunger; from time to time they would present them a victim, that they would take away as soon as the dogs would want to throw themselves to devour him/her; finally, the fatal moment arrives when some men or women are going to be delivered to them for good; these wretched were attached to posts, in the presence of commissioners who restrain them from escaping or defending themselves. The massifs were released; they hasten to their prey; in an instant the victim are ripped apart, their pulsating flesh in pieces, their blood streams from all directions; we only hear the squeal of the pain and the horrible agony; the victims at bay implore the pity of those monsters; in vain they ask for death as a last favor, pointless prayer; nothing can move the heart of those tigers; *they have rid themselves of all human sentiments; to the lamentable cry of their miserable victims they only respond with a sardonic laugh and continue to incite the massifs to better devour their prey.* Meanwhile, the victims' voice dies out, one barely hears their groaning, and their devoured cadavers still pulsate; the massifs panting, are tired; they are sated of flesh and human blood: in vain the butchers continue to incite them, they refuse to continue their horrible scramble; they remove [the dogs] to have them return to their den, *and the monsters in human faces continue, with knives, to finish the lives of their wretched victims.* From one end of the island to the next the French were committing the same kinds of cruelties.)[51]

4) Je le répète, que Mazères se compare et se juge s'il veut, par analogie, avec les ânes et les chiens, je ne l'en empêche pas; il peut exister entre lui et ces quadrupèdes quelques analogies; les chiens, par exemple, ont été auxiliaires des ex-colons, qui les ont aidé à détruire et à dévorer les noirs; ils peuvent donc très-bien sympathiser ensemble; mais je soutiens que l'homme intelligent, espèce unique, ne peut être comparée et jugée qu'avec l'homme semblable, et les animaux avec les individus de leur espèce.[52]
Si l'injustice, la mauvaise foi, les cruautés de tous genres, donnent des droits à ceux qui les ont éprouvés, contre ceux qui les ont exercés, quel peuple a jamais eu plus de droit à l'indépendance que le peuple haytien?[53]
(I repeat, Mazères can compare and judge himself analogously to the donkeys and the dogs if he wants to, I don't stand in his way; it is possible that there are some analogies between those quadruped and him; the dogs, for example, were auxiliaries to the ex-colonists, which helped them destroy and devour the Blacks; they can very well sympathize together. But I maintain that the intelligent man, unique species, can only be compared and judged in relation to his [human] kind, and the animals in relation to individuals of their species.)[54]
(If injustice, ill-will and cruelties of all kinds give rights to those who experienced them against those who committed them, then what nation has had more right to independence then the nation of Haiti?)[55]

5) Lassés de tant de crimes et de forfaits, nous courûmes aux armes; nous nous mesurâmes avec nos bourreaux; nous nous battîmes corps à corps, homme pour homme, à coup de pierres et de bâtons ferrés, *pour conserver notre liberté, notre existence, celles de nos femmes et de nos enfans.* Après avoir versé des flots de notre sang, confondu avec celui de nos tyrans, nous restâmes les maîtres du champ de bataille. Que Mazères, ce colon féroce et de mauvaise foi, qui a été le témoin et un des instigateurs des cruautés de tous genres, que ses compatriotes ont exercées sur nous, les repasse dans son imagination; qu'il se rappelle combien de victimes il a fait immoler ou qu'il a égorgées de ses propres mains, alors il verra si nous avons des droits à la liberté et à l'indépendance, que nous avons conquises aux prix de tant de sang et de sacrifices![56]

(Weary of so many crimes and infamies, we hastened to arms; we measured ourselves up to our butchers; we fought hand-to-hand, man for man, with rocks and metal rods, *to preserve our freedom, our existence, the freedom and existence of our women and children.* Having shed streams of blood, mixed with the blood of our tyrants, we prevailed as masters of the battlefield. That Mazères, this ferocious and ill-willed colonist who was the witness and one of the instigators of cruelties of all kinds that his compatriots exerted on us, replays them in his imagination; that he recollects the number of victims that he had sacrificed or that he had slain with his own hands, then he will realize that we have rights to the liberty and the independence that we have conquered with the price of so much blood and sacrifices.)[57]

In eight pages of panoramic details, De Vastey describes just two incidents; the 113 pages of *Réflexions* report and detail numerous examples of European inhuman barbarity in Saint-Domingue. His precisions allow the reader to see for oneself—in a palpable manner—the unimaginable cruelties leading to the thirteen-year revolution and the Africans' eventual self-liberation from physical slavery. Later, in 1853, William Wells Brown's novel *Clotel; or, the President's Daughter: A Narrative of Slave Life in the United States* recounts similar atrocities against the African Americans. It was published during the enslavement of Africans on the soil of the United States, and the "fictional" approach made it possible for the abolitionist W.W. Brown to lay out truths of terror, with lesser repercussions than he would have encountered with a straightforward account or manifesto. René Maran's 1921 novel, *Batouala*, which illustrates the colonial horrors of Ubangi-Shari in French Equatorial Africa, is described by Donald E. Herdeck as the work that "helped prepare the intellectual groundwork for the anti-colonial revolt which was to sweep the post-World War II world."[58] Similar to Césaire and Dr. John Henrik Clarke, in his preface René Maran also addresses the notion of civilization in relation to colonization. He notes:

Civilisation, civilisation, orgueil des Européens, leurs charniers d'innocents . . . Tu bâtis ton royaume sur des cadavres. Quoi que tu veuilles, quoi que tu fasses, tu te meus dans le mensonge. A ta vue les larmes de sourdre, et la douleur de crier. Tu es la force qui prime le droit. Tu n'es pas un flambeau mais un incendie. Tout ce à quoi tu touches, tu le consumes.[59]

(Civilization, civilization, pride of the Europeans, and their burying-ground for innocents . . . You build your kingdom on corpses. Whatever you may want, whatever you may do, you act with deceit. At your sight, gushing tears and screaming pain. You are the might which exceeds right. You aren't a torch, but an inferno. Everything you touch, you consume.)[60]

Comparable to Vastey, however, Césaire opted for the straightforward factual accounts in his *Discours sur le Colonialisme.* Admittedly, Césaire published during the post-slavery era not only in the French colonies but across the Americas. He wrote a century later than William Wells Brown and thirty years later than René Maran; his work appeared during a period of relatively growing intellectual and political freedom, in comparison to the preceding eras. That De Vastey, along with Henry Christophe and Jean-Jacques Dessalines, categorically wrote and published against the horrors of the slavery era—during the slavery era—is a testament to the significance of their acquired physical and psychological freedom. Their categorical "*j'accuse*" prepared the ground for succeeding defenders of human rights. In *Discours*, Césaire argues that though the record and recollection of such reprehensible and indefensible acts—as described in the monographs, manifestos, slave narratives, and novels of African descendants—will not please everyone, it is psychologically and socially detrimental to keep those historical skeletons buried in silence while the lasting impacts remain blatantly and loudly evident. The manipulative efforts to mask and silence what is glaringly present, contribute to social chaos and social neurosis. To unveil a few reprehensible historical truths of the twentieth century, Césaire points to specific French officials. He quotes colonel de Montagnac's boasting fact: "to get rid of the thoughts that sometimes besiege me, I have heads cut off, not heads of artichokes, but heads of humans."[61] ("Pour chasser les idées qui m'assiègent quelquefois, je fais couper des têtes, non pas des têtes d'artichauts, mais bien des têtes d'hommes.")[62] Césaire further quotes Comte d'Herisson, Saint-Armand, and commandant Gérard, who admitted:

> Les tirailleurs n'avaient ordre de tuer que les hommes, mais on ne les retint pas; enivrés de l'odeur du sang, ils n'épargnèrent pas une femme, pas un enfant. . . . A la fin de l'après-midi, sous l'action de la chaleur, un petit brouillard s'éleva: c'était le sang des cinq mille victimes, l'ombre de la ville, qui s'évaporait au soleil couchant. Oui ou non, ces faits sont-ils vrais?[63]
>
> ([T]he soldiers had orders to only kill men, but we didn't hold them back; intoxicated by the smell of blood, they didn't spare not a woman, not a child. . . . At the end of the afternoon, due to the heat, a fog arose: it was the blood of five thousand victims, the shadow of the town, that was evaporating at sunset. Yes or no, are these facts true?)[64]

Césaire's ultimate question—"Yes or no, are these facts true?"—emphasizes, on the one hand, the process of unearthing and unmasking such accounts of terror and, on the other hand, brings attention to the calumnious long-standing attributes of "savagery" and "barbarism" imputed to the Africans.

Notes

1. Author's translation. De Vastey's full statement is translated in Chapter 1 of this present work, under the subtitle "On Existence: Redefining Humanity and the Concept of Civilization."
2. Author's translation.

3. Pompée Valentin Baron De Vastey, *Réflexions sur une Lettre de Mazères, Ex-Colon Français, Adressée à M.J.C.L. Sismonde de Sismondi, sur les Noirs et les Blancs, la Civilisation de l'Afrique, le Royaume d'Hayti, etc.* (Cap-Henry: Chez P. Roux, imprimeur du Roi, 1816), 93.
4. De Vastey, *Réflexions*, 93. Emphasis added.
5. Author's translation. Emphasis added.
6. It is noteworthy that in 1963 Aimé Césaire published the play *La Tragédie du Roi Christophe*. Césaire's fictional work (based on sound research) was one of the first twentieth-century writings to give voice to Baron De Vastey. In the play De Vastey solidifies Césaire's historical analysis on Haiti's role and challenges as the Black republic of the Americas, surrounded by an anti-African and anti-Black world structure. Furthermore, *La Tragédie* inspired many scholars to acknowledge De Vastey's body of work.
7. Author's translation.
8. Aimé Césaire, *Discours sur le Colonialisme* (Paris: Présence Africaine, 1955), 23–24.
9. Author's translation.
10. Césaire, *Discours sur le Colonialisme*, 13.
11. Author's translation.
12. I use *beingness* within similar framework as Dr. John Henrik Clarke, in his documentary *A Great and Mighty Walk*: that is, one's existence, one's humanness, one's "human beingness."
13. Frantz Fanon, *Peau Noire Masques Blancs* (Paris: Éditions du Seuil, 1952), 10–11. "La civilisation blanche, la culture européenne ont imposé au Noir une déviation existentielle. Nous montrerons ailleurs que souvent ce qu'on appelle l'âme noire est une construction du Blanc." ("White civilization, European culture have imposed an existential deviation on the Blacks. We will demonstrate elsewhere what is often called the black soul is a construction of the Whites." Author's translation.
14. Alioune Diop was the founder of *Présence Africaine*. The journal was founded as a venue where Black intellectuals can more genuinely ponder and question consequential topics related to Africa and African descendants. The journal remains a vital publication organ in African/Black intellectualism and culture, from 1947 to our present day. Alioune Diop was an influential figure in the Négritude Movement because of his abilities as an intellectual, a writer, and an editor. In 1956 he was the prime organizer for the 1st International Congress of Black Writers and Artists.
15. Author's translation. Emphasis added.
16. Pascal Blaise, *Pensées* (Paris: Garnier-Flammarion, 1976), 75. Emphasis added.
17. Fanon, *Peau Noire*, 151.
18. Author's translation.
19. Arthur A. Schomburg, "The Negro Digs Up His Past," *The New Negro* (New York: Touchstone Book, 1997), 231, 237. Emphasis added.
20. John Henrik Clarke, "The Influence of Arthur A. Schomburg on My Concept of Africana Studies," *Phylon* 49, no. 1 & 2 (1992): 5.
21. Carter G. Woodson, *The Mis-Education of the Negro, 1933* (Washington, DC: The ASALH Press, 2005), 7.
22. Pompée Valentin Baron De Vastey, *Le Système Colonial Dévoilé* (Cap-Henry: Chez P. Roux, Imprimeur du Roi, 1814), vii–viii. Emphasis added.
23. Author's translation. De Vastey's reference to his "faibles écrits" ("my poor writings") is an a priori disclaimer for those who would choose to focus on his writing style (such as syntax) in an effort to avert his contents. He further emphasized that his goal is not "to aspire to the glory of being a man of letters" but to educate members of the race and others.
24. Woodson, *The Mis-Education*, 76.
25. De Vastey, *Réflexions*, 2. Emphasis added.
26. Author's translation.

27. De Vastey, *Réflexions*, 3.
28. Author's translation.
29. De Vastey, *Réflexions*, 4. Emphasis added.
30. Author's translation.
31. De Vastey, *Réflexions*, 109–110.
32. Author's translation.
33. Césaire, *Discours sur le Colonialisme*, 21.
34. Author's translation. Emphasis added to "transforms himself."
35. De Vastey, *Réflexions*, 105.
36. Ibid., 105.
37. Author's translation.
38. C.L.R. James, *The Black Jacobins* (New York: Vintage Books, 1989), 32.
39. Ibid., 31.
40. De Vastey, *Réflexions*, 112.
41. Author's translation.
42. De Vastey, *Réflexions*, 5–6.
43. Author's translation.
44. De Vastey, *Réflexions*, 7.
45. Ibid., 97–99.
46. Author's translation.
47. Michel Marie Claparède was an officer of Napoléon Bonaparte's expedition to San-Domingo, led by Charles Victoire Emmanuel Leclerc.
48. De Vastey, *Réflexions*, 97–99.
49. Author's translation.
50. De Vastey, *Réflexions*, 100–101. Emphasis added.
51. Author's translation.
52. De Vastey, *Réflexions*, 16.
53. Ibid., 91.
54. Author's translation.
55. Author's translation.
56. De Vastey, *Réflexions*, 103. Emphasis added.
57. Author's translation. Emphasis added.
58. René Maran, *Batouala,* translated by Barbara Beck and Alexandre Mboukou (London: Heinemann, 1987), 5.
59. René Maran, *Batouala, Véritable Roman Nègre* (Paris: Albin Michel, 1921), 11.
60. Author's translation.
61. Author's translation.
62. Césaire, *Discours sur le Colonialisme*, 19.
63. Ibid., 19–20.
64. Author's translation.

3

THE WORDS OF J.J. DESSALINES AND H. CHRISTOPHE

An Appeal to the Nations and Citizens of the World

While the published words of Jean-Jacques Dessalines were drafted to promulgate his allegiance and commitment to the newly formed nation of Haiti, and to caution posterity of the political, social, and economic dangers that lay ahead, the succeeding words of King Christophe were formulated as both a record of the abominable enterprise of slavery and an appeal to the humanity of the world, in order to help safeguard the natural and human rights of new nation's citizenry. Cognizant of the fact that the business of slavery retained its full impact and cruelty outside of the new Black republic, cognizant of the extent to which such system had enclosed African descendants in powerlessness, King Christophe, similar to his military and diplomatic predecessor, Toussaint Louverture, insistently appealed to liberal thinkers and philanthropists in Europe and the entire world. However, after years of military battles and diplomatic strategies, to assure the liberty of Blacks and Mulattoes, the Black generals—Louverture, Dessalines, and Christophe—could not succeed in convincing the world of the benefits of equality and racial harmony. In vain, Louverture unremittingly endeavored to persuade Napoléon Bonaparte that the end of the slavery system was the best method for lasting peace in Saint-Domingue and for humane cooperation between the colonies and the metropole. The lucrativeness of enslavement was too powerful, and of primary importance, to disrupt in the name of *genuine* enlightenment and humanity. "Prosperity is not a moral question and the justification of San Domingo was its prosperity," C.L.R. James reminds his readers in *The Black Jacobins*. "Never for centuries had the western world known such economic progress."[1] Ahead of his time, it was precisely the belief that humanity and enlightenment would prevail over inhumane extortion that eventually led Louverture to his demise. James succinctly underlines Toussaint's failure as "the failure of enlightenment, not of darkness. . . . [I]t is easy to see to-day, as his generals saw after he was dead, where he had erred. It does not mean that they or any of us would have done better in his place."[2] Indeed, there is no guarantee that any of us, if placed in his position—in the midst of the politico-economic impuissance of African descendants and the social terror of his time—would have done differently in all efforts to re-equilibrate human relations by liberating the descendants of Africa. Dessalines, on the other hand, "could see clearly and simply, it was because the ties that bound this uneducated soldier to French civilization were of the slenderest."[3] Dessalines did not carry the burden of the European enlightenment philosophies that were in stark contradictions with the atrocious realities the African descendants endured. In that regard, unlike Louverture, Dessalines was psychologically *free* to operate from *what was/what is* in lieu of what he philosophically and morally analyzed *ought to be.*

With insightful objective, not muddled by illusions, from 1804 to 1806, Dessalines' primary goal was to simultaneously reassure the people of Haiti of their rights to freedom and independence as well as to psychologically prepare them for the onerous path ahead. On November 18, 1803, the military victory of the *Bataille de Vertières* (Battle of Vertières) guaranteed the end of chattel slavery in Saint-Domingue. Dessalines sagaciously understood, with utmost clarity, that the momentous and destiny-altering victory was the beginning of a liberation process that will require steadfast commitment, integrity, and sacrifices. In his "Procès-Verbal de la Proclamation de l'Indépendance d'Haïti," signed on January 1, 1804, Dessalines articulated concise and constructive principles for the new nation—a nation that Dessalines described as *the* empire of liberty ("l'empire de la liberté"). Following the final battle of independence, the Proclamation became an act of "national authority," drafted to cultivate an "empire of liberty in the country of our birth."[4] "Il faut par *un dernier acte d'autorité nationale*, assurer à jamais l'empire de la liberté dans le pays qui nous a vu naître."[5] By October 8, 1804, Jean-Jacques Dessalines would stand as Jacques 1er, Empereur d'Haïti, and straightforwardly asseverate:[6]

> Eh quoi! Victimes pendant quatorze ans de notre crédulité et de notre indulgence; vaincus, non par des armées françaises, *mais par la piteuse éloquence des proclamations de leurs agents.* . . . Indigènes d'Haïti! J'ai veillé, combattu, quelquefois seul, et si j'ai été heureux que de remettre en vos mains le dépôt sacré que vous m'avez confié, *songez que c'est à vous maintenant à le conserver.* . . . Et toi, peuple trop longtemps infortuné, témoin du serment que nous prononçons, souviens-toi que c'est sur ta constance et ton courage que j'ai compté quand je me suis lancé dans la carrière de la liberté pour y combattre le despotisme et la tyrannie, contre lesquels tu luttais depuis quatorze ans . . . *que mon nom est devenu en horreur à tous les peuples qui veulent l'esclavage, et que les despotes et les tyrans ne le prononcent qu'en maudissant le jour qui m'a vu naître*; et si jamais tu refusais ou recevais en murmurant les lois que le génie qui veille à tes destins me dictera pour ton

> bonheur, tu mériterais le sort des peuples ingrats. Mais loin de moi cette affreuse idée; tu seras le soutien de la liberté que tu chéris, l'appui du chef qui te commande.[7]
>
> (What! Victims of our credulity and our leniency for fourteen years; defeated not by the French army but by the cheap eloquence of their agents' proclamations. . . . Natives of Haiti! I stood guard, I fought, sometimes alone, and if I am only delighted to put back in your hands the sacred trust that you confided to me, *remember that it is now your turn to preserve it*. . . . And you, a people who has experienced misfortune for too long, witness of the sermon that we utter, remember that it is on your constancy and courage that I relied when I embarked on the career for liberty, in order to combat the despotism and the tyranny against which you fought for fourteen years. . . *that my name has become horror to all the nations that want slavery, and that the despots and the tyrants only pronounce it to curse the day that I was born*; and if ever you refuse or mutteringly receive the laws that the spirit who keeps watch over your destiny has commanded me for your happiness, you would deserve the fate of ingrate nations. But enough of this frightful thought; you will be the fulcrum of the liberty that you cherish, the support of the chief who leads you.)[8]

Most salient in the Proclamation is the position of accountability in leadership and national responsibility, embedded in his communication. Dessalines remained aware of their former enslavers' unmitigated barbarity and duplicity; in fact, he reminded the new nation of such fiendish inhumanity throughout the Proclamation. However, with his emphasis on "victims of our [own] credulity and leniency" the message Dessalines sought to convey, at that juncture of their history, was one of self-assertion, through collective introspection, cerebral clarity, and empowerment, in order to prevent the nation—its citizenry—from dupery and more torments from their exploiters.

Nascent Black Political Thought

Two of the prevalent modes of dupery the enslavers employed in revolutionary Saint-Domingue were: one, the seed of division and, two, deceitful promises of equality in political, economic, and social dealings. Thus, from 1804 until his death in 1806, Dessalines led with the conviction that it is the leader's responsibility, along with the ruling class, to engage with precision, integrity, and steadfast fairness on behalf of the nation. In his 1814 *Manifeste du Roi*, King Christophe also recollects the reality and consequences of falling prey to unsuspecting fourberie. "We can no longer be duped," he admonished the citizens, "we know the pervertedness of our enemies."[9] ("Nous ne pouvons plus être trompés, nous connaissons la perversité de nos ennemis.")[10] Similar to the emperor, King Christophe brought the nation's attention to its own responsibility to learn from past errors, in terms of the masked intentions of the enslavers and colonists who sought to perfidiously accomplish what was difficult to achieve overtly. Within that context, King Christophe also called to mind one of the most notable schemes of division, connived by the French general Hédouville. It was the plot to turn General André Rigaud against the Governor General Toussaint Louverture, in a stratagem to weaken the latter's work toward liberty and equality in Saint-Domingue. In his scheme, Hédouville granted the young Mulatto officer permission to disobey any order from the African governor general, in an effort to use the politics of color and power to create discord and to sabotage their common goal of autonomy in Saint-Domingue.[11] "This agent," King Christophe wrote, "succeeded in disturbing everything by shaking the firebrands of *discord*, and by igniting the torches of civil war among us."[12] ("Cet Agent parvint à tout bouleverser, en secouant parmi nous les brandons de la *discorde*, et en allumant les torches de la *guerre civile*.")[13] In reference to French enslavers as a whole, King Christophe further remarks: "it was not enough to come armed, in addition they had to employ perfidious and shameful measures, in order to better assure the success of the expedition; they had to sow *disunity* and operate a beneficial *diversion* for their destructive projects."[14] ("Ce n'était pas assez de venir à main armée, il fallait encore pour mieux assurer le succès de l'expédition, employer des moyens perfides et honteux; il faillait semer parmi nous la *désunion* et opérer une *diversion* salutaire à leur projets destructeurs.")[15]

In a letter sent to France during his final months alive, Leclerc admitted his repeated approach of manufactured conflicts of division among Black officers: "not being strong enough to finish up with Dessalines, Maurepas and the others, *I use one against the other*."[16] Cognizant of the impact of such destructive tactics employed in colonial Saint-Domingue, in his Proclamation, Jean-Jacques Dessalines warned against the continuance of those stratagems in the new Republic of Haiti. As prescriptions, he stressed the principles that are indispensable to the survival and prosperity of the nation: namely, the principle of individual and communal commitment to the well-being of the nation as an entity, the principle of mutual support and unity, confidence in self (as individuals and as a nation-state), respect for and valorization of the ancestral past and traditions, as well as the continuous remembrance of the ancestors who endured or perished under enslavement and those who died for freedom and posterity. Such remembrance is the foundation of a people's historical consciousness, without which the nation will remain adrift, unaware of its *true* strengths as well as its damaging weaknesses. As examined in Chapter 1 of the present work, without the knowledge of self (individual and national) and without the fortitude and conviction that grow from such knowledge, a nation or community will tend to give up on its future and its collective objectives; furthermore, it will compromise—if not gravely damage—its well-being and dignity for generations to come. In 1904, for the centenary remembrance of Haiti's independence, the national anthem was adopted.[17] The anthem, recorded as *La Dessalinienne* (hymne national), underlines

Dessalines' main principles. The first few lines of the initial musical stanza assert: "For the country, For the Ancestors, Let us walk united, Let us walk united. In our ranks there shall be no traitors! Of our land let us be the only masters."[18] ("Pour le Pays, Pour les Ancêtres, Marchons unis, Marchons unis, Dans nos rangs point de traîtres! Du sol soyons seul maîtres.")[19]

Dessalines' forewarnings, commemorated and recorded as the nation's anthem a hundred year after the Proclamation of 1804, remain prophetic statements. Historical accounts reveal that from the consecutive presidency of Alexandre Pétion and Jean-Pierre Boyer onward (more boldly after the death of Henry Christophe forth), the warnings of the Proclamation, solidified in the Constitution of 1805, have been disregarded and violated by the ruling class of the nation-state; they have been disregarded and violated by external powers, either forcefully or in complicity with the ruling class of the nation-state. After an assessment of the nineteenth and twentieth centuries, as well as the developments of the dawn of the twenty-first century, it is worth pondering Dessalines' 1804 national forewarning that called for integrity, courage, and service in national leadership as well as dignity, and caution in political and international affairs. Before the emperor's assassination, he undertook two weighty processes to eradicate disunity and establish the creed of union and fraternity. First, he sought to extirpate conflicts rooted in skin color among the descendants of Africa—an unchanging reality since enslavement. Article 14 of the Imperial Constitution of 1805 required that all Haitians (regardless of hue) be known by the generic denomination "Black": "les Haïtiens ne seront désormais connus que sous la dénomination générique de Noirs."[20] The precision on the word "generic" underlines Dessalines' understanding on the ways in which common denominations such as race and color function in the political, social, and economic realms. The generic "Black" denomination was not to be interpreted as an essence but a term of reference to their common national historical circumstances. Anyone who opted to live in the Republic, regardless of hue and geographical origin, had to remain conscious of the nation's particular history and must work to help forge an equitable future for its citizens. In so doing, Dessalines attempted to eradicate the practice of racism and colorism, and the embedded claims of economic entitlement such mindset fosters. Through that process, he hoped to avert political conflicts between Mulattoes, full-blooded Blacks, and the various gradations of color in between. A common national well-being would make them indivisible and more equipped to safeguard their political and economic autonomy from outside forces. Second, he aimed for an egalitarian distribution of the new nation's resources among its citizens, whose ancestors collectively fought and died for freedom. Ultimately, Emperor Jacques 1er endeavored to remedy the color and the class dynamics endemic in the nation's recent origin of enslavement and unabated extortionate exploitation. In his April 28, 1804, Proclamation—"Liberté ou La Mort. Proclamation. Jean-Jacques Dessalines, Gouverneur Général aux Habitans D'Haïti"—Dessalines described harmony among the citizens as the only route to the nation's happiness and salvation: the guarantor of their success. Concord, he entreated, was "the secret of being invincible." "Keep this precious concord, this successful harmony among you; it is the pledge to your happiness, to your salvation, to your success; it is the secret to being invincible."[21] ("Maintenez cette précieuse concorde, cette heureuse harmonie parmi vous; c'est le gage de votre bonheur, de votre salut, de vos succès; c'est le secret d'être invincibles.")[22] Strength in unity was the formula and mindset that led to the victory of the Africans in Saint-Domingue.

In an effort to prevent the repetition of errors from the past—from colonial Saint-Domingue—during his years of governance, Dessalines warned the officers of treachery from within their ranks as well as from foreigners' divisive and exploitative pressures. The role of the leaders, as he viewed it, must be the protection and defense of the nation. If the leadership gives way to unscrupulous national and international politicians, such corrupted beings will be "*the schemers of our troubles and of our divisions*."[23] ("et que s'ils trouvent un asile parmi nous, ils seront *les machinateurs de nos troubles et de nos divisions*.")[24] In his forewarning, Dessalines refers not only directly to the French but also—by extension—to all governments maintaining slavery in the Americas and to all governments that continue absolute economic exploitation within or without the slavery system. In his "[and] what a dishonoring absurdity to be victorious only to be slaves. Slaves!"[25] ("[et] quelle déshonorante absurdité que de vaincre pour être esclaves. Esclaves!"),[26] the caution at that historical juncture was not only against physical reenslavement and the reconquering of the territory of Haiti but also—and perhaps more so—against economic and political re-enslavement. His exclamatory repetition of "Esclaves" stresses the absurdity in allowing such possibility. In this context Dessalines advised that no colonist or European should set foot on the territory as master or proprietor. If a succeeding chief of state violates this prescript—which became law in the Constitution of 1805—he would be digging his own grave and the grave of the citizens of Haiti. ("Jamais aucun colon ni européen ne mettra le pied sur le territoire, à titre de maître ou de propriétaire . . . Que d'autres chefs, après moi, creusent leur tombeau et celui de leurs semblables, en tenant une conduite diamétralement opposée à la mienne.")[27] As a method of international relations, Dessalines wanted to maintain Haiti's independence in peace and in equitable commercial exchange with all nations of the world.

Abominably, the subsequent murder of the Liberator in 1806 shattered his efforts of concord; furthermore, it unveils the deep politico-economic antagonism and social fissure that was widening between the ruling class along with the elite class and the majority of the people, at the very moment the nation's Coat of Arms—"L'Union Fait La Force"—was adopted.[28] Moreover, Dessalines' assassination is regrettably tied to his egalitarian approach of resource distribution. His most powerful opponent and author of his assassination was the faction led by Alexandre Pétion, who opposed the verification of land titles and other policies geared toward social equality for the masses. By 1807 the country was divided into two factions, with Henry Christophe governing in the North and

Alexandre Pétion presiding in the South; it would re-unify in 1820, after Christophe's death.[29] After Dessalines' assassination, Alexandre Pétion and Jean-Pierre Boyer "granted monopolies to foreign traders and limited the bargaining power of Haitian middlemen. They redistributed the peasant surplus among their cronies, and they provided luxuries to their families and friends."[30] To maintain support for his own presidency in the South, during Christophe's presidency and subsequent Kingdom in the North, Pétion distributed small plots from less desired lands to the masses. Such lands, the peasantry used for subsistence cultivation.[31] Moreover, through his policies and political maneuvers, Alexandre Pétion would ultimately prove to be more invested in European cultural assimilation and the stamp of approval from American and European powers of the time rather than in the nation's sustainable advancement. As an established practice, the foreign merchants benefited from the ruling class' extravagant and squandering spending and the state's growing financial dependence on foreign governments. As a consequence, foreign merchants, with the support of their respective governments, controlled Haiti's finances to the detriment of the nation's economy. One defining example of Pétion's acquiescence to foreign powers' self-entitled requests was the occurrence with New York merchant Jacob Lewis. Pétion invited Lewis—who left in bad terms with Emperor Dessalines—back to Haiti. As a condition, Lewis demanded money that he claimed the state owed him for what the emperor had recovered from him. In compliance, "Pétion issued a presidential decree ordering that all export crops from the plantations of Dessalines' widow be turned over to Lewis."[32] Pétion's compliance and complicity, which was the norm in his relations with foreign merchants, presaged Haiti's economic future. In the final analysis, Pétion was the first to disregard the forewarnings of the Liberator; he discounted the rudimentary precepts that should have guided the protection, the advancement, and the well-being of the nation.

One could analytically conclude that such blind quest for international validation—perhaps based on warped esteem of self and the nation—contributed to Pétion's acceptance of France's indemnity. Pétion's acceptance and Boyer's acquiescence to sign, in 1825, the indemnity France imposed on the new Black Republic set the nation-state on the road to economic dependence and ensuing political and social unrest. With Pétion's presidency—then Boyer—commenced overt exploitation by foreign powers and rampant corruption within the state. Such politico-economic modus operandi would prove to be a lasting and devastating practice. In *Walker's Appeal to the Coloured Citizens of the World, but in Particular, and Very Expressly, to Those of the United States of America*, Article II, titled "Our Wretchedness in Consequence of Ignorance," David Walker entreated African Americans to "remember the divisions and consequent sufferings of *Carthage* and of *Hayti*. Read the history particularly of Hayti."[33] David Walker's recommendation aimed to encourage African Americans to read and learn the history of Haiti's leadership pitfalls, given the circumstantial connections between

African descendants of the Americas. De Vastey's *Le Cri de la Patrie* (The Cry of the Nation), published in 1815, focuses solely on Pétion's complicity with the French. "Withered by ambition and hardened by crimes"[34] ("Flétri par l'ambition et endurci dans le crime"),[35] De Vastey argued, Pétion has always been a traitor to the African descendants in Saint-Domingue and a traitor of the Haitian people.[36] De Vastey considered that by unveiling the venal practices of the state—which include the complicity of the chief of state with external forces—the nation would be better equipped to safeguard its interests. "By unveiling the ills, we will be able to find the cure; and, an immediate and efficacious cure that could save us."[37] ("En découvrant le mal, nous pourrons en trouver le remède, et un remède prompt et efficace qui puisse nous sauver.")[38] While courage, integrity, and service were fundamental leadership precepts to Dessalines, he was aware of the forces and pressures with which the newly formed nation-state would have to contend. As such, he viewed his task of leading the new Black Republic as an equally onerous service and honorable responsibility. "By accepting this onus," he admitted, "as onerous as it is honorable, is also to hold myself responsible of the good and the bad that will come from my administration; however do not forget that it is during the most tempestuous times that you entrusted me with the rudder of the vessel of the State."[39] ("En acceptant enfin ce fardeau, aussi onéreux qu'honorable, c'est me charger de la somme du bien et du mal qui résultera de mon administration; mais n'oubliez pas que c'est dans les temps les plus orageux que vous m'avez confié le gouvernail du vaisseau de l'État.")[40]

Through his philosophies and actions, time has proven that Jean-Jacques Dessalines was a visionary. One of his most perspicacious and prophetic lines articulated in the "Procès-Verbal de la Proclamation de l'Indépendance d'Haïti" of 1804 remains: "We dared to be free, let us *dare to remain* free by us and for us."[41] ("Nous avons osé d'être libres, osons l'être par nous-mêmes et pour nous-mêmes.")[42] Stated differently, the message was: against all odds, the Africans accomplished the seemingly impossible and "dared" to take their freedom. On the one hand, it was Dessalines' response to the enslavers who believed they had the self-arrogated authorization to enslave Africans and exterminate those who refused to succumb to enslavement. That response foreshadows and sheds light on the price that Haiti continued to pay for "daring" to be free, in 1804. Above all, Dessalines wanted to convey the principles and practices of collective self-assertion, self-valorization, and self-confidence that conscientious succeeding figures of the Black Diaspora would continue to herald: "let us dare to *be/ remain* free by us and for us." The revolution and the eventual independence of the Africans and Mulattoes in Saint-Domingue were the manifestation of the "world's first radical democracy of transnational scope," Nick Nesbitt remarks in "The Idea of 1804." Haiti "presented freedom to the world as an absolutely true logic, one that must be made, in turn, universal reality: no humans can be enslaved."[43] I would modify Nesbitt's statement to assert: no human community will accept enslavement without indefatigable efforts toward freedom. As a case in point, during the Nat Turner Rebellion in August 1831 (in Southampton, Virginia),

> Nat Turner was fighting against what the Founding Fathers of [his] nation said they were fighting against—tyranny! He was fighting for what the Founding Fathers at least implied they were fighting for—Liberty and Justice for All—which ironically did not include Black people in its scope.[44]

Dessalines emerged as a leading general from the recurring liberation battles of the 13-year revolution in Saint-Domingue. As a young man, he first learned the arts of war and healing from Adbaraya Toya (Victoria Montou), an enslaved woman whom, in the tradition of African diasporic kinship in the Americas, Dessalines referred to as his aunt. Within the enslaved community, she was known as *Gran Toya* (short for Grandma Toya) or *Man Toya* (Mother—*Manman*—Toya). She was a skilled warrior who mastered the art of hand-to-hand combat and the throwing of knives during combats. She organized and led a few rebellions in Saint-Domingue, before the 1791 *Cérémonie du Bois-Caïman*. As a midwife and a healer, she taught Dessalines the wisdom of life and the importance of revolutionary disobedience, including resistance and persistence. Akin to *Man Toya*, Dessalines was strong-willed, astute, and with an innate opposition to subjugation. His commitment to liberty and justice led him to escape the plantation life a few times to live as a maroon. He was always found and brought back to the plantation, where he endured cruel punishments. Such unjust and brutal punishments only emboldened his conviction to secure the human and natural rights due not only to him but to his fellow Africans. For her lasting influence on Dessalines, Adbaraya Toya shall be remembered as the grandmother, mother, and aunt-figure who helped prepare the Liberator of African descendants enslaved throughout the Americas. Under the leadership of Toussaint Louverture, Dessalines further mastered his military acumen. As Dessalines fought for the ideals and fruition of freedom, he remained attentive to the perpetual danger the Blacks would endlessly face in losing their acquired freedom. In the months leading to Louverture's exile and subsequent death, Dessalines fortified his stand against the French scheme of re-enslavement, and manifested his characteristic consistency and fearlessness in the last strategies and battles for freedom. As Gérard M. Laurent accurately notes in his *Six Études sur J.J. Dessalines*, published in 1950, Dessalines further brought "dissimulation, fortitude, discipline, prudence, tact, and intelligence."[45] It was with his characteristics along with his methodic military organization that Dessalines conditioned himself and his followers to victory. Gérard Laurent's work examines the character and eminent accomplishments of Jean-Jacques Dessalines with an academic seriousness hitherto neglected. In the preface to his work, he lays bare the importance of studies on the philosophies and methods of Jean-Jacques Dessalines—the nation's Liberator. "A study of the organization of the second phase of the war of independence," Laurent explains, "evidences the delicate role Dessalines played, and the finesse of his intelligence. . . . The Liberator was not only a fiery warrior but also a leader rich in brilliant intellectual qualities."[46] ("Une étude sur l'organisation de la seconde phase de la guerre de l'Indépendance met en relief le rôle délicat joué par Dessalines et la finesse de son intelligence. . . . Le Libérateur ne fut pas uniquement un foudre de guerre, mais aussi un meneur riche de brillantes qualités intellectuelles.")[47]

In *The Second Crucifixion of Nat Turner*, John Henrik Clarke examines early White writers' disparaging and criminalizing constructions of the most influential Black revolutionaries such as Nat Turner, Jean-Jacques Dessalines, Marcus Garvey, and Malcolm X, among others. *The Second Crucifixion*, an edited text first published in 1968, gave voice to Black intellectuals who sought to revive Nat Turner from the assassination of his character, in the 1800s, and from the oppressors' manipulated and lasting narratives of criminalization in the 1900s. In the 1997 edition of *The Second Crucifixion* Clarke ponders the authentic role and mission of Nat Turner, who, similar to Dessalines,

> [early] in life . . . saw himself as a person with a mission—a mission to change the condition of slavery or destroy it if the means to do so were at his disposal. This mission was *part of his total existence*. . . . In a way, his resolve was a self-proclaimed priesthood . . . read the same bible his oppressors read, but gave it a new interpretation. . . . He concluded finally that a strike against slavery was an act of holiness.[48]

The numerous rebellions throughout the Americas, including Nat Turner's uprising and the revolutionary battles of Saint-Domingue, were inevitable responses to the conditions within which the Africans and their descendants were coerced and violently kept. Thus—as Dr. Clarke frames it—the "conflict did not grow out of their situation; conflict was inherent in the situation. That which was human in the slave *was always at war* with that in the master that breached the bounds of the human."[49] Similar to Dessalines, Turner endured the most inhumane treatments his enslavers could concoct. Their relentless acts of cruelty "inflamed the young slave, and he resolved upon having revenge."[50] From the narrative of those who new Nat Turner, William Wells Brown reports in *The Black Man: His Antecedents, His Genius, and His Achievements* that

> in his childhood Nat was of an amiable disposition; but circumstances in which he was placed as a slave, brought out incidents that created a change in his disposition, and turned his kind and docile feeling into the most intense hatred to the white race.[51]

The Strategies to Freedom

In 1814 King Christophe thought that it would be difficult for future generations to fathom the level and the unimaginable types of brutality the Africans endured from European enslavers. He wrote

> L'avenir aura peine à comprendre que dans un siècle de lumière où la philanthropie est généralement répandue parmi les hommes, une entreprise aussi abominable ait eu lieu; c'est du sein d'une nation éclairée *qu'est parti un essaim de barbares dans l'intention criminelle de détruire toute une nation civilisée et tranquille, ou de la replonger dans les fers de l'esclavage pour jamais.*[52]
>
> (Posterity will find it difficult to grasp that in a century of enlightenment, where philanthropy is generally spread among men, an enterprise so abominable took place; it is from the bosom of an enlightened nation *came a swarm of beasts with the criminal intention to destroy an entire civilized and peaceful nation, or to force it back into the irons of enslavement forever.*)[53]

It was with the resolve to break off the iron shackles of enslavement that the Africans in Saint-Domingue devised their strategies to liberation.

By 1792, roughly one year after the *Cérémonie du Bois-Caïman*, and roughly 35 years after the Makandal's uprising,[54] the revolted enslaved Africans returned to the hills and joined their temporary Spanish "allies." As the Europeans utilized the Africans as a means to establish their respective dominance, the Africans made use of the Europeans' feigned alliances as their own reverse strategy in their fight toward freedom. The alliances were formed based on which European power was conditionally providing assistance, bearing in mind that each European government's ephemeral assistance to the Africans was a scheme to gain or maintain control over competing European powers. In the midst of political maneuvers, the unrest in Saint-Domingue proved to the Whites, particularly to the French commissioner Léger-Félicité Sonthonax, the Africans' determination to put an end to their enslavement. Thus, "hemmed in on all sides and looking for support against the enemy at home and the enemy abroad," that is the Whites of the counter-revolution/the royalists, Sonthonax declared the abolition of slavery in his emancipation proclamation. "It was his last card and he could not help himself."[55] Sonthonax professed his declaration on August 29, 1793; the decree was sent to France for ratification and was indeed ratified in 1794 by the Assembly. However, most planters did not follow the legal abolition of slavery in Saint-Domingue, thus maintained Blacks in de facto enslavement; in addition, the economic and political structures remained intact components of the slavery system. "You say that you are free," a colonist derided. "Yet you are going to be forced to come back to my house and there I shall treat you as before and shall show you you are not free."[56] In the midst of social agitation, divisions, and contradictions, Sonthonax attempted to rally all the African descendants on his side, for the sake of his success as the commissioner; in political polemics, Sonthonax reminded the Africans of the Spaniards' duplicity. In his rhetoric, he associated slavery directly and solely to kingdoms, though slavery was in operation in all the colonies of the Americas: "Kings are only pleased in the midst of slaves," he claimed, "[The Spaniards] promise themselves to burden you with irons as soon as your services are no longer needed . . . they express liking today; they will become your first executioners."[57] ("Les rois ne se plaisent qu'au milieu des esclaves. [L'espagnol] se promet bien, au contraire, de vous charger de fer sitôt que vos services lui seront inutiles . . . ils vous caressent aujourd'hui; ils deviendraient vos premiers bourreaux.")[58] As the political manipulations continued, the Spaniards and the British negotiated to have the ex-slaves fight on their side for respective imperial power, with the false promise of safeguarding their freedom. The politic of the Spaniards, the French, and the British was the continuous use of the Blacks' manpower in battle, in order to gain imperial/expansive control of the colonies on the American continent. That method is the blueprint of the lasting approach of utilizing Blacks as *numbers* to political power and *means* to economic ends. The African officers were aware of the Europeans' scheme and tactically navigated their way out of slavery and subsequently safeguarded their own freedom.

In 1801 Toussaint Louverture published a constitution for Saint-Domingue, in which he asserted slavery as de facto and forever abolished. Sonthonax's proclamation did not offer true freedom for the Africans and their descendants, though it called for some modification in their treatments. A comparative perusal of excerpts from the two documents sheds light on their respective contents and implications.

Sonthonax's 1793 *Proclamation*:

> **Article IX.** Les nègres actuellement attachés aux habitations de leurs anciens maîtres, seront tenus d'y rester; ils seront employés à la culture de la terre.
>
> (The Negroes who are currently bonded to the plantations of their former masters, must stay there; they will be used to work the soil.)[59]
>
> **Article XI.** Les ci-devant esclaves cultivateurs seront engagés pour un an, pendant lequel temps ils ne pourront changer d'habitation que sur une permission des juges de paix, dont il sera parlé ci-après, & dans les cas qui seront pour nous déterminés.
>
> (The heretofore slave laborers will be committed for one year during which time they will not be able to change plantation unless the judges of peace grant a permission, that will be talked about afterwards, and in cases that will be determined by us.)
>
> **Article XXIX.** Les cultivateurs ne pourront être contraints de travailler le dimanche: il leur sera laissé deux heures par jour pour la culture de leur place. Les juges de paix régleront, suivant les circonstances, l'heure à laquelle les travaux devront commencer et finir.

(The laborers cannot be constrained to work on Sundays: they will be given two hours per day for the cultivation of their plot. The judges of peace will work out, depending on the circumstances, the time the labors should commence and end.)[60]

Toussaint Louverture's *Saint-Domingue Constitution of 1801*:

Article 3. Il ne peut exister d'esclaves sur ce territoire, la servitude y est à jamais abolie. Tous les hommes y naissent, vivent et meurent libres et Français.

(There can no longer be slaves on this territory; servitude is forever abolished. All who are born [on this territory] are to live and die free and French.)[61]

Article 4. Tout homme, quelle que soit sa couleur, y est admissible à tous les emplois.

(All men, regardless of skin color, are permitted to all positions.)

Article 5. Il n'y existe d'autre distinction que celle des vertus et des talents, et d'autre supériorité que celle que la loi donne dans l'exercice d'une fonction publique. La loi est la même pour tous, soit qu'elle punisse, soit qu'elle protège.

(There cannot be further distinctions other than those of virtues and talents, nor any other superiority than what the law grants in order to exercise a public function. The law is the same for all, whether it punishes or protects.)[62]

In 1802, after the Treaty of Amiens, Napoléon Bonaparte set out to reestablish slavery in the French colonies of America. Having lost his chances for India, Bonaparte prepared to reestablish slavery in Saint-Domingue. Toussaint's Constitution, a declaration of humanity and autonomy, solidified Bonaparte's plans of re-enslavement. Bonaparte prepared and published in 1802 *Loi: Relative à la traite des Noirs et au régime des colonies* (Law: Regarding the slave trade and the government of the colonies).[63] The articles unequivocally set out to relegitimize the enslavement of the Africans and their descendants.

Art. I. Dans les colonies restituées à la France en exécution du traité d'Amiens, du 6 germinal an X, l'esclavage sera maintenu conformément aux lois et réglemens *antérieurs à 1789*.[64]

(In all the colonies that were given back to France, as implementation of the treaty of Amiens, in March of 1802, slavery will be maintained in accordance with the laws and regulations *prior to 1789*).[65]

II. Il en sera de même dans les autres colonies françaises au-delà du Cap de Bonne-Espérance.

(It will be the same in the other French colonies beyond Cap de Bonne-Espérance.)

III. La traite des noirs et leur importation dans lesdites colonies, auront lieu, *conformément aux lois et réglemens existans avant ladite époque de 1789.*

(The slave trade and the importation [of Africans] to the said colonies will take place *in accordance with the laws and regulations existing before the said epoch of 1789.*)

IV. Nonobstant toutes les lois antérieures, le régime des colonies est soumis, pendant dix ans, aux réglemens qui seront faits par le Gouvernemens.

(Notwithstanding all previous laws, the regime of the colonies is acquiescent, for ten years, to the regulations drawn up by the Government.)

Bonaparte sent Leclerc as the commander of the expedition employed to destroy the Africans' revolution, by any means. Leclerc was instructed to initially treat Louverture, Dessalines, and Moïse with feigned respect and to coax the generals who have displayed some level of admiration for European culture, among whom was Christophe. Bonaparte did not believe that the three leading generals—Louverture, Dessalines, and Moïse—would fall prey to Leclerc's duplicity. In the event of such skepticism and resistance, Bonaparte instructed that those men be treated as traitors. They should be "hunted down by 'a war to the death,' and if captured shot within 24 hours. This would end the second period."[66] He further instructed that anyone a French official deems *suspicious*—whether in perception or reality—was to be arrested. After all the African generals are killed or deported, and the gendarmerie was comprised of only Whites, then the colony would be ready for the "special laws" of re-enslavement.[67] In *Manifeste du Roi*, Christophe reflects on the Machiavellian mindset and actions of the French enslavers:

Ils n'ont rien négligé pour atteindre leur exécrable but . . . il nous disait: *Vous êtes tous égaux et libres devant Dieu et devant la République.* Tandis que les instructions du général Leclerc étaient formelles pour l'esclavage. Ce n'était pas assez de prendre les hommes à témoins de son parjure, il fallait encore insulter la Divinité, en l'interpellant par un horrible blasphème.[68]

Pour mieux y parvenir, *on résolut d'arrêter le gouverneur Toussaint Louverture; on fabriqua une correspondance (inventée par des rédacteurs mercenaires et machiavéliques)* . . . dans l'instant où il reposait sur la foi des traités; chargé de chaînes, il fut jeté avec sa famille à bord du vaisseau le Héros, et transporté en France. L'Europe entière est instruite comment il termina sa carrière infortunée dans les supplices et les horreurs des cachots du Château de Joux en Franche-Comté. Telle fut la récompense qui lui était réservée pour son attachement et pour les grands et éminens services qu'il avait rendus à la France et aux colons.[69]

[T]ous ceux qui avaient montré de la force d'âme, de l'érudition ou du caractère *à l'époque où nous avons revendiqués les droits de l'homme*, furent les premiers arrêtés; ils n'épargnèrent pas même les traîtres qui avaient le mieux favorisés le succès des armées françaises.[70]

(They didn't neglect anything to attain their execrable goal . . . they would tell us: *You are equal and free to God and the Republic.* At the same time general Leclerc's instructions for enslavement were official. It was not enough to hold men witness to their perjury, but they also had to insult Divinity, by convoking it into a horrible blasphemy.[71]

To better reach the goal, *they resolved to arrest the governor Toussaint Louverture; they fabricated a correspondence (invented by mercenary and Machiavellian writers)* . . . in the very moment that he puts his faith in the treaties, he was enchained and thrown, with his family, aboard the ship the Héros, and transported to France. All of Europe was informed about how his unfortunate career ended in tortures and the horrors of the dungeons of the Château de Joux in Franche-Comté. That was the recompense that was reserved for his commitment and for the outstanding and eminent services that he rendered to France and to the colonists.

All those who showed fortitude, erudition or character during *the epoch that we demanded the rights of men* were the first to be arrested; they didn't even spare the traitors that best helped further the success of the French army.)[72]

The traitors to whom King Christophe referred were the *gens de couleur* generals, André Rigaud, Alexandre Pétion, and Jean-Pierre Boyer, who arrived with Leclerc's expedition with the expectation of assuming favorable positions within the colony of Saint-Domingue's racist and colorist hierarchy. Once Rigaud, Pétion, and Boyer realized Bonaparte's ultimate plan for all African descendants irrespective of skin color, and once they gauged the strength of Dessalines' leadership (military acumen and bravery), Pétion and Boyer joined Dessalines' ranks, and Rigaud returned to France. Dessalines had assumed leadership of the battles for freedom immediately after Toussaint's arrest and deportation. Leclerc died after months of arduous battles, loss of soldiers, sickness, and desperation; as his replacement, Bonaparte sent Vicomte de Rochambeau. While Bonaparte was in France with his negative conception of Blackness, Leclerc was in Saint-Domingue with his lived experiences of the African descendants' psychological disposition and physical strength. Similar to Sonthonax, Leclerc grasped the Africans' unyielding resolve for their human freedom. Before his death, Leclerc wrote to France to assert that a war of extermination was the approach that will force the remaining African descendants into re-enslavement; given that re-enslavement was Bonaparte's ultimate mission, the French commanders and soldiers arrived with the decision to exterminate. The war of extermination that Bonaparte Napoléon undertook in Saint-Domingue exemplifies the enslavers' mindset that two African descendant figures—Marcus Mosiah Garvey and Carter G. Woodson, among others—would later theorize. In 1920 Garvey wrote, "[they] subjugate first, if the weaker peoples will stand for it; then exploit, and if [the weaker people] will not stand for SUBJUGATION nor EXPLOITATION, the other recourse is EXTERMINATION."[73] In 1933, in reference to the practice of lynching during the slavery and post-slavery era in the United States, Woodson underlined the enslavers' perspective and actions: "why not exploit, enslave or exterminate a class that everybody is taught to regard as inferior?"[74]

From 1802 to 1803, Rochambeau, the manslayer who embodied unimaginable fiendishness, was the ideal headman for the war of extermination on the African descendants in Saint-Domingue. In a trenchant description recorded in *Manifeste du Roi*, King Christophe recounts Napoléon's barbarity and Rochambeau's fiendishness:

> Au gouvernement de Leclerc, succéda celui de Rochambeau, ce montre agent de Bonaparte, digne complice des colons, se souilla de tous les crimes; il n'épargnera ni le sexe, ni l'enfance, ni la vieillesse; il surpassa en cruauté les plus profonds scélérats des temps antiques et modernes, les gibets élevés de toutes parts, les noyades, les bûchers, les plus horribles supplices furent mis en exécution par ses ordres; au lieu de bateaux à soupapes, il en inventa d'une autre espèce, où les victimes des deux sexes, entassées les unes sur les autres, expiraient étouffées par les vapeurs du soufre.[75]
>
> (To the governance of Leclerc succeeded Rochambeau's, this monster agent of Bonaparte and worthy accomplice of the colonists, tainted himself with all crimes; he did not spare gender, nor childhood, nor old age; in cruelty, he surpassed the most villainous scoundrels of antiquity and modern times; the gallows were erected everywhere, the drownings, the stakes, the most horrible tortures were executed from his orders; in lieu of boats with valves, he invented another type, where the victims of both sexes, piled up one on top of the other, died suffocated by the vapors of the sulfur.)[76]

Recollecting the atrocities of Rochambeau, who was determined to exterminate a race that refused to be enslaved, Dessalines wrote with unwavering conviction in his Proclamation, *Liberté ou la Mort*: "Yes, we have rendered these *true cannibals*, war for war, crimes for crimes, outrage for outrage."[77] ("Oui, nous avons rendu à ces *vrais cannibales*, guerre pour guerre, crimes pour crimes, outrages pour outrages.")[78] The emphasis on "*true cannibals*" (the original/true cannibals) is crucial as it addresses—as examined in Chapter 2 of the present work, in reference to Aimé Césaire and Joy DeGruy—the extent to which European enslavers projected their own barbaric behaviors onto the Africans and concocted lasting stereotypes of the so-called "African barbarity." Dessalines' "Procès Verbal," Baron De Vastey's *Le Système Colonial Dévoilé* (The Colonial System Unveiled) and *Réflexions sur une Lettre de Mazères* (Reflexions on a Letter from Mazères), and King Christophe's *Manifeste du Roi* (along with the enslavers' and colonists' own records of the slavery system), all unveil the utter bestiality—the diabolic nature—of the enslavers and colonists of the fifteenth century to the twentieth century. As Rochambeau fought on behalf of French economic greed and impudence, Dessalines fought for human freedom and dignity. Dessalines asserted,

> Oui, j'ai sauvé ma patrie; j'ai vengé l'Amérique . . . Qu'importe le jugement que prononceront sur moi les races contemporaines ou futures? J'ai fait mon devoir, ma propre estime me reste; il me suffit. Mais que dis-je? La conservation de mes malheureux frères, le témoignage de ma conscience ne sont pas ma seule récompense.[79]
>
> (Yes, I have saved my country; I avenged America . . . What is it to me the judgement that contemporary and future generations will express? I completed my duty; I am left with my self-respect; that is enough for me. What am I saying? The preservation of my wretched brothers, and the affirmation of my conscience, are they not my only recompense.)[80]

Dessalines' pronouncement further sheds light on his courage, confidence, humility, and integrity; having acknowledged that he met his responsibility and has saved his patrimony, the judgment of others—contemporary or future—does not matter. The preservation of his race and the peace with his conscience were, to him, of significance; for, he responded to and completed his life's purpose or mission.

Building on Dessalines' own affirmation of "the laws the spirit who keeps watch over [the African descendants'] destiny has commanded [him] for [their] happiness,"[81] Laurent notes in his chapter "L'Âme d'un Libérateur" (The Soul of a Liberator) of *Six Études*, "Destiny assigned a mission to Jean-Jacques Dessalines that he had to accomplish: give freedom back to the Blacks . . . to complete that goal he had to be tenacious and intrepid, ferocious and indomitable."[82] ("Jean-Jacques Dessalines avait à remplir une mission que lui assigna le destin: rendre indépendants les noirs . . . pour atteindre ces fins il lui fallait être téméraire et intrépide, épouvantable et indomptable.")[83] In the same vein, C.L.R. James remarks in *The Black Jacobins* that Dessalines "deserves his place among the heroes of human emancipation. He was a soldier, a magnificent soldier, and had no other pretensions."[84] James further analyzes that "Dessalines was a one-sided genius, but he was the man for the crisis, not Toussaint. He gave blow for blow."[85] In *De L'Égalité des Races Humaines*, Firmin studies not only the contribution of ancient Africa to world evolution but also the contributions of African descendants. Jean-Jacques Dessalines stands as the first successful defender and liberator of an entire race. "We must honor the memory of that iron man who was endowed with unparalleled bravery as well as the temperament of a defender and the heroism of a liberator."[86] ("Il faut bien honorer la mémoire de cet homme de fer qui unissait à une bravoure sans égale le tempérament du justicier et l'héroïsme du libérateur.")[87]

While Dessalines' military valiance and leadership brilliance deserve lasting honor and acknowledgment, it remains irrefutably clear that the descendants of Africa in the Americas owe their freedom to the collective commitment and methods of both Toussaint Louverture and Jean-Jacques Dessalines, as well as to all the fighters of the revolution—men and women. Dessalines' and Louverture's differing temperaments and approaches led to the dismantlement of the enslavement system. Saint-Domingue became the ground of a race war raged out of Bonaparte's rapaciousness, audacity, and fiendishness. "Thousands of brave black soldiers were dead for no other crime than that of refusing to be slaves once more."[88] In *Réflexions*, De Vastey sums up the absurdity and, most importantly, the inhumanity of such carnage. He wrote:

> [Si] les hommes se sont arrogé le droit de réduire d'autres hommes dans le plus barbare esclavage, ceux-ci n'auraient-ils pas le droit de briser leurs fers? Quoi? Vous pourriez me priver de la liberté, me ravir le plus précieux de tous les biens; vous pourriez me charger d'indignes fers, et moi, votre frère et votre semblable, je ne pourrai me revendiquer les droits que je tiens de Dieu seul, que nul ne peut me ravir . . . quelle logique abominable! quelle affreuse moralité! Que de vouloir admettre en principe que la liberté est un mal, et que l'esclavage est un bien; de vouloir persuader aux hommes que les uns auraient le droit de réduire les autres dans un perpétuel esclavage, sans que ceux-ci n'auraient le droit de pouvoir jamais en sortir![89]
>
> ([If] some men arrogated the right to reduce other men into the most barbaric slavery system, wouldn't the latter have the right to dismantle their irons? What? You could deprive me of my freedom, rob me of the most precious of all gifts; you could burden me with undignified irons, and I, your brother and your fellow-man, could not reclaim the rights I received from God only, of which no man can rob me. . . . What an abominable logic! What an atrocious morality! To want to assume that, in principle, liberty is bad and that slavery is a gift; to want to persuade mankind that some had the right to reduce others to a perpetual enslavement with the latter not having the right to ever liberate themselves!)[90]

In 1829–1830, in *Appeal to the Coloured Citizens of the World*, David Walker posed a series of questions that reinforced De Vastey's 1814–1816 published reflections. "Are We Men!!," Walker questioned:

> O my brethren! Are we MEN? Did our Creator make us to be slaves to dust and ashes like ourselves? Are they not dying worms as well as we? Have they not to make their appearance before the tribunal of Heaven, to answer for the deeds done in the body, as well as we? Have we any other

> Master but Jesus Christ alone? Is he not their Master as well as ours?—What right then, have we to obey and call any other Master, but Himself? How we could be so *submissive* to a gang of men, whom we cannot tell whether they are *as good* as ourselves or not, I never could conceive. However, this is shut up with the Lord, and we cannot precisely tell—but I declare, we judge men by their works.[91]

The many battles and wars the African descendants fought, then, as Nat Turner reminded his followers during the speech that psychologically prepared his followers before their actions, "is not for robbery and to satisfy [their] passion; it is a struggle for freedom." "Ours," he impressed, "must be deeds, and not words."[92]

King Christophe's Appeal to the World

1) Nous espérons que le retour des pensées libérales et restauratrices qui animent les puissances européennes, les porteront à reconnaître l'indépendance d'un peuple qui ne demande qu'à jouir de la paix et du commerce, qui est le but et la fin de toutes les nations civilisées. . . . Nous ne pouvons plus être victimes de notre crédulité et de notre bonne foi; nous ne pouvons oublier que l'on a déjà voulu nous ravir la liberté . . .[93]
   (We hope that the return to the liberal and restorative thoughts that drive the European powers will lead them to recognize the independence of a nation that only demands peace and commerce, which is the goal and the end of all civilized nations. . . . We can no longer be victims of our credulity and our good faith; we cannot forget that they have already wanted to rob us of our freedom. . .)[94]
2) Nous en appelons aux philantropes de toutes les nations, à tous les hommes enfin, à l'univers entier, quel peuple après vingt-cinq ans de combats et de sang répandu, ayant conquis la liberté et son indépendance, consentirait à déposer les armes pour devenir encore le jouet et la victime de ses cruels oppresseurs? Nous le demandons, quel peuple souscrirait à cet excès d'avilissement? . . .[95]
   (We call on philanthropists of all nations, on all men, ultimately, on the entire universe; after twenty-five years of battles and bloodshed, and having conquered its freedom and independence, what nation would consent to put down its arms in order to become, once again, the toy and victim of its cruel oppressors? We ask, what nation would accept this level of abasement? . . .)[96]
3) C'est dans les circonstances favorables où les pensées libérales et restauratrices semblent prévaloir sur ces temps désastreux, où les peuples gémissaient sous l'oppression où nous voyons les souverains de l'Europe s'occuper maintenant du bonheur de leurs peuples, que nous croyons devoir *faire entendre notre voix, pour justifier, au tribunal des nations, la légitimité de notre indépendance.* Un simple exposé de faits, une simple narration des événemens qui nous amenés

à l'indépendance, suffiront pour démontrer jusqu'à l'évidence, nos droits et la justice de notre cause à l'univers entier.[97]

(It is in the favorable circumstances when liberal and innovative thoughts seem to prevail over those disastrous times, when nations were groaning under oppression, that we see the sovereignties of Europe focusing on the happiness of their own people, we believe we should *make our voice heard, to justify, to the tribunal of nations, the legitimacy of our independence.* A simple unveiling of the truths, a simple narration of the events that led us to independence, will suffice to prove with evidence, to the entire world, our rights and the justice of our cause.)[98]

4) Nous ne pouvons plus être trompés, nous connaissons la perversité de nos ennemis; nous avons sous nos yeux les mémoires et les projets des nommés Malouet, Barré de Saint Venant, des Pages et des Brulley, et de tant d'autres colons; *la religion politique de ces marchands de chair humaine*, de ces conseillers de malheurs, nous est bien connus, *l'esclavage et la destruction.* Nous n'ignorons pas les trames criminelles et les moyens honteux de ces apôtres du crime et du mensonge; ils nous ont assez enseignés par leurs écrits, plus que par les tortures mêmes que nous avons endurées, que la seule solide garantie de nos droits politiques, *de notre existence même*, tient à la conservation de notre indépendance.[99]

(We can no longer be duped; we know the pervertedness of our enemies. We have before our eyes the memories and the projects of such men as Malouet, Barré de Saint Venant, the Pages and the Brulleys, and so many other colonists; we are well aware of *the religion of politics for these merchants of human flesh*, for these counselors of trouble, *slavery and destruction.* We are aware of the criminal associations and the ignoble methods of these apostles of crime; they have sufficiently taught us, more so through their writings than even through the tortures that we have endured, that the only and solid security of our political rights, *of our existence even*, is the preservation of our independence.)[100]

The writings of such figures as Louverture, Dessalines, Christophe, and De Vastey (to stay within the context of the newly formed Black Republic's first decade of the 1800s) uncover the facts of their *own* condition and offer their *own* examinations as "témoin[s] oculaire et auriculaire" ("ocular and auricular witness").[101] Their works relate their lived condition to the contemporary circumstances of Africans throughout the Americas. Rooted in accounts of lived experiences, the rudimentary study of those writings lays bare the origins of contemporary hierarchies. Without such knowledge, there will remain the persistent vacuum in the understanding of current sociopolitical structures and policies. In his 1814 manifesto (*Manifeste du Roi*), King Christophe explains:

La *faction* orgueilleuse et liberticide des colons et des vendeurs de chair humaine. . . . C'est cette *faction* enfin qui a fait couler des flots de sang de

> nos compatriotes; c'est elle qui a été l'instigatrice des supplices inouïs que nous avons éprouvés; *ces supplices affreux ne pouvaient être inventés que par des colons, endurcis et habitués dans tous les genres de crimes*; c'est aux colons à qui la France est redevable de la perte d'une nombreuse armée, qui a terminé ses destins dans les plaines et les mornes d'Hayti; c'est enfin à ceux à qui elle est redevable de cette honteuse entreprise qui a imprimé une tache indélébile au nom français.[102]
>
> (The arrogant and *liberticide faction* of the colonists and traffickers of human flesh. . . . It is that *faction*, alas, who have shed floods of the blood of our compatriots. It is that group who was the instigator of the unprecedented torture inflicted on us; *these abominable tortures could only be invented by colonists, hardened and accustomed to all types of crimes*; it is to the colonists that France owes the loss of a numerous army, that met its destiny in the plains and mountains of Hayti; it is finally because of them that France owns this shameful undertaking that has imprinted an indelible stain on the name of the French.)[103]

At the outset, one would note King Christophe's sagacious observations in his discerning examination of the types of French and, by extension, the various types of Europeans. His keen and precise analysis—an approach notable in the writings of Black intellectuals such as De Vastey, C.L.R. James, and Césaire, to name a few—is contrary to the racial generalizations found in the writings of Europeans (and European descendants) of their era. Most importantly, the incisive written words of King Christophe and Baron De Vastey are recorded as the first African responses—in the genre of manifesto—to the unremitting terror and defamatory writings against Africans and their descendants. In *The Black Jacobins*, C.L.R. James reminds his readers of the enslavers' foremost ideology and objective: prosperity. Thus, the relentless calumnious writings had as the main objective the justification of terrorizing extortion. Akin to *Réflexions* and *Le Système Colonial Dévoilé*, the purpose of King Christophe's manifesto is to simultaneously reveal and document.[104] Without the awareness of, accessibility to, and the perusal of the memoirs, speeches, letters, manifestos, and monographs of the advocators of natural rights and human rights in the Americas (of *all* humans' rights), the existential dilemma of African descendants will continue to be perplexing and seemingly irreversible. Historical knowledge has proven that the purported irreversibility of current conditions is the manifestation of insatiable economic interests and the lack of good will to repair and resolve centuries of devastation. Ultimately, it was to counter such destructive mindset and fiendish practices that the earlier fighters of human rights advocated that above economic interests and politically motivated allegiances to race, nation, religion, and gender *ought to be* the essential allegiance to humankind, the allegiance to the well-being of humankind. In *De L'Égalité*, Firmin calls to attention the revolutionary and transformative effects of Haiti's Proclamation of Independence. One can affirm, Firmin declares, that

> la proclamation de l'Indépendance d'Haïti a positivement influé sur le sort de toute la race éthiopienne, vivant hors de l'Afrique. Du même coup, elle a changé le régime économique et moral de toutes les puissances européennes possédant des colonies; sa réalisation a aussi pesé sur l'économie intérieure de toutes les nations américaines entretenant le système de l'esclavage.[105]
>
> (the proclamation of Haiti's Independence has positively influenced the circumstance of the entire Ethiopian race, living outside of Africa. At the same time, it has changed the economic and moral regime of all the European powers withholding colonies; its realization has also weighed on the internal economy of all the American [continent] nations that are continuing with the slavery system.)[106]

Notes

1. C.L.R. James, *The Black Jacobins* (New York: Vintage Books, 1989), 45.
2. Ibid., 288.
3. Ibid., 288.
4. Author's translation.
5. Jean-Jacques Dessalines, "Procès-Verbal De La Proclamation De L'Indépendance D'Haïti," *Mémoires Pour Servir à L'Histoire D'Haïti*, edited by Louis Boisrond-Tonnerre (Paris: France, Libraire, 1851), 3.
6. In December 1804—two months after Dessalines' coronation—Napoléon Bonaparte crowned himself the emperor of France, the first emperor of the French people. However, Napoléon had declared himself emperor since May 1804, four months before Dessalines declared himself emperor of Haiti.
7. Dessalines, "Procès-Verbal," 3–7. Emphasis added.
8. Author's translation. Emphasis added.
9. Author's translation.
10. King Henry Christophe (Roi Henry 1er), *Manifeste du Roi* (Cap-Henry: Chez P. Roux, Imprimeur du Roi, 1814), 15.
11. Further accounts of various plots of division can be read in James, *The Black Jacobins*, 202, 222–223, and 350.
12. Author's translation. Emphasis added.
13. King Christophe, *Manifeste du Roi*, 3.
14. Author's translation. Emphasis added.
15. King Christophe, *Manifeste du Roi*, 5. Emphasis added.
16. James, *The Black Jacobins*, 350. Emphasis added.
17. Haiti's national anthem is the poetic composition of Justin Lhérsison and the musical composition of Nicolas Géffrard.
18. Author's translation.
19. Justin Lhérisson and Nicolas Géffard, *La Dessalinienne* (Haiti, 1903).
20. Jean-Jacques Dessalines, *Constitution Impériale de 20 Mai, 1805.* (Le Cap: Chez P. Roux, Imprimeur du Gouvernement, 1805).
21. Author's translation.

22. Jean-Jacques Dessalines, *Liberté ou La Mort. Proclamation. Jean-Jacques Dessalines, Gouverneur Général Aux Haibitans D'Haïti* (Le Cap: Chez P. Roux, Imprimeur du Gouvernement, 1804).
23. Author's translation. Emphasis added.
24. Dessalines, "Procès-Verbal," 4. Emphasis added.
25. Author's translation.
26. Dessalines, "Procès-Verbal," 5.
27. Dessalines, *Liberté ou La Mort.* Readers may also consult *Article 12* of the Imperial Constitution of 1805.
28. The Coat of Arms (*L'Union Fait La Force*) was adopted in 1807, after Dessalines' assassination.
29. Henry Christophe began to reign as King Henry 1er from 1811 until his death in October 1820.
30. Michel-Rolph Trouillot, *Haiti: State Against Nation, The Origins and Legacy of Duvalierism* (New York: Monthly Review Press, 1990), 64.
31. The prosperity and challenges of Christophe's governance is examined in *Literary and Sociopolitical Writings of the Black Diaspora*, Chapter 7.
32. Trouillot, *Haiti: State*, 70.
33. David Walker, *Appeal, in Four Articles; Together With a Preamble, to the Coloured Citizens of the World, but in Particular, and Very Expressly, to Those of the United States of America* (Bedford: Applewood Books, 1830), 23.
34. Author's translation.
35. Pompée Valentin Baron De Vastey, *Le Cri De La Patrie* (Cap-Henry: Chez P. Roux, Imprimeur du Roi, 1815), 7.
36. Ibid., 7.
37. Author's translation.
38. De Vastey, *Le Cri*, 7.
39. Author's translation.
40. Dessalines, "Procès-Verbal," 10.
41. Author's translation. Emphasis added.
42. Dessalines, "Procès-Verbal," 5.
43. Nick Nesbitt, "The Idea of 1804," *Yale French Studies*, The Haiti Issue: 1804 and Nineteenth-Century French Studies no. 107 (2005): 7–8.
44. John Henrik Clarke, *The Second Crucifixion of Nat Turner* (Baltimore: Black Classic Press, 1968, 1997), Introduction, 3.
45. Gérard M. Laurent, *Six Études sur J.J. Dessalines* (Port-au-Prince: Les Presses Libres, 1950), 22.
46. Author's translation.
47. Laurent, *Six Études*, 7.
48. Clarke, *The Second Crucifixion of Nat Turner*, Introduction, 4. Emphasis added.
49. Ibid., 4. Emphasis added.
50. William Wells Brown, *The Black Man: His Antecedents, His Genius, and His Achievements* (Boston: James Redpath, Publisher, 1863), 59.
51. Ibid., 59.
52. King Christophe, *Manifeste du Roi*, 4–6. Emphasis added.
53. Author's translation. Emphasis added.
54. François Mackandal was known as a *bossal*; that is, he was born in Africa and transported—on the slave ship—to the continent of America. In 1758 he was tortured and executed by the French, after he led an uprising against enslavement.
55. James, *The Black Jacobins*, 128–129.
56. Ibid., 262.
57. Author's translation.

58. Léger-Félicité Sonthonax, *Proclamation* (Cap-Français: Imprimerie de P. Gatineau, 1793).
59. Author's translation.
60. Sonthonax, *Proclamation*.
61. Author's translation.
62. Louis Joseph Janvier, *Les Constitutions d'Haïti 1801–1885* (Paris: C. Marpon et E. Flammarion, 1886).
63. Author's translation.
64. Napoléon Bonaparte, Premier Consul, *Loi du 30 Floréal An X. Relative à la traite des Noirs et au régime des colonies* (Paris, 1802). Emphasis added.
65. Author's translation. Emphasis added.
66. Janvier, *Les Constitutions d'Haïti*, 292.
67. Ibid., 293.
68. King Christophe, *Manifeste du Roi*, 5. Emphasis added.
69. Ibid., 6. Emphasis added.
70. Ibid., 6–7. Emphasis added.
71. Author's translation. Emphasis added.
72. Author's translation. Emphasis added.
73. Marcus Garvey, *The Philosophy and Opinions of Marcus Garvey* (Dover: The Majority Press, 1986), 13.
74. Carter G. Woodson, *The Mis-Education of the Negro* (Washington, DC: The Association for the Study of African American Life and History, 1933), 4.
75. King Christophe, *Manifeste du Roi*, 11.
76. Author's translation.
77. Author's translation. Emphasis added.
78. Dessalines, *Liberté ou La Mort*. Emphasis added.
79. Ibid.
80. Author's translation.
81. Dessalines, "Procès-Verbal," 3–7.
82. Author's translation.
83. Laurent, *Six Études*, 15.
84. James, *The Black Jacobins*, 353.
85. Ibid., 361.
86. Author's translation.
87. Anténor Firmin, *De L'Égalité Des Races Humaines: Anthropologie Positive* (Paris: Librairie Cotillon, 1885), 544.
88. James, *The Black Jacobins*, 355.
89. Pompée Valentin Baron De Vastey, *Réflexions sur une lettre de Mazères, ex-colon français, adressée à M.J.C.L. Sismonde De Sismondi, sur les Noirs et les Blancs, la Civilisation de l'Afrique, le Royaume d'Hayti, etc.* (Cap-Henry: Chez P. Roux, Imprimeur du Roi, 1816), 93.
90. Author's translation.
91. Walker, *Appeal*, 19.
92. Brown, *The Black Man*, 64.
93. King Christophe, *Manifeste du Roi*, 14.
94. Author's translation.
95. King Christophe, *Manifeste du Roi*, 15.
96. Author's translation.
97. King Christophe, *Manifeste du Roi*, 2. Emphasis added.
98. Author's translation. Emphasis added.
99. King Christophe, *Manifeste du Roi*, 15. Emphasis added.
100. Author's translation. Emphasis added.

101. De Vastey, *Réflexions*, 97.
102. King Christophe, *Manifeste du Roi*, 8–9. Emphasis added.
103. Author's translation. Emphasis added.
104. Pompée Valentin Baron De Vastey, *Le Système Colonial Dévoilé* (Cap-Henry: Chez P. Roux, Imprimeur du Roi, 1814).
105. Firmin, *De L'Égalité*, 590.
106. Author's translation.

4

AFRICA'S LEGACY OF INGENUITY AND BEAUTY IN THE WRITINGS OF MARTIN DELANY, ANTÉNOR FIRMIN, AND CHEIKH ANTA DIOP

The affirmation of the Black aesthetics, of the late twentieth century onward, was built on centuries of historical and cultural restoration on the parts of intellectuals, scholars, artists, and activists. The "Black Is Beautiful" Movement and the Black Arts Movement of the 1960s derived from both the cultural and political legacies of the first half of the 1900s: namely, the New Negro Renaissance, the Pan-African Movement, the Garvey Movement, the Négritude Movement, and the Black Internationalist philosophy. The historical, anthropological, and philosophical works of such figures as Martin Delany (the United States), Anténor Firmin (Haiti), and Cheikh Anta Diop (Sénégal) provided the foundational research, analyses, and ensuing knowledge that were necessary to reclaim the African past and contribute to the intellectual regeneration of African descendants. In 1879 (with a revised edition in 1880), Delany published *Principia of Ethnology: The Origin of Races and Color, With an Archeological Compendium of Ethiopian and Egyptian Civilization, From Years of Careful Examination and Enquiry*. Firmin published *De L'Égalité des Races Humaines: Anthropologie Positive* in 1885 (*Of the Equality of the Human Races: Positive Anthropology*).[1] Diop published *Nations Nègres et Culture* in 1954 (*Negro Nations and Culture*)[2] and subsequently published *Antériorité Des Civilisations Nègres: Mythe ou Vérité Historique* in 1967 (*Anteriority of the Negro Civilizations: Myth or Historical Truth*).[3] In addition to the comprehensive anthropological, ethnological, historical, and philosophical methods of Delany's and Firmin's body of work, the later cultural anthropological works of Jean Price-Mars (Haiti) and Zora Neale Hurston (the United States)—with their particular focus on language, spiritualism, and religion—began to assert the representation of folk culture in the literary and academic realms. Among other writers engaged in the cultural redemption of the African heritage in the Americas, Price-Mars and Hurston began to transmit the authentic voice and traditions of the masses, by illustrating the various aspects of their lives. Their works unveil: one, that the customs of African traditions are apparent in the Americas in the African descendants' spirituality and their creolized manifestation of the mysteries of the African continent, in their linguistic rhythm and expressions, in their dance, food, their wisdom, and the general philosophies of life; two, Price-Mars' and Hurston's writings honor the efforts of African descendants to rise from economic and cultural subjugation, in order to fulfill their potential as valued citizens; and three, for the purpose of psychological recalibration and lasting social transformation and progress, their texts also present the adverse cultural behaviors developed from the circumstances of enslavement and systems of exploitation.[4] From the works of the aforementioned, the global sociopolitical and arts movements of the 1960s were armed with the truths that were studied and revealed by their predecessors. Such studies unveiled the long historical trajectory of African descendants, from ancient Africa to their contemporary conditions.

This chapter focuses on the pioneering and formative publications of Martin Delany, Anténor Firmin, and Cheikh Anta Diop, in connection with the continuous reclamation of the African past and the rehabilitation process of African descendants. The highlight that Delany, Firmin, and Diop draw on Black Egypt civilization was not to negate the invaluable social, political, and cultural contributions of the other regions of the continent; instead, their focus was part of the necessary process of reclamation and repossession of the African past. Given that the ancient Egyptians were Negroes, "the moral fruit of their civilization is to be counted *among the assets* of the Black world."[5] Ancient Egypt is/was not the only asset to world contribution and to the legacy of African descendants, but it is part of their complete historical past. It is with complete knowledge that one can have "genuine retrieval" of oneself. "To his great surprise," the African "will discover that most of the ideas used today to domesticate, atrophy, dissolve, or steal his 'soul,' were conceived by his own ancestors."[6] The scholarly works of Delany, Diop, and Firmin paved the way for: one, the philosophies of reclamation and the assertion of the Africans' undeniable intelligence in all facets of life, from the construction of monuments to military acumen, as well as their intellectualism evidenced in their philosophies and publications, from antiquity to our contemporary era; two, the aesthetic attestation of the Africans and their descendants, conspicuous in their physical being and various art forms, from antiquity to present time.

Delany's Contribution to the Reclamation of the African Past

In *Principia of Ethnology* Martin Delany traces and presents hieroglyphic records, a detailed review of the anatomy of the human skin, biblical and historical references on the common origin of human beings, and the equality of the races. His report on the anatomy of the human skin focuses particular attention on the dermis, epidermis, and the hypodermis. In his chapter "Special Explanation on Color," Delany offers a physiological examination of the circulatory system and its role on the appearance of skin color: that is, the functions of "the cuticle or epidermis at the surface; the rete mucosum immediately next and below; the cutis vera, corium, dermis, or true skin lying at the base of all."[7] In "Special Explanation on Color," Delany continues the study on the circulatory and cellular composition of human beings to examine the multifaceted diversity in color among the species.[8] Delany underlines the elemental but disregarded reasoning:

> [I]t is in accordance with the economy of the Creator to give a general and unerring reproductive system, to each race, whereby it should be known by its own peculiar characteristics; as also it was part of His economy to give each individual of the same race, a particular reproductive system of temperament, whereby the same parents as father and mother, produce children of different temperaments and different color of eyes and hair as before mentioned, as may be seen in almost every family of the white race.[9]

Delany had commendable aptitude in science and worked with established abolitionist doctors, as an apprentice, to learn as much as possible about general medicine, particularly physiology within the human biological system. In 1850 he applied to and was accepted to Harvard Medical School. After a group of racist White students petitioned his removal from the school, Delany was in fact expelled from Harvard Medical School. The political significance of his color within long-standing politics of education and social advancement was the factor for his expulsion, coupled with the Whites' petty jealousy. His own abominable experiences from a racist structure, in addition to the horrors his ancestors suffered and that his contemporaries continued to endure, bolstered Delany's commitment to contribute to the elevation of the race. He worked to expose the intentions of racism and the relentless measures to bar African descendants from the quality of education and training that would lift the race and establish the social and economic equality of the races. Having scientifically demonstrated the unquestionable unity of the human species, as well as the reasons for the variation of color, from the "purest white" to the "purest black," Delany establishes a simple comparison between the vegetable kingdom, the animal kingdom, and the human races, to appeal to the good sense of the most racist but schooled individual. For, as Firmin posits in *De L'Égalité*, "à des hommes instruits et intelligents il suffit d'indiquer un ordre d'idées, pour que la vérité qui en découle brille à leurs yeux avec une éloquente évidence"[10] ("to educated and intelligent men it suffices to indicate an order of ideas for the truth that ensues to shine in their eyes with an impressive evidence").[11] Certainly, in addition to their intelligence must be a level of humanness, amity, and abated avarice that would permit the acknowledgment of such truth. Firmin was well aware of the contradictions of the so-called educated or schooled Europeans; his statement was meant to indirectly convey to the pseudo-intellectuals the blinding extent of their race prejudice. Delany and Firmin were cognizant of the fact that Europeans had purposefully falsified truths and invented—and were further inventing—hypotheses, theories, and conclusions manufactured to continually and remorselessly dehumanize and enslave, in all aspects of life. Thus, in his statement, Firmin philosophically and strategically aimed at their ego, for possible humane introspection. In "Special Explanation on Color," Delany concludes that if one concedes the aesthetic and temperament diversity within the human species, then "we shall have incontrovertibly established the unity of races and color of the whole human family."[12] In his efforts to access the good sense and humanity of those who held economic, political, and armament power, Delany laid bare the most basic analogy between the vegetable kingdom, the animal kingdom, and humans. He explains:

> That like the vegetable kingdom, every seed, from that of a grain of mustard to a cocoanut, there is but one uniform plan and structure for reproduction—the substance of the seed which is the kernel, consisting of nothing more than the impacked leaves of whatever tree or plant produced it—and as in the animal kingdom, in the anatomical structure of all vertebrates, from fish to man, the Divine Creator had but *one plan*, so in the human races, running through all the *various shades of complexion*, there is but *one color*, modified and intensified from negative to the extremest positive, as seen from the purest white, in *all intermediate colors*, to the purest black.[13]

The "liberal use" of the Bible as one major source, in the first five sections of Delany's study, is the utmost distinction between his examination of the races and the subsequent historical and anthropological publications of Firmin and Diop—particularly Diop's research.[14] The first five sections titled: "The Origin of Races and Color," "The Creation of Man," "The Original Man," "The Family of Noah," "How Color Originates," and the eighth section "The Progress of the Races," which traces the migration and reproduction of Noah's sons with a focus on Ham, are grounded in the Old Testament.

> The African branch of this family [Ham's sons—Cush, Mizraim, and Phut][15] is that which was the earliest developed, taking the first strides in the progress of the highest civilization known to the world, and for this cause, if for no other, it may be regarded as the oldest race of man, having, doubtless, centuries prior to the others, reared imperishable monuments of their superior attainment.[16]
>
> Nimrod, the son of Cush—"Kush," in Ethiopian—commenced as previously mentioned, his grand, intellectual, moral . . . physical, and topographically structural improvements, which left their impress on two of the mightiest empires known to antiquity—Assyrian and Babylonian.[17]

After a detailed biblical and scientific exposition of the common origin of all human beings, Delany employed hieroglyphic record and the historical references of the most reputable and renowned historians of antiquity to prove the Black African origin of Ancient Egypt and the true geographical position of Egypt. In his ninth section, "Progress of the Black Race," and his tenth section, "Builders of the Pyramids," Delany quotes historians and philosophers as Herodotus, who is known as the father of history (c. 484 BC); Strabo (63 BC); and Pliny the Elder (23 AD). From those records, Delany particularly underlines Herodotus' assertion that "[t]he Egyptians have black skin and wooly hair" and Strabo's confirmation that "the Ethiopians are black and whooly haired."[18] Ultimately, Delany articulates the purpose of his study not only for his era but for posterity. He explains, "Our compendium"

> is designed to illustrate not what had been attained by great efforts and the high civilization of the ancient Africans, *but that which is now required and demanded of the people of the present day of that race.* A continent and race are to be redeemed and regenerated; this can only be accomplished by their own efforts, under the guidance of an all-wise Providence and His grace.[19]

Among Delany's other publications, *The Condition, Elevation, Emigration and Destiny of the Colored People of United States* (1852) and *Blake; Or the Huts of America* (1859–1862) also stand as seminal works for the education of African descendants. *Principia of Ethnology* is part of Delany's total body of work dedicated to knowledge, reclamation, and rehabilitation. Delany's aim is relevant for readers of the twenty-first century—that is, his appeal to discern what is currently required for the race to accomplish up to the level of its potential. In an article published in 2008, professor emeritus Dr. Théophile Obenga remarked that the social and scholarly call to read and study the works of Martin Delany, Anténor Firmin, and Cheikh Anta Diop is motivated by their enduring significance for Africans' and African descendants' phenomenological perspective. Obenga emphasized that the encouragement "is supported, in part, by the urgencies of the present moment for the African's phenomenological consciousness, the Black Pan-African awakening and the solidarity of the immense African population so Africa can build itself, from the values of dignity and collaboration, on a continental scale."[20] ("est en fait soutenu, de part en part, par les urgences du moment présent de la phénoménologie de l'esprit africain, de la conscience noire panafricaine et la solidarité de tout l'immense peuple africain pour que l'Afrique se construise, selon des valeurs de dignité et de partage, à l'échelle continentale.")[21] Firmin was indeed aware of the urgency of the time; the urgency to counter the unimaginable racist theories and practices and their daily destruction on African descendants. "Le temps presse" ("time is of essence"), he wrote in the preface of *De L'Égalité*,

> et j'ignore si parmi mes congénères de la race noire, il s'en trouve qui offrent la somme de bonne volonté et de patience accumulée qu'il a fallu

> mettre en œuvre pour élaborer, combiner et présenter les arguments et les recherches de la manière que je me suis évertué de le faire.[22]
>
> (I am not aware if among my congeners of the Black race there are those who offer the sum of good will and accumulated patience that I had to put into effect in order to elaborate, combine and present the argumentations and the research in the manner I have striven to do it.)[23]

Whether or not there were other African descendants assiduously engaged in the same level of scholarly output in the 1800s—historical, anthropological, and philosophical—it is clear that for a long time to come, there will be a considerable need for academic workers with serious intellectual commitment and good will, in order to "wash the race from the unjust imputation that weighs on her for so long."[24] In the 1800s Africans and African descendants were in dire need—the exigency continues in the twenty-first century—for the writings and the voices that would begin to free them from the defamatory publications of racist Europeans.

Firmin's Contribution to the Anthropological, Historical, and Philosophical Methodologies of Black Thought

Most European writers, before and after the publication of *De L'Égalité des Races*—from the 1800s to the early 1900s—resolutely denied the influence of ancient Egypt on Western development and rebuffed, with a more passionate fervor, the legacy of Black Africa in Egypt as well as the Black African influence on Western development, thought, and culture. In "Hommage à Anténor Firmin (1850–1911), égyptologue haïtien," Théophile Obenga detailed the momentous significance of Firmin's work and its methodological influence on physical and cultural anthropology in the research of Price-Mars and Diop. Published in 1885, years after the first advanced decipherment of the hieroglyphs, Firmin's voluminous research is grounded in irrefutable historical facts, hieroglyphic scripts, and anthropological studies. The first hieroglyph scripts, deciphered between the first years of the 1800s and 1822, were inscribed on the Rosetta stone found in the Nile Delta. The stone was unexpectedly found in 1799 during an expansion project of a fort near the town named *Rashid* (translated as Rosetta), in the course of the French expedition in Egypt—from 1798 to 1801. After the French capitulation in Alexandria, Egypt, in 1801, the British gained possession of the Rosetta stone in 1802. It has been in the British Museum since that year. The British scientist and multidisciplinary scholar Thomas Young began the decipherment of the stone's hieroglyphs in the early 1800s. Jean-François Champollion built on and advanced the decipherment of the Rosetta stone by 1822. Jean-François Champollion's expertise in philology as in Eastern languages and cultures facilitated the successful decipherment of the hieroglyphs inscribed on the stone.

It is weighty to ponder that the enslavers' and colonists' visceral animus increased in their defamatory writings and denigrative propagation against Africans, under the pretense of a supposed "inferiority," after the Africans' triumph in Saint-Domingue in 1803, after the Louis Delgrès' rebellion movement in Guadeloupe in 1802, the Denmark Vesey's rebellion in South Carolina in 1822, the Nat Turner rebellion in Virginia in 1831—among countless unnamed African rebellions and *marronage* throughout the Caribbean—and, very significantly, it is after the disclosure of the Africans' glorious past, with Champollion's decipherment of the hieroglyphs, which corroborate the reports of earlier European scholars such as Herodotus and Volney. It is also during the early 1800s that important texts such as the following were published: the Saint-Domingue Constitution of 1801 (under the leadership of Toussaint Louverture), and Louverture's numerous letters to Napoléon Bonaparte, underlying the inhumanity in human commerce and enslavement, Jean-Jacques Dessalines' proclamations, King Christophe's *Manifeste Du Roi*, Pompée Valentin De Vastey's writings such as *Le Système Colonial Dévoilé* and *Réflexions*, David Walker's *An Appeal*, Frederick Douglass' *The North Star*, Martin Delany's *The Condition*, and so on—the list is considerably long and remarkable, particularly given that the enslavement system was in full force.

I posit, then, that the incensed and vilifying publications of the enslavers and colonists were not because they truly believed the Africans were "inferior"; it is rather because from the late 1700s to the early 1800s, they have read and witnessed irrefutable proofs of the Africans' intelligence, intellectual abilities, military acumen, resolve, and endurance. The brainwash of the world through calumnious propaganda against the Africans, the physical terrors, and the unfathomable measures adopted to keep the Africans and their descendants thwarted and in perpetual destitution *all* intensified during the 1800s, from the realization of the Africans' aptitudes and fortitude. The enslavers' conscious efforts to believe themselves as "superior" and the measures enforced to prevent the manifestation of the Africans' true aptitudes and abilities led to centuries of unimaginable inhumane acts and imprisoning policies.[25] It is important to recall in this context that after nominal "freedom," Africans and their descendants were prohibited to read, learn, and converse in groups. One can reasonably propound the following examination: if the Africans were indeed inferior in intelligence and intellect, all the measures to stop them from learning, conversing in groups, and evaluating their circumstances would not have been so violently enforced. If the Africans supposedly could not absorb intellectual material and could not ponder ideas to devise solutions, all the liberation movements and efforts from figures such Olaudah Equiano, Toussaint Louverture, Sojourner Truth, and Fredrick Douglas—to only name a few—could not have been possible. It was in fact the fear and rancor against the Africans' relative success—against all odds—which the enslavers anticipated could lead to the end of economic enslavement, that incessantly propelled the enslavers' remorseless and terrorizing inhumane acts. In his *Réflexions* (1816), De Vastey remarked such fact regarding the enslavers' and colonists' resentment and malevolence against the Africans' aptitudes, abilities, and strengths. In *The Philosophy*, Garvey expounded a similar observation and analysis. "As Mazères contemplates our progress in civilization, his rage augments . . ." It is worth restating De Vastey:

> A mesure que Mazères contemple de nos progrès dans la civilisation, sa rage s'augmente; dans l'impuissance où il est de ne pouvoir se venger, se baigner encore dans notre sang, il exhale toutes ses fureurs par des injures les plus ignobles; les expressions les plus viles, les plus dégoûtantes, échappent de la plume de cet homme qui se dit *si poli*. . . . Quels désappointemens pour un ex-colon! Violà les véritables causes des fureurs de cet énergumène, et qui ont valu tant d'injures et de sottises . . .[26]
>
> ([in] his impuissance whereby he is unable to take revenge, to bathe again in our blood, he breathes all of his furies through the most ignoble insults; the most vile and the most revolting expressions, come from the pen of this man who claims to be *so polite*. . . . What disappointments for the ex-colonist! Here are the true sources of this maniac's fury that prompted so many insults and nonsense . . .)[27]

Similarly, in the 1920s Garvey put forth his observation and examination on the manifestation of jealousy. His view was that the oppressor was cognizant of the oppressed abilities and capabilities; it is precisely that awareness that inflames his anger. It was because of the awareness that the oppressed may one day unfasten the shackles to intellectual and psychological liberation that systems of below-standard education and miseducation were worked out to sabotage his access to formal knowledge. "If the Negro is inferior," Garvey questioned, "why circumvent him; why suppress his talent and initiative; why rob him of his independent gifts; why fool him out of his rights of country; why imprison his intelligence and exploit his ignorance; why keep him down by the laws of inequality?[28] Furthermore, he added:

> The white world has always tried to rob and discredit [the Negroes] of our history. They tell us that Tut-Ankh-Amen, a King of Egypt, who reigned about the year 1350 B.C. (before Christ), was not a Negro, that the ancient civilization of Egypt and the Pharaohs was not of our race, but that does not make the truth unreal . . . Negro professors at that time taught in the universities in Alexandria, then the seat of learning; that ancient Egypt gave to the world civilization.[29]

Without formal access (from the education system) to the Negro past, Garvey entreated parents to teach their children about their African social genesis. He reasoned that it is because of their perceived strengths and their capabilities for great achievements that they are "kept down by a jealous and prejudiced contemporary world."[30] Chronologically, going further back in time in publication production—preceding *The Philosophy*—in 1829–1830, David Walker offers a historical behavioral synopsis of the Africans' enslavers. He underlines jealousy and avarice as parts of the fervor fueling unabated exploitation. He understood bloodthirstiness as the merciless measure used to maintain the exploitative motives and the underlying sentiments of hatred and jealousy. In Article I of *Appeal*, "Our Wretchedness in Consequence of Slavery," Walker outlines a historical trajectory, from the conquest of Egypt to the transatlantic slave trade. Walker assessed:

> The whites have always been an unjust, jealous, unmerciful, avaricious and blood-thirsty set of beings, always seeking after power and authority.—We view them all over the confederacy of Greece, where they were first known to be any thing (in consequence of education) we see them there, cutting each other's throats—trying to subject each other to wretchedness and misery—to effect which, they used all kinds of deceitful, unfair, and unmerciful means. We view them next in Rome, where the spirit of tyranny and deceit raged still higher. We view them in Gaul, Spain, and in Britain.—In fine, we view them all over Europe, together with what were scattered about in Asia and Africa, as heathens, and we see them acting more like devils than accountable men. But some may ask, did not the blacks of Africa, and the mulattoes of Asia, go on in the same way as did the whites of Europe. I answer, no—they never were half so avaricious, deceitful and unmerciful as the whites, according to their knowledge.[31]

In comparable analysis to De Vastey's, Walker's, and Garvey's works, Dr. John Henrik Clarke examines in *A Great and Mighty Walk* the reasons the European writers of the 1800s were overwhelmingly adamant about denying Africa's influential past; the reasons European writers were unrelenting in their agenda to falsify or bury Africa's history and ideologically—in their falsification of facts and words—removing Black Africans out of Egypt, and then abstractly removing Egypt out of Africa. Firmin's *De L'Égalité* succeeded in methodically exposing the approaches European enslavers used to concoct "erroneous but dominant and omnipresent anthropological theories"[32] ("des théories anthropologiques erronées mais dominantes, omniprésentes").[33]

Firmin's insight and meticulous arguments are steadily developed in *De L'Égalité* in order to systematically present historical facts in relation to dominant contemporary ideologies. That Firmin not only dedicated the time and energy to lay out ancient historical foundation for the purpose of the African descendants' epistemological consciousness but was also transparent about the psychological weight of such task is inspiring to future students and scholars. In his preface, he admits the depressive psychological impact the entrenched and dominant racist ideologies exerted on him, while in Paris, and the commitment and fortitude that bolstered his work in the midst of an intellectually oppressive environment. His commitment to expose the truth and to contribute to the psychological and intellectual liberation process of African descendants was the force that sustained him and unrelentingly guided his research and publication. Firmin's frankness about both the weight of environmental pressures on his state of mind, and his efforts to confront oppressive pseudo-science and pseudo-history, confirms that the reconstruction and reclamation of the African past require conscious and conscientious intellectual work and psychological perseverance. As to the lasting influence of his output, Firmin questioned the extent to which his work contributes to such process of recovery. "Ai-je réussi, dans une certaine mesure, à répandre dans mon livre la clarté, la précision, tous les attraits qui captivent l'esprit et font le charme des ouvrages destinés à propager des idées justes, mais encore contestées et méconnues?" ("Did I succeed, to a certain extent, in transmitting in my book, the clarity, the precision, all the allures that captivate the mind and constitute the charm of the types of work geared to promulgate reasonable ideas that are still contested and unacknowledged?") *De L'Égalité des Races Humaines* is a momentous encyclopedic work—of 685 pages—grounded in conclusive historical facts and sound reasoning that contradicted, in 1885, haphazard racist mis-information grounded in avarice. *De L'Égalité* emphasized the unity of the human species and extolled the diversity within the species as a universal strength. It is the innermost understanding of this unity that renders a human being "sacred." Without references to "notions of speculative morality that are vague, irregular, incoherent, with changing criteria based on time and surroundings"[34] ("des notions de morale spéculative, vagues, irrégulières, incohérentes, changeant de critérium, selon les temps et les milieux"),[35] the most consequential understanding of the unity, interconnection, and interdependence of the species *is* the recognition for the practice of unfailing humanity.

Firmin thoroughly examines the basis for the unfathomable anti-philosophical and pseudo-scientific doctrines of the 1800s, which set out to facilitate and justify the sanguinary exploitation of mankind, using the Africans as their most exploitable group.[36] Comparing the approaches between Europeans and Euro-Americans, Firmin argues that the American school of pseudo-scientists did not hide the capitalist interests they were advocating; the European pseudo-humanists/scientists, on the other hand, were concurrently interested in advancing their rhetorical tactic with a façade of intellectualism (pseudo-humanitarian philosophies) while exploiting the Africans. Firmin admits,

> Pour moi, toutes les fois que je lis ces passages enlevés, ce style grave et pompeux où, tout en flétrissant ma race sur le front de laquelle on semble imprimer le sceau de la stupidité, on proteste éloquemment contre l'immoralité de l'esclavage, je ne puis m'empêcher de crier au pharisaïsme.[37]
>
> (As for me, each time that I read those passages, the stern and pompous style, where while debasing my race and seem to imprint the seal of stupidity on its forehead they eloquently protest against the immorality of enslavement, I am obliged to call out the phariseeism.)[38]

In Chapter "Hiérarchisation Factice des Races Humaines," and the subsection "Difficultés de Classer les Aptitudes" of *De L'Égalité* ("The Factitious Hierarchization of the Human Races," "Difficulties to Hierarchize Aptitudes"), Firmin exposes the Black Egyptian origin of mathematics. However, before he develops his analyses, he discusses an important factor that remains relevant to twenty-first-century preoccupations: that is, mathematical intelligence was not/is not the only genre of intelligence to be lauded, for intelligence and intellectual productions in other aspects of human sciences and life are also significant.

> [Il] faut convenir que beaucoup de savants, sans être des mathématiciens, occupent une place plus élevée dans les carrières de l'intelligence, où ils ont cueilli des palmes autrement importantes. . . . Je conviens, tout le premier, qu'il faut pour devenir un bon mathématicien, avoir des habitudes intellectuelles que tous les hommes ne cultivent pas et peut-être ne peuvent cultiver; mais en est-il différemment pour les autres sciences d'une complexité supérieure? Non. Pourquoi doit-on alors voir dans l'aptitude au calcul un signe naturel de la supériorité organique du cerveau?[39]
>
> D'ailleurs, ce n'est pas à la race blanche que revient l'honneur d'avoir inventé ni la science des nombres ni la mesure de l'étendue. L'origine de mathématiques remonte à la noire Égypte, la patrie de Pharaons. Tous les savants qui se sont occupés de l'histoire des sciences exactes sont unanimes à reconnaître que les anciens Égyptiens ont été les créateurs de la géométrie. Plus de trois mille ans avant l'ère chrétienne, alors que les nations européennes étaient encore à l'état barbare, les Chamites qui habitaient les bords du Nil faisaient déjà des calculs géométriques sur l'aire de diverses espèces de surface.[40]
>
> (One must admit that many savants, without being mathematicians, hold very elevated positions in the professions of intelligence, where they achieved brilliant success. I am the first to admit that to become a good mathematician one must have intellectual traits that not all cultivate or perhaps cannot cultivate; but is it different for the other sciences of high complexity? No. Then, why should we see in the aptitude for calculation a natural sign of organic superiority of the brain?
>
> Besides, it is not to the white race that belong the honor of having invented the science of numbers and the science of area measurement. The origin of mathematics dates back to Black Egypt, the nation of the Pharaohs. All the savants who have taken charge of the history of the exact sciences are unanimous in recognizing that the ancient Egyptians were the creators of geometry. More than three thousand years before the Christian era, when the European nations were still in the state of barbarism, the Hamites who inhabited the coast of the Nile were already devising geometrical calculations on diverse aspects of surface area.)[41]

While Firmin discerns the importance of all sciences that study—with truth and integrity—human beings and their environments, he concedes that the geographical origin and social evolution significance of mathematical concepts and formulas must be acknowledged. With that objective, Firmin's work systematically reports and analyzes the imprint of ancient Africa on modern society and scholarship.

> [La] Grèce, la première nation de la race blanche occidentale qui soit parvenue à un développement sérieux de civilisation, doit incontestablement à l'Égypte toutes les premières notions de mathématiques qu'elle a perfectionnées en continuant l'évolution scientifique. . . .
>
> Le premier savant Grec qui se fût occupé des mathématiques avec quelque éclat est Thalès de Milet; mais il avait acquis en Égypte la meilleure partie de son savoir. . . . Platon, qui s'occupa des mathématiques avec succès et qui a principalement contribué à leur donner le prestige qu'une routine aveugle continue encore à y voir, ne se contenta pas de les étudier avec les pythagoriciens, mais il alla lui-même en Égypte, comme pour en puiser la lumière à sa propre source.[42]
>
> (Greece, the first nation of the white occidental race that reached a serious development of civilization, indisputably owes to Egypt all the first notions of mathematics that it developed while continuing its scientific evolution. . . .
>
> The first Greek savant who engaged in mathematics with some brilliance is Thales of Miletus; but he had acquired the foundation of his knowledge in Egypt. . . . Plato, who engaged in mathematics with success and who principally contributed to the prestige of mathematics that a blind routine continues to perceive, not satisfied with merely studying with the Pythagoreans, went, himself, to Egypt, to siphon knowledge from the source.)[43]
>
> Deux causes ont empêché les anciens Égyptiens de jouir de toute la gloire qui leur revient dans cette sphère comme en tant d'autres. La première est qu'ils se servaient d'une langue dont la grammaire était assez développée, mais dont l'écriture était tellement compliquée et difficile que tous les documents scientifiques et littéraires qui en sont sortis ont demeuré des semaines de siècles sans avoir pu être interprétés. . . .
>
> La seconde cause qui a, en quelque sorte, empiré les désagréments de la première, est l'esprit exclusif des prêtres, qui étaient les principaux détenteurs de la science. Ils faisaient un mystère de toutes leurs acquisitions scientifiques et ne les enseignaient que dans un milieu restreint, à un petit nombre d'élus, constituant une école fermée et appelée seule à la possession complète de la doctrine ésotérique.[44]
>
> (Two factors hampered the ancient Egyptians from benefiting the glory that belongs to them in this sphere as in others. The first is that they utilized a language which the grammar was well developed, but the writing was so

complicated and difficult that all the scientific and literary documents that were produced remained, for centuries, without the possibility of being interpreted and translated. . . .

The second factor which, to some extent, worsened the difficulties of the first is the mindset of exclusivity of the priests, who were the principal keepers of the science. Their scientific acquisitions remained a mystery and only taught them in a restricted space, to a selected few, establishing a closed school solely dedicated to the complete possession of the esoteric doctrine.)[45]

In his chapter "L'Égypte et la Civilisation," Firmin inserts citations from Champollion's research, posthumously published in 1836, to support his 1885 research and analyses. In *Grammaire Égyptienne, ou Principes Généraux de L'Écriture Sacrée Égyptienne* Champollion reminded his readers that it was not only during his era that Europe sought erudition in Egypt. European exploration and appropriation of knowledge from antiquity started before the Christian era. "[It] is not only during our time that Egypt has become the object of research for modern erudition,"[46] Champollion wrote. ("[Ce] n'est pas de notre temps seulement que l'Égypte est devenue un objet de recherches pour l'érudition moderne.")[47] "[And] if the modern nations can take pride—deservedly—for their knowledge and their material well-being," he continued,

> on ne devra point l'oublier, c'est aux obscurs et longs travaux des lettrés, infatigables investigateurs des ruines du temps passé, que les sociétés européennes doivent la possession d'un précieux héritage, les leçons de l'expérience des peuples nos devanciers, la connaissance des principes fondamentaux des sciences, des arts et de l'industrie, que nous avons approfondis et développés d'une manière si merveilleuse.[48]
>
> (one must not forget that it is to the long and obscure works of the *savants*, the indefatigable investigators of the ruins of antiquity, that European societies owe the possession of a precious heritage, the lessons of experience of our predecessors, the knowledge of the fundamental principles of the sciences, the arts and industry, that we have deepened and developed so marvelously.)[49]

Champollion presents history as the primary discipline for the study of the achievements of antiquity and the acknowledgment of the pioneer contributors. However, the discipline of history alone cannot accomplish the task; it must engage all the other disciplines of human life.

> L'histoire, dont le but marqué, le seul digne d'elle, est de présenter un tableau véridique des associations humaines qui marchèrent avant nous dans la carrière de la civilisation, embrasse une telle immensité de faits d'un ordre

> si différent et d'une nature si variée, qu'elle emprunte forcément le secours de tous les genres d'études, de celles même qui forment, en apparence du moins, des sciences tout à fait distinctes.[50]
>
> (History, which the distinct goal, the only worthy goal, is to present a truthful picture of the family of humans that walked before us in the career of civilization, embraces such an immensity of facts, of an order so different and of a nature so diverse that it necessarily enlists the help of all the genres of study, particularly of those that form, at least in appearances, the sciences that are completely different.)[51]

Among the major sciences that helped decode different facets of Egyptian history were the understandings of philology and archeology. Philology made possible the study of the mechanism of ancient languages within Egypt and linguistic comparisons to neighboring nations. The grasp of philology also allowed modern researchers access to the Egyptians' secrets on social ideas, as well as religious thought and philosophical opinions. Archeology made possible the direct testimonials—so to speak—of hieratic and hieroglyphic inscriptions, artistic productions, and the events of their political existence. Unaltered, the scripts evidenced and communicated Egypt's ancient past. The auxiliary functions of ancient historical accounts (from Greek historians themselves), philology, and archeology collectively assisted in the decipherment of ancient Egyptian society and its foundational racial component. In *De L'Égalité*, Firmin underlines the race component and reports Champollion's assertion:

> Les anciens Égyptiens appartiennent à une race d'homme tout à fait semblable aux *Kennous* ou Barabras, habitants actuels de la Nubie. On ne retrouve chez les coptes de l'Égypte aucun des traits caractéristiques de l'ancienne population égyptienne. Les Coptes sont le résultat du mélange confus de toutes les nations qui successivement ont dominé sur l'Égypte. On a tort de vouloir retrouver en eux les traits de la vielle race.[52]
>
> (The ancient Egyptians belong to a race of beings completely indistinguishable to the Kennous or Barabras, current inhabitants of Nubia. One does not find in the Copts any characteristic traits of the ancient Egypt population. The Copts are the result of the indeterminate mixture of all the nations that successively dominated Egypt. It would be an error to try to find in them the traits of the old race.)[53]

To further evidence the Black African presence in Egypt and its foundational influences in ancient Egypt, Firmin also references Volney's 1787 publication, which documents his explorations and research during the said decade. In his *Voyage en Syrie et en Égypte, Pendant Les Années 1783, 1784 et 1785*—Tome Premier (*Voyage in Syria and in Egypt, During the Years 1783, 1784 and 1785*—Volume I), Constantin-François Volney reported findings on Egypt's environmental and natural composition, geographical settings and surroundings, its inhabitants and their culture (particularly their linguistic structures and their system of religiosity), and Egypt's ancient demography and physical racial traits. In *Voyage*, Volney details his reaction to sighting a great Sphinx: "Upon seeing this head characterized Negro in all its traits, I recollect this remarkable passage from Herodotus, where he says" ("En voyant cette tête caractérisée nègre dans tous ces traits, je me rappelai ce passage remarquable d'Hérodote où il dit"):

> Pour moi, *j'estime que les Colches sont une colonie des Égyptiens, parce que, comme eux, ils ont la peau noire et les cheveux crépus*; c'est-à-dire, que les anciens Égyptiens étaient de vrais Nègres, de l'espèce de tous les naturels d'Afrique; et dès lors, on explique comment leur sang, allié depuis plusieurs siècles à celui des Romains et des Grecs, a dû perdre l'intensité de sa première couleur, en conservant cependant l'empreint de son moule original.[54]
>
> (For me, I believe that the Colchians are an Egyptian population, because like them, they have black skin and wooly hair; this is to say that the ancient Egyptians were true Negros, the type that is original in Africa; and since then we have explained how their blood, mixed to that of the Romans and the Greeks for many centuries, must have lost the intensity of the first color, while preserving, however, the imprint of its original source.)[55]

The Truth Is Eternal

Firmin gauged it significant to note that after Volney's sojourn in the United States between 1795 and 1798 (in the midst of the enslavement system), and after Champollion's death in 1832, Volney increasingly defended the interests of European and Euro-American enslavers who remained unwavering in their propaganda to negate the Black African foundation of Egypt and, relatedly, persisted in the dehumanizing violence and extortion against African descendants in the Americas. In spite of the textual assertions and confirmations of ancient European scholars such as Homer, Herodotus, Diodorus of Sicily, and a number of other Greek savants, and in spite of the subsequent decipherment of the hieratic and hieroglyphic inscriptions, European and Euro-American enslavers/colonists refused to admit that the Black race was capable of producing an influential civilization. Such enslavers or colonists—racist "publicists,"[56] to use Anténor Firmin's term—incessantly manufactured new absurd arguments to advance calumnious platitudes.[57] One could ponder, then, the reasons why a few French scholars decided to report the findings of ancient historians regarding Egyptian civilization and the Black African base of ancient Egypt? An examination of the lasting periods of European conflicts and competitions for national hegemony/imperialism suggests that it would seem important for French scholars to publicize that the Greeks' and Romans' respective civilizations were in fact built on African civilization. To promote France as the hub of intellectualism and enlightenment, exposing the truth about the so-called Greek and Roman civilizations was vital. Later in the 1800s, however, with the revolutionary rise of African descendants against the commerce and debasement of human beings, it then became more crucial to form a European alliance geared to more brazenly erase Black Africans from the history of human civilization. This reasoning is consistent with the European strategy—very early on—of employing Africans' aptitudes to their benefit at opportune moments and circumstances, only to more resolutely debase and terrorize such Africans at the economically and politically convenient opportunities.

"The truth is eternal" ("La vérité est éternelle"), Firmin affirms. "It must remain absolute across time and space, without which logic rejects its validity. . . . Thus, in declaring that the Black race is inferior to all others, it had to be proven that the fact is current and perpetual."[58] ("Elle droit se maintenir entière à travers les temps et les lieux, sans quoi la logique lui refuse toute sanction. . . . En déclarant donc que la race noire est inférieure à toutes les autres, il a fallu prouver que le fait est actuel et perpétuel.")[59] Yet, historical trajectory reveals the complete opposite. From ancient Africa to the enslavement system of the Americas and beyond, the African descendants have proven, in space and time, a level of irrefutable genius in all human aspects, from academic to military, even though the majority has been and remain intellectually and industrially paralyzed by the lasting impacts of such debilitating forces as: enslavement, Code Noir (French Caribbean colonies in 1685 and Louisiana in 1724), Black Codes (the United States 1865), Jim Crow laws (the United States in 1870s), European and American exploitative trade systems with Black nations, prohibition of education, substandard education, global systems of miseducation, disinformation, mass incarceration, global abject poverty, and so on. In the latter chapters of *De L'Égalité*, "Rapidité De L'Évolution Dans La Race Noire" ("The Rapidity of Evolution Within the Black Race") and "Rôle De La Race Noire Dans L'Histoire De La Civilisation" ("The Role of the Black Race in the History of Civilization"), Firmin commends the accomplishments of some of the illustrious contemporary figures of his era. He calls attention to the role of ancient Black Africa on Europe and the influences of African descendants' philosophies and practices in the Americas and on contemporary European thought. Of particular attention are the Africans who arose as capable and shrewd soldiers. Firmin sought to underscore the wretched conditions within which the Africans fought the various battles, and the absolute fortitude they had to muster in order to carry on and persevere. "What must one think of those men who," ("Que doit-on penser de ces hommes qui,")

> privés aussi de tout, même des armes de combat, n'ayant ni arsenal, ni magasin, ni ambulance, faisant des trentaines de kilomètres par jour, sans ration, le plus souvent déguenillés, disputant aux ronces les lambeaux de leur chair, trouvèrent pourtant en leurs âmes la force de persévérer dans leur noble entreprise, de résister aux meilleures troupes de l'Europe

et de les chasser enfin du sol haïtien lavé pour jamais de la souillure de l'esclavage![60]

(deprived of everything, even combat armament, not having neither arsenal, nor magazine, nor ambulance, traveling overlong kilometers a day, without ration, most often in rags, wrangling their tattered flesh from thorny branches, found in their souls, in spite of it all, the strength to persevere in their noble enterprise, to resist the best European troops and to finally chase them off Haitian soil, forever cleaned from the defilement of enslavement!)[61]

The psychological aspect of the Africans' triumph, undeterred by their scant material resources, is attestation of their fortitude. The merits of the human species do not solely lie in intellectual production, moral and psychological virtues such as "bravery, energetic will, constancy in the struggle, in battles, all these active forces"[62] ("toutes les vertus morales, tells que la bravoure, la volonté énergique, la constance dans la lutte, toutes ces forces actives)"[63] *are* integral characteristics. Henry Christophe's military intelligence and organizational competence, Dessalines' military acumen and unshakable confidence in his abilities and the capabilities of his soldiers, Louverture's illustrious record as a diplomatic negotiator and leader are all evidence—among innumerable Black leaders, revolutionaries, and intellectuals—of the caliber of the Africans and their descendants. Significantly, the seminal works of such figures as Delany, Diop, and Firmin (himself) are further manifestation of the Black genius, though socially fettered to a considerable extent.

In 1863—16 years before Delany's *Principia* and 22 years before Firmin's *De L'Égalité*—William Wells Brown published *The Black Man: His Antecedents, His Genius, and His Achievements*; his work demonstrated, early on, that the truth of the African genius and achievements is indeed eternal. In *The Black Man*, Brown details the struggles and attainments—against all the brutal social and systemic oppression of the 1700s and 1800s—of 57 of the most notable African descendants of the Diaspora. For the pedagogical intention of this work, it is worth listing the names of the antecedents of this current generation and posterity, in order to encourage direct readings of their accomplishments, from *The Black Man* or elsewhere.

Benjamin Banneker, Nat Turner, Madison Washington, Henry Bibb, Placido, Jeremiah B. Sanderson, Toussaint L'Ouverture, Crispus Attucks, Dessalines, Ira Aldridge, Joseph Cinque, Alexandre Dumas, Henri Christophe, Phillis Wheatley, Denmark Vesey, Henry Highland Garnett, James M. Whitfield, Andre Rigaud, Frances Ellen Watkins, Ex-President Roberts [Joseph Jenkins Roberts], Alexandre Petion, Martin R. Delany, M.D., Robert Small, Frederick Douglass, Charles L. Reason, Charlotte L. Forten, William H. Simpson, James M'Cune Smith, M.D., Bishop Payne, William

> Still, Edwin M. Bannister, Leonard A. Grimes, President Geffrard, George B. Vashon, Robert Morris, William J. Wilson, John Mercer Langston, William C. Nell, John Sella Martin, Charles Lenox Remond, George T. Downing, Robert Purvis, Joseph Jenkins, John S. Rock, William Douglass, Elymas Payson Rogers, J. Theodore Holly, James W. C. Pennington, A Man Without A Name, Samuel R. Ward, Sir Edward Jordan, Joseph Carter, James Lawson, Capt. Cailloux, Capt. Joseph Howard.[64]

In "The Negro Digs Up His Past," 1925, Arthur A. Schomburg also records some of the notable achievements of African descendants. Schomburg's study, in that particular essay, brings to light the works that date back to the 1500s, with Juan Latino (born Juan de Sessa), to the 1700s, with Jacobus Elisa Capitein and Gustavus Vassa (Olaudah Equiano), to the 1800s, with Denmark Vesey, David Walker, and Nat Turner, to the 1930s, with the social and intellectual works of Carter G. Woodson.[65] *The Black Man* expressly describes Nat Turner and Madison Washington—among others—as being of unmixed African descent.[66] Of Turner, Brown reports the words of those who knew him and admitted, in spite of their prejudice and hate, that Nat Turner was "honest and sincere . . . he certainly never had the advantages of education; but he can read and write, and for *natural intelligence and quickness of apprehension*, is surpassed by few men I have ever seen."[67] Of Madison Washington, Brown reports: "Born of African parentage, with no mixture in his blood, he was one of the handsomest of his race. His dignified, calm, and unaffected features announced at a glance that he was *endowed with genius*, and created to guide his fellow-men."[68] Throughout the text, Brown specifically points out those of unmixed African parentage in order to fully dispel delusions of African "inferiority" and to fully invalidate the definition and representation of black beauty from a European standard; that is, Blacks who are closer to a European aesthetic—an aspect we will continue to explore in the next section of this chapter. In the preface of *The Black Man: His Antecedents, His Genius, and His Achievements*, Brown expresses the objective of his work, which resonates with his own antecedents, contemporaries, and successors. He wrote that the "calumniators and traducers of the Negro race," who manifest anger in actions and in publications, "are to be found, mainly, among two classes."

> The first and most relentless are those who have done them the greatest injury, by being instrumental in their enslavement and consequent degradation. *They delight to descant* upon the "natural inferiority" of the blacks, and claim that we were destined only for a servile condition, entitled neither to liberty nor the legitimate pursuit of happiness. The second class are those who are ignorant of the characteristics of the race, and are the mere echoes of the first. *To meet and refute these misrepresentations*, and to supply a deficiency, long felt in the community, of a work containing *sketches of individuals who, by their own genius, capacity, and intellectual development, have*

> *surmounted the many obstacles which slavery and prejudice have thrown in their way*, and raised themselves to positions of honor and influence, this volume was written.[69]

John Henrik Clarke underlines that contemporaneously "there is still concerted effort in the academic community of the Western world not to recognize a Black man as a hero in history."[70] In *The Second Crucifixion of Nat Turner*, Clark presents Turner a prime example of, first, calumnious attack, then, disregard or erasure. Significantly, Clarke entitled the compilation of essays *The Second Crucifixion of Nat Turner* for two reasons: one, the literal death of Turner at the gallows and, two, Turner's character assassination by White writers who not only vilified his sacrifices for liberation but continued "to play down his rebellion and preclude recognizing him as a genuine radical."[71] However, the truth is eternal: for, Turner will remain one who was crucified for defending the freedom of the human body, the human soul, and the human mind. "Nat Turner is not considered a hero in the general literature of the United States," Clarke reminds us, "for the same reasons that other great Black rebels, both men and women, have not been given their due in the literature of the world."[72] Nonetheless, it is essential to bear in mind that

> [perhaps] the greatest achievement of African people away from home is not that they survived but that they prevailed and went on to produce great literature and music and to build institutions of lasting value. . . . To have survived slavery and all its cruelty *removes from Black people forever the stamp of inferiority*. What frightens their enemies is that they have transcended simple survival and have proved themselves at critical moments of history when all of the odds were against them. That Black people could move beyond mere survival and teach heroic lessons is indeed frightening to their enemies. The true Nat Turner story says this for the time that he lived in and the message resounds for all time. Nat Turner's story is part of our revolutionary heritage.[73]

Continuing the research and commitment of earlier Black thinkers such as Brown, *De L'Égalité* stands as one of the influential works that traced the evolution of the entire human species, with a particular focus on the achievements and contributions of Africa and its descendants. It is a work of intellectual activism to the extent that it sought to transform the way African descendants view and value themselves, as well as the way others perceive them. Firmin's intellectual successor on ancient and contemporary Africa, Cheikh Anta Diop, is the anthropological and historical link for twenty-first-century students and researchers. Diop's works evidence the fully developed consciousness of an African intellectual who evolved from the double consciousness that Africans and African descendants performed since the transatlantic slave trade. *Nations Nègres et Culture* and *Antériorité Des*

Civilisations Nègres: Mythe ou Vérité Historique expose the contribution of the entire African continent—from North to South, East to West. Diop's works unveil to the world the significance of African civilization and the prominence of the African aesthetic, from an African standard of being. In such capacity, *Nations Nègres* and *Antériorité* are indeed the continuation and elaboration of not only Firmin's and Delany's research but also the philosophical and historical continuation of earlier writers such as David Walker and William Wells Brown.

Cheikh Anta Diop: The Legacy of the African Aesthetic and Culture

Nations Nègres et Culture, first published in 1954, reports additional ocular observations from Herodotus on the origin and racial make-up of Egyptians. Herodotus' reputation as an esteemed Greek historian further gave credence to facts that other European travelers and historians would later confirm and that nineteenth-century and twentieth-century researchers would prove conclusive. In his chapter "Who Were the Egyptians?" ("Qu'Étaient Les Égyptiens?"), Diop reminds his readers that in his writings, Herodotus "insists, on many occasions, on the Negro characteristic of the Egyptians."[74] ("Hérodote, à plusieurs reprises, insiste sur le caractère nègre des Egyptiens.")[75] Diop commands the straightforwardness of ancient Greek savants that later Europeans tried to conceal. He points out that Herodotus:

> Après avoir rapporté son témoignage oculaire qui nous apprend que les Égyptiens étaient des Nègres, démontre ensuite, avec une rare honnêteté (quand on sait qu'il était Grec) que la Grèce a pris à l'Égypte tous les éléments de sa civilisation, jusqu'au culte des Dieux, et que c'est l'Égypte qui est le berceau de la civilisation.[76]
>
> After having reported his ocular testimony that teaches us that the Egyptians were Negroes, he then demonstrates with a rare honesty (when we know that he was Greek) that Greece took from Egypt all the elements of its civilization, including the cult of the gods, and that Egypt is the cradle of civilization.[77]

In *Antériorité des Civilisations Nègres: Mythe ou Vérité Historique*, 1967, Diop methodically studies: the primitive history of humanity, the Negro origin of ancient Egyptians and the civilization of Egypt, the anteriority of Upper Egypt in relation to the Delta, the culture of Pharaonic Egypt, the evolution of the Greco-Roman world since Alexander III of Macedon conquered Egypt, the transmission of Egyptian cultural values and knowledge to Greece, and the transference from Greece to the world—ultimately, the contribution of Black Egypt to world civilization. The Sphinx as well as the hieratic and hieroglyphic inscriptions remain direct testimonials of Africa's earliest history; the juxtaposition of images of ancient and contemporary Africans—that Diop inserted in the latter part of *Antériorité*—further evidences the racial African aesthetics from antiquity to present time. It comprises (roughly) 104 pages of comparison between ancient and contemporary African images, monuments, and various social and religious artifacts. Image xiii is a cave (or rock) painting of Sahara, illustrating an African woman. Image xvi is the image of Narmer, a "typical Negro," the first Pharaoh of Egypt who unified Upper Egypt and Lower Egypt for the first time. Such are the material facts "that no science can destroy at this time,"[78] according to Diop ("Telle est la matérialité des faits qu'aucune science ne peut détruire à l'heure actuelle").[79] Image xvii exhibits Djezer, a "typical Negro," Pharaoh of the IIIrd Dynasty. He inaugurated the grand architecture of carved stones. Images xxxv to xliii juxtapose portraits of contemporary Africans and sculptured images of ancient Africans.

Diop's oeuvre rigorously studies Africa's past for informed understanding and clearer sociopolitical programs for the future, as well as its cultural legacy. His research commitment is motivated by the conviction that the consciousness of the modern human being cannot verily progress unless it is resolved to recognize the falsifications in texts and the interrelation between texts and lived experiences. By the 1950s, progressive African intellectuals had grasped, beyond any doubt, the danger inherent in studying their past and their society from mendacious works of propaganda. "It has thus become indispensable," Diop explained in *Nations Nègres*, "that the Africans lean toward their own history and their civilization and study those in order to better know themselves."[80] ("Il devient donc indispensable que les Africains se penchent sur leur propre histoire et leur civilisation et étudient celles-ci pour mieux se connaître.")[81] By the time Diop further researched various components of Africa's ancient history and social structures, an intellectual commitment was diasporically established. One could submit that the political impetus of the Garvey Movement, particularly the dedication to aesthetic representation, further bolstered Diop's anthropological and historical foundations. Throughout his activist career, Garvey consistently called for the study and teaching of Africa's history and cultural legacy to counteract Europeans' textual falsifications.

> We should expect but very little by way of compliment from the pen of other races. We are satisfied to know, however, that our race gave the first great civilization to the world. . . . White historians and writers have tried to rob the black man of his proud past in history, and when anything new is discovered to support the race's claim and attest to the truthfulness of our greatness in other ages, then it is skillfully rearranged and credited to some other unknown race or people. . . . Every falsehood that is told by the historian should be unearthed, and the Negro should not fail to take credit.[82]

Cheikh Anta Diop would, from 1954 onward, provide such data as a trained archeologist, Egyptologist, historian, and linguist. The socio-cultural African

Diasporic movements that emerged in Harlem, Port-au-Prince, and Paris "advocated the reclamation and valorization of African heritage and culture . . . to liberate themselves from centuries of constructed and imposed identity, Africans and persons of African descent ought to seek to affirm and define their own identity."[83] Within the context of the cultural repossession, the 1954 publication of George Granville Monah James—*The Stolen Legacy*—deserves attention for its analysis on the origin of philosophy and religion (the African Mystery system). The focus of James' work was on the origin of philosophical thought, the Mystery system, and mathematical precedence. In the process of giving back to Africa its true legacy, James called for a New Philosophy of African Redemption, which advocated that both races (Black and White) combine their efforts

> to not only preach and teach the truth that the Mystery system of the African Continent gave the world philosophy and religion, and the arts and sciences, but they must see that all false praise of the Greeks be removed from the textbooks of ours schools and colleges: for this is the practice that has blind-folded the world, and has laid the foundations for the deplorable race relations of the modern world.[84]

James' detectable frustration regarding the misguided and long-lasting African denigration as well as his direct and unapologetic words surely led to the marginalization of his work.

The African system of Mystery and the African aesthetic, restored in the publications and social movements of African descendants, were/are indispensable components against centuries of cultural aggression and denigration. The African/Black beauty, in addition to the African/Black genius, became an important aspect of examination in the works of African descendants form the early 1800s onward. In 1816, utilizing the accounts of European voyageurs, Pompée Valentin De Vastey exhibited the very perceptions of such travelers to support assertions of African beauty, evident in the Americas. Moreover, in *Réflexions*, De Vastey presents the writing of earlier European travelers to challenge the propaganda of a so-called "superior" race and the illusions of an "inferior" race aesthetic. On the perception of beauty in regard to the Nègres and Négresses of Africa, De Vastey wrote:

> Bosman vante la beauté des négresses de Juïda; Ledyard et Lucas celle des nègres de Jalofes; Lobo celle des abyssins; "ceux du Sénégal, dit Andansson, sont les plus beaux hommes de la Nigritie; leur taille est sans défaut, et parmi eux, on ne trouve point d'estropiés."[85]
>
> (Bosman boasts of the beauty of the Negresses of Juïda; Ledyard and Lucas boast of the Negroes of Jalofes; Lobo of the Abyssinians; "those of Sénégal, said Andansson, are the most handsome men of Nigritie; their height is flawless, and among them one could not find any disabled.")[86]

De Vastey continues with four pages of excerpts on the Africans' aesthetic, taken from European accounts. On the ways the Africans—who were not accustomed to seeing Europeans—reacted to their appearance, De Vastey reports:

> "Les femmes de la Nubie, dit Bruce, en voyant la blancheur de ma peau, firent un cri d'horreur, et semblèrent la considérer plutôt comme l'effet d'une maladie, que comme une couleur naturelle." D'autres femmes se moquèrent de Bruce, sur son nez long et pointu. Chaque peuple a ses préjugés; nous trouvons la couleur noire plus belle que la blanche; nos peintres haytiens peignent la divinité, les anges en noirs, les mauvais génies et les diables en blanc.[87]
>
> ("The women of Nubia, said Bruce, at the sight of the whiteness of my skin, let out a cry of horror, and seemed to consider it as an effect of an illness than a natural color." Other women mocked Bruce for his long and pointy nose. Each people/group has its prejudices; we find the color black more beautiful than the color white; our Haitian painters paint divinity and the angels in black, the bad spirits and the devils in white.)[88]

Continuing the affirmation and representation of the African aesthetic, Diop provides numerous portraits and sculptures in his works, more specifically in *Nations Nègres et Culture* and *Antériorité des Civilisations Nègres*—to serve as contemporary and posterity research sources. From the publications of De Vastey to Firmin, to Garvey, and to Diop, the African aesthetic is evidenced. Thus, the late-twentieth-century Black and Beautiful Movement of African Americans and the African Diaspora was framed from long-standing works of cultural recovery, particularly the restitution of the African aesthetic—the Black aesthetic. Such works of recovery were imperative and remain essential constituents of the psychological and social as well as the political and economic processes of the twenty-first century. Mercer Cook's compilation and translation of selected Diop's publications into English—titled *The African Origin of Civilization: Myth or Reality*—substantially aided in the dissemination of the historical, scientific, and aesthetic data of ancient Africa, for the integral psychological reconditioning of Africans and African descendants. Collectively, the works of African descendant intellectuals and activists—particularly, the works of Delany, Firmin, and Diop in this chapter—aimed to contribute to the process of reeducation. Diop connects cultural–psychological awakening to politico-economic progress. "The ancient Egyptians were Negroes," Diop reminds his readers in the 1973 preface to Mercer Cook's translation of *Nations Nègres* and *Antériorité*. In the preface, "The Meaning of Our Work," Diop continues to explain that "[instead] of presenting itself to history as an insolvent debtor, that Black world is the very initiator of the 'western' civilization flaunted before our eyes today."[89] Thus, it is imperative that contemporary Africans—and African descendants—study the stages of African sociopolitical structures, in order to gauge and influence Africa's future. It is therefore crucial to "master that historical process by knowledge, rather than simply to submit to it."[90] "With a world enlightened as to the real truth about the place of the African Continent in the history of civilization," George G.M. James advanced in 1954,

> false tradition and belief should cease to be effective, disrespect and prejudice should tend to disappear, and race relations should tend to be normal and peaceful . . . cultivate race pride in Black people themselves and offer to them a New Philosophy of African Redemption as the Modus Operandi of achieving racial reformation.[91]

In *Cheikh Anta Diop: An Intellectual Portrait*, Molefi Kete Asante continues the articulation for a new philosophy and extends its application to the political sphere and the socioeconomic well-being of African descendants. "It was Diop's belief, as it had been the belief of Dubois, Blyden, and other major African intellectuals," Asante examines,

> that it was impossible to be fully engaged in the contemporary world without utilizing one's mental gifts to work toward the liberation of the African people. It had occurred to Diop very early that the condition of African people would not change unless one put into practice the political ideas.[92]

Diop's oeuvre not only influenced the political thought of African intellectuals and activists on the continent but also influenced the intellectual works, political thought, and actions of Blacks across the African Diaspora. Among such figures, one would note: John Henrik Clarke, Théophile Obenga, Chancellor Williams, Asa Hilliard, Charles S. Finch III, and Maulana Karenga[93]—among a long list of notable scholars. Indeed, in 1973, in his conclusion of "The Meaning of Our Work," Diop urged African descendants to contribute to the restoration of African history in Africa and in the Diaspora. He wrote, "I should like to conclude by urging young American scholars of good will, both Blacks and Whites, to form university teams and to become involved, like Professor Lawrence . . . the American contribution to this final phase could be decisive."[94] In 1962 Professor Harold G. Lawrence published the article "African Explorers of the New World,"[95] a brief precursor to Professor Ivan Van Sertima's more developed research expounded in *They Came Before Columbus: The African Presence in Ancient America*.[96]

Notes

1. Author's translation.
2. Author's translation.
3. Author's translation.

4. For developed analyses of the author on the contributions of Price-Mars and Hurston, readers may consult *Literary and Sociopolitical Writings of the Black Diaspora in the Nineteenth and Twentieth Centuries*, chapters 4 and 6.
5. Cheikh Anta Diop, *The Origin of African Civilization: Myth or Reality*, translated by Mercer Cook (Chicago: Lawrence Hill & Co., 1974), xiv.
6. Ibid., xv.
7. Martin Delany, *Principia of Ethnology: The Origin of Races and Color, With an Archeological Compendium of Ethiopian and Egyptian Civilization, From Years of Careful Examination and Enquiry by Martin Delany* (Philadelphia: Harper & Brother Publishers, 1879), 32–33.
8. Ibid., 33–42.
9. Ibid., 35–36.
10. Anténor Firmin, *De L'Égalité des Races Humaines* (Paris: Librairie Cotillon, 1885), Dedication, xi-xii.
11. Author's translation.
12. Delany, *Principia of Ethnology*, 40.
13. Ibid., 40–41.
14. Ibid., 9–10.
15. Canaan, the 4th son, in Asia, p. 42–43.
16. Delany, *Principia of Ethnology*, 44.
17. Ibid., 46–47.
18. Ibid., 32.
19. Ibid., 93. Emphasis added.
20. Author's translation.
21. Théophile Obenga, "Hommage à Anténor Firmin (1850 to 1911), égyptologue haïtien," *ANKH Égyptologie, Histoire de l'Afrique, Sciences* (www.ankhonline.com, 2008), 142.
22. Firmin, *De L'Égalité*, xi.
23. Author's translation.
24. Firmin, *De L'Égalité*, xvi. Author's translation.
25. For further examination of the concepts and illusions of "superiority" and "inferiority," refer back to Chapter 1 of this present work.
26. Pompée Valentin Baron De Vastey, *Réflexions sur une Lettre de Mazères, Ex-Colon Français, Adressée à M.J.C.L. Sismonde de Sismondi, sur les Noirs et les Blancs, la Civilisation de l'Afrique, le Royaume d'Hayti, etc.* (Cap-Henry: Chez P. Roux, imprimeur du Roi, 1816), 109–110. For further examination consult Chapter 2 of this present work.
27. Author's translation.
28. Marcus Garvey, *The Philosophy and Opinions of Marcus Garvey* (Dover: The Majority Press, 1986), 82–83, Volume II.
29. Ibid., 19.
30. Ibid., 82.
31. David Walker, *Appeal to the Coloured Citizens of the World, but in Particular, and Very Expressly, to Those of the United States* (Boston: Revised and Published by David Walker, 1830), 20.
32. Author's translation.
33. Obenga, "Hommage à Anténor Firmin," 135.
34. Author's translation.
35. Firmin, *De L'Égalité*, 124.
36. Ibid., 204.
37. Firmin, *De L'Égalité*, 205.
38. Author's translation.
39. Firmin, *De L'Égalité*, 250.
40. Ibid., 250–251.
41. Author's translation.

42. Firmin, *De L'Égalité*, 251.
43. Author's translation.
44. Firmin, *De L'Égalité*, 251.
45. Author's translation.
46. Author's translation.
47. Jean-François Champollion, *Grammaire Égyptienne, ou Principes Généraux de L'Écriture Sacrée Égyptienne* (Paris: Typographie de Firmin Didot Frères, Imprimeurs de L'Institut de France, 1836), iij.
48. Ibid., iij.
49. Author's translation.
50. Champollion, *Grammaire Égyptienne*, iij.
51. Author's translation.
52. Firmin, *De L'Égalité*, 337.
53. Author's translation.
54. Constantin-François Volney, *Voyage en Syrie et en Égypte, Pendant Les Années 1783, 1784 et 1785*, Tome Premier (Paris: Volland, Libraire, Quai des Augustins, 1787), 74–75.
55. Author's translation.
56. Firmin, *De L'Égalité*, 459.
57. Ibid., 342–343.
58. Author's translation.
59. Firmin, *De L'Égalité*, 333.
60. Ibid., 543.
61. Author's translation.
62. Author's translation.
63. Firmin, *De L'Égalité*, 543.
64. William Wells Brown, *The Black Man: His Antecedents, His Genius, and His Achievements* (Boston: James Redpath, Publisher, 1863), 7–9.
65. Arthur A. Schomburg, "The Negro Digs Up His Past," *The New Negro* (New York: Touchstone Book, 1997), 233–236.
66. Brown, *The Black Man*, 59, 75.
67. Ibid., 72. Emphasis added.
68. Ibid., 75. Emphasis added.
69. Ibid., 5–6. Emphasis added.
70. John Henrik Clarke, *The Second Crucifixion of Nat Turner* (Baltimore: Black Classic Press, 1968, 1997), 3.
71. Ibid., 1.
72. Ibid., 4.
73. Ibid., 5.
74. Author's translation.
75. Cheikh Anta Diop, *Nations Nègres et Culture* (Paris: Éditions Africaines, 1955), 21.
76. Ibid., 24.
77. Author's translation.
78. Cheikh Anta Diop, *Antériorité des Civilisations Nègres: Mythe ou Vérité Historique?* (Paris: Présence Africaine, 1967), xvi. Author's translation.
79. Ibid., xvi.
80. Author's translation.
81. Diop, *Nations Nègres et Culture*, 8.
82. Garvey, *The Philosophy*, 82, Volume II.
83. Kersuze Simeon-Jones, *Literary and Sociopolitical Writings of the Black Diaspora in the Nineteenth and Twentieth Centuries* (Boulder: Lexington Books, 2010), 138.
84. George G.M. James, *The Stolen Legacy* (Trenton, NJ: Africa World Press, Inc., 1992), 156.

85. De Vastey, *Réflexions*, 22.
86. Author's translation.
87. De Vastey, *Réflexions*, 21–22.
88. Author's translation.
89. Diop, *The Origin of African Civilization*, xiv.
90. Ibid., xv.
91. James, *The Stolen Legacy*, 157–158.
92. Molefi Kete Asante, *Cheikh Anta Diop: An Intellectual Portrait* (Los Angeles: University of Sankore Press, 2007), 10.
93. Ibid., 124–126.
94. Diop, *The African Origin of Civilization*, xvii.
95. Harold G. Lawrence, *African Explorers of the New World* (Los Angeles: John Henry and Mary Louisa Dunn Bryant Foundation, 1962).
96. Ivan Van Sertima, *They Came Before Columbus: The African Presence in Ancient America* (New York: Random House, 1976).

5

THE PHILOSOPHIES OF PSYCHOLOGICAL AND STRUCTURAL LIBERATION

From M.M. Garvey and C.G. Woodson to M.L. King

"To learn to think,"[1] that is, to learn *and* to think, are the fundamentals and objectives with which Carter Woodson and Marcus Garvey developed the philosophies, theories, and arguments expounded in *The Mis-Education of the Negro* and *The Philosophies and Opinions of Marcus Garvey*. The questioning of existing epistemology and the application of newly found and newly developed knowledge into liberating, progressing, and enriching living conditions are the nucleus of Garvey's and Woodson's writings. Moreover, attention is called to the national and international nuances of the Black world. However, such nuances can only be thoroughly discerned through systematic studies and pondering of the various national structures within which African descendants navigate daily. Without such discernments, for the purpose of solidarity and corrective actions, the established global structures and hierarchies will, generally, remain unchanged. The inveterate exploitation and disregard of African descendant communities will continue uninhibited. When Garvey and Woodson posit—in *The Philosophies* and *The Mis-Education*—that the Negro is his own worst enemy, the motivation was certainly not to undermine the nocuous psychological impact and the lasting dire economic outcome ensued from centuries of systemic racial subjugation and exploitation. Instead, the motivating force was the call to collective introspection grounded in profound knowledge, for group empowerment and viable resolutions to long-standing problems. With the objective to exhibit in order to reconstruct, Woodson exposes the afflictions and hindrances of African descendant communities within the context of the United States of America. While Woodson's informative examples are extracted from the lived experiences of African descendants in the United States, his theories contribute to the demystification of various group-mindset among African descendants, European descendants, and others, all developed from the cumulative actions and behaviors dated from the

1400s to his era. *The Mis-Education* unveils the historical genesis and trajectory of the twentieth century's and the twenty-first century's very tangible socioeconomic ills, as well as the lasting psychological aftereffects. Learned behaviors of indirection and venality in the political and social dealings of the purported leadership of Black communities were additional detriments to the momentous and quasi-insurmountable external factors.

Psychological Liberation: Garvey and Woodson on the Concept of Leadership

When any individual accepts a position of leadership, it ought to be with the understanding of rendering service to the community he or she would serve and, by extension, to the greater world. When an African descendant accepts a position of leadership for a Black community or a predominantly Black nation, it ought to be as service and as sacrifice to help rectify the long-standing historical afflictions; it ought to be with the understanding that his or her "valuable time is required . . . to respond to the call as a matter of duty, for his [or her] usefulness is otherwise assured."[2] From such being, Woodson reasoned we may expect "sound advice, intelligent guidance, and constructive effort for the good of all elements of our population."[3] Regrettably, Black communities and nations of the twentieth century onward have had to contend with what Woodson terms "misleaders." Thus, Woodson's second objective in *The Mis-Education* was to identify the destructive comportments of misleaders. In his chapter "The Need for Service Rather than Leadership," Woodson redefines the concept of leadership, which has been misinterpreted and maladapted. To counterbalance the ruinous implications and disastrous practices of a globally maladapted term and approach, Woodson proposes a new mindset with the use of a new term, "service."[4] If one could successfully translate the idea and practice of leadership into service, Woodson maintains, "we may soon find it possible to lift the Negro to a higher level."[5] In his examination of the concepts of leadership in relation to service, Woodson cautions against unending strife and opposition in the constant battle for access to predatory leadership in lieu of constructive service. Though African descendants have the potential to be empowered with their abilities and capabilities, they are rendered helpless by the dealings of misleaders and are thus unable to secure and protect their wellness. Woodson describes the chaos that is ensued from the quest for venal power:

> The one has the job that the other wants; or the one is a leader of a successful faction, and the other is struggling to supplant him. Everything in the community, then, must yield ground to this puerile of contest. . . . [T]he other is persistently struggling to undo everything accomplished by his opponent. The one is up today, and the other in ascendancy tomorrow. . . . To present a sane proposition to the community through one of these leaders

> means local warfare rather than an effort to work together for the common good. . . . Little thought is given to social uplift, and economic effort is crushed by factional wrangling.[6]

Selfish ambitions of misleaders incapacitate the development of the masses. One could seamlessly apply Woodson's observations of destructive politics within organizations—including the churches of the African American communities of his era—to the politico-economic "leadership" realities of the Republic of Haiti throughout the twentieth and twenty-first centuries, thus far, particularly, Woodson's observation that "the other is persistently struggling to undo everything accomplished by his opponent." Discerningly, Woodson further underlines that no consideration is given to social uplift and economic adjustment for the masses. Any effort in the direction of productive reorganization and necessary redistribution is "crushed by factional wrangling." Thus, concurrent with the disregard of misleaders against the same mass on behalf of whom they are expected to advocate and lead, their selfishness and greed partly account for the economic and social stagnation of the African descendants. Unbridled selfishness and excessive greed are indeed global phenomena and have been the modus operandi for centuries; however, such mode of operation is momentously more catastrophic for African descendant communities who started life in the Americas in forced destitution. The various modes of venality rob such misleaders of their soul and humanity and consequently harden them to the inhumane plight of the masses. Furthermore, Woodson examines that without knowledge in race history and without a focus on community needs or national objectives—in the case of predominantly Black nations—the predatory leaders "figure out that there is no hope for the masses; and they decide, then that the best thing they can do is to exploit these people for all they can and use the accumulations selfishly."[7] Remarkably, Woodson's observation that "potentially the colored people are strong although they are actually weak" points to the heart of the matter, for it zooms into the need for indispensable psychological recalibration that will facilitate the path to viable social change.

It is impossible for the community or the nation to progress "when the majority of those who should know better *have chosen* to go backward, but this is exactly what most our misleaders do."[8] Woodson's examination on choice—in "have chosen"—correlates to his observation of the community's stagnation due to psychological weakness. Here, choice relates to two mutually inclusive practices. On the one hand, the misleaders should have enough good will *to choose* to further educate or reeducate themselves in community-building and nation-building. The practice of appropriate self-education for positive leadership has been a long-standing method in Black communities; Marcus Garvey and Malcolm X (among others) individually accomplished it and imparted such knowledge to their national and global communities. On the matter of in-depth education, Woodson relied on ancient wisdom to underline the merits of advancing and deepening one's knowledge. "Philosophers have long conceded . . . that every man has two educations," Woodson distinguished, one that is given and one that is acquired. The education that one develops for self is most meaningful, for "all that is most worthy in man he must work out and conquer for himself. It is that which constitutes our real and best nourishment."[9] Garvey reasoned that education "is the medium by which a people are prepared for the creation of their own particular civilization, and the advancement and glory of their own race."[10] Moreover, "to spiritually regulate one's self is another form of the higher education that fits man for a nobler place in life, and still, to approach your brother by the feeling of your own humanity, is an education that softens the ills of the world and makes us kind indeed. Many a man was educated outside the school room."[11]

On the other hand, and in addition to one's resolve for adequate and holistic education, for the purpose of full human development and incorruptible governance, Woodson's emphasis on *choice* as it relates to those who *have chosen* to mislead underlines the attention he accords to the concept of "sacrifice" in the praxis of conscionable leadership. The external economic exploitation and structural impediments—from outside of the Black communities—are factual. Notwithstanding, for the masses of Black communities and Black nations to have a chance at securing basic human needs (adequate food, housing, education, health care, etc.), those who hold the positions to speak and negotiate on behalf of the masses cannot prioritize accruing their own excessive wealth by further exploiting the masses' labor and resources to the benefit of external forces. Hence, the extent to which misleaders will refrain from rapacious actions *is* a choice and/or a "sacrifice"—depending on the level of external pressures or threats. However, from the perspective of *choice*, Woodson sternly rests the unbridled external exploitation of the masses on the misleaders of the race. "The exploiters of the race are not so much at fault as the race itself," Woodson argued, and "[if] Negroes *persist in permitting* themselves to be handled in this fashion they will always find some one at hand to impose upon them. The matter is one which rests largely with the Negroes themselves. The race will be free as soon as it decides to do so. No one else can accomplish this task for the race. It must plan and do for itself."[12] The argument that "the exploiters of the race are not so much at fault as the race itself" is certainly a debatable and contentious assertion. However, this degree of accountability that—perhaps unbalanced out of exasperation of the trajectory—Woodson ascribes to the Black race, particularly its leaders, is meant to further encourage a level of collective introspection and empowerment, for long-term vision, commitment, fortitude, and sacrifice. Dr. John Henrik Clarke would later expound a similar thought that is also debatable, but the very fact that such thought raises more questions is ground for forthright discussions that should lead to individual self-examination and candid group-examination. In "A Great and Mighty Walk" Dr. Clarke maintains that "only the slave can abolish slavery." He continues to elaborate his perspective with a symbolic illustration and explains "if someone is on your back, you have to bend a little to balance them on your back . . . the best move, if you want them off of your back, is to stand straight up."[13] Spoken in 1996, that Dr. Clarke uses the present tense indicates that he is referring to mental and economic slavery. I receive Dr. Clarke's symbolism of standing upright as the starting point; for, while standing, a perpetrator can still tightly clasp his or her hands around the neck of the target or prey. Stated differently, standing "straight up" will not immediately unclasp the hands and arms strongly wrapped around the neck, obstructing air. The individual who stands up must continue to struggle, with every bit of strength, in order to undo the forces around his or her neck. The world's many Black communities have stood up for centuries, at different times in history, yet they continue to struggle for air, for breath, and for life. The forces perpetuating abject poverty continue to *choke the life out of them*, from birth to the classrooms (if accessible), to the workforce (if available), to servitude, to the vast prison systems (depending on the society within which they live), and to brutal death.

All factors considered, nonetheless, if the African descendants who have accessed positions of governance would do away with predatory leadership or misleadership and create collective opportunities for the masses to contribute their time and energy in various social organizations and institutions, "the race might accomplish something."[14] "[Properly] awakened," Woodson asserts, "the Negro can do the so-called impossible . . . and thus help to govern rather than merely be governed."[15] If Garvey and Woodson could weigh in the current state of affairs in the twenty-first century, they would question the extent to which the leaders of Black communities—globally—have governed with accountability and efficiency or have been directly and/or indirectly governed by mercenary agents. The concept of well-organized governments and the practice of responsible governance—for the well-being of the people—were at the root of the Garvey Movement and philosophy. The practice of misleadership is treason, according to Garvey, whether such predatory practice is against a community, a nation, or a race. It is treachery to imperil the rights, the safety, the well-being, and the prosperity of a people.[16] In *The Philosophy*, Garvey explains that oppressed people are often betrayed by traitors from their own group, "those who are generally susceptible to bribery for the selling out of the rights of their own people."[17] As for African descendants, he wrote:

> I believe [the Negroes] are more encumbered in this way than any other race in the world, *because of the lack of training and preparation for fitting us for our place in the world among nations and races*. The traitor of other races is generally confined to the mediocre or irresponsible individual, but, unfortunately, the traitors among the Negro race are generally to be found among the men highest placed in education and society, the fellows who call themselves leaders.[18]

The lack of comprehensive education and the systemic barriers to the business, political, and economic realms—along with one's own rapacious mental disposition—render misleaders susceptible to bribery and unscrupulous complicity. Two interrelated structural and psychological hindrances are thus at play: circumscribed and/or substandard education yield to what Woodson identifies as the resultant lack of "mental power." Similar to Garvey, Woodson psychoanalytically correlates misleadership to the lack of integrity and knowledge; it is the manifestation of drained or devoid "mental power." Stated differently, Woodson discerns "ill-fed brains" as the root-cause of the symptomatic behaviors of misleaders: underhandedness, lack of dignity, lack of vision for oneself and the community, and lack of character. "Inasmuch as the education of the Negro has come from without," he explains, "we can clearly see that he has received *only a part of the development* which he should have undergone or he has developed negatively. *The Negro lacks mental power, which cannot be expected from ill-fed brains*."[19] *Only a part of the development* refers to inadequate or restricted education, limited human preparation in self-knowledge, self-awareness, and fundamental ignorance of the community he or she is called to lead. In *Nations Nègres et Culture*, Cheikh Anta Diop underlines the extent to which the schooling and conditioning that were based on the defamation of Africans "deeply affected the personality of the Negro."[20] The "climate of isolation," where the Africans' achievements were not only omitted in all written accounts but that the world was simultaneously accustomed to the violent denigration and alienation of Africans and their descendants, *leads* the misleader to subconscious self-disparagement as well as contempt and disregard for Black communities. Akin to Woodson's observations, Diop confirmed that the majority of those who were schooled in a system of vilifying propaganda against Africans were doubly isolated—that is, isolated from the Black community, of which they have become ashamed due to their euro-centric miseducation, and isolated from the White community, which disregard them and demean their Africanness. Hence, the misleader is self-denigrated in his/her own psyche and denigrated by others. As a result, "it often happens that the Negro intellectual loses confidence in his own possibilities and in those of his race . . . especially the educated Black who had had an opportunity to become conscious of the world opinion about him and his people."[21] Woodson argues that in the final analysis, African descendants must be further educated not only in history but also in all the disciplines of the humanities, the social sciences, and the natural sciences. Once thoroughly educated, they will be able to discern whether the forces of the education that were imposed on the race served "to bless [them] or to bless [their] oppressor. After learning the facts in the case the Negro must develop the power of execution to deal with these matters as do people of vision."[22] Woodson asserted that the Association for the Study of Negro Life and History has no specific ideology and "no special brand for the solution of the race problem *except to learn to think* . . . what will help a Negro in Alabama may prove harmful to one in Maine. . . . *A thinking man, however, learns to deal wisely with conditions as he finds them*.[23]

Woodson's conclusion in *The Mis-Education*, titled "The Study of the Negro," is elucidative; it explains his frustrations with the ill-fed, dormant-minded, complicit-minded, and predatory-minded Blacks. The conclusion develops his position—introduced in the chapter "The Need for Service Rather Than Leadership"—that part of the accountability lies with the Negros, in spite of the Whites' established coercive and violent systems of subjugation. "In a manner [the oppressors of the race] deserve to be congratulated for taking care of their own interests so well," Woodson reasoned. On the other hand, "[the] Negro needs to become angry with himself because he has not handled his own affairs wisely. In other words, the Negro must learn from others how to take care of himself in this trying ordeal. He must not remain content with taking over what others set aside for him."[24] It is significant that the conclusion, "The Study of the Negro," follows the chapter "Higher Strivings in the Service of the Country"; for, it is in "Higher Strivings" that Woodson first uses the term "the New Negro"—a term that pointed to a new mindset for Afro-Americans, early in the 1900s. Having meticulously examined the roots of the psychological, economic, political, and social ills for the African descendants in the United States, "Higher Strivings" offers recommendations for viable advancement. Ultimately, Woodson's overarching message is that African Americans — and by extension African descendants in the United States and abroad—must take control on matters significant to their progress; they must handle "their own affairs," concurrent with radical structural/systemic adjustments. The African descendant, then,

> should endeavor to be a figure in politics, not a tool for the politicians. . . . Real politics, the science of government, is deeply rooted in the economic foundation of the social order. To figure greatly in politics the Negro must be a great figure in politics. A class of people slightly lifted above poverty, therefore, can never have much influence in political circles. . . . *The New Negro* in politics will see his opportunity not in thus restricting himself but in visioning the whole social and economic order with his race as a part of it.[25]

Without systemic industrial, economic, political, and consequential sociopsychological change, the majority of African descendants will remain relatively enslaved or controlled beings; that is, subjected to the wills of those with collective material power. In the first half of the twentieth century, Woodson and Garvey reasoned that if comprehensively educated and properly awakened, the African descendants—along with all others who wish for the well-being of humankind—can succeed in readjusting their position in the world. There is a critical and foundational history lesson that Garvey defined as crucial for both individual and group psychological readjustment, for African descendants and others. Taking the British colonies as examples, Garvey remarked: "we have *been camouflaged* into believing that we were made free by Abraham Lincoln. That we were made free by Victoria of England, but up to now we are still slaves, we are industrial slaves, we are social slaves, we are political slaves, and the new Negro desires a freedom that has no boundaries, no limit."[26] The word choice *Camouflaged* thrusts the pretense of freedom—a pseudo-freedom—into the light of scrutiny. The nominal freedom African descendants were given by the enslaving White power, by the second half of the 1800s, was blatantly void of the substance necessary to secure their human rights and full rights to national citizenship; equally important, it was void of the resolution to redress the material imbalance created from centuries of violent and legalized plunder, as it was void of any intention to establish systemic socioeconomic and sociopolitical equality. "[Take] away industry from a race; take away political freedom from a race, and you have a group of slaves."[27] Analogous to Garvey's observation, in his chapter titled "The Negro Revolution" (*Why We Can't Wait*), Martin Luther King, Jr. examines the dissimulation embedded in the 1862–1863 emancipation proclamation. In essence, the 1963 plans to celebrate the centennial of the "Negro's liberation from bondage" were simply a masquerade. In disappointment King underlined a number of facts:

> But alas! All the talk and publicity accompanying the centennial only served to remind the Negro that he still wasn't free, that he still lived a form of *slavery disguised* by certain niceties of complexity. As the then vice-President, Lyndon B. Johnson, phrased it: "emancipation was a proclamation but not a fact." The pen of the Great Emancipator had moved the Negro into the sunlight of physical freedom, *but actual conditions had left him behind in the shadow of political, psychological, social, economic and intellectual bondage*. . . . The Negro also had to recognize that one hundred years after emancipation he lived on a lonely island of economic insecurity in the midst of a vast ocean of *material* prosperity. Negroes are still at the bottom of the economic ladder. . . . He is deprived of normal education and normal social and economic opportunities. When he seeks opportunity, he is told, in effect, to lift himself by his own bootstraps, advice which does not take into account the fact that he is barefoot.[28]

King's remark on the Whites' habitual reference to the symbolic "bootstraps" is astute. He lays bare the displacement of responsibility that such reference entails; and, in his analysis, he emphasizes and reminds the government as well as the nation that the African American is symbolically "barefoot" and, in too many circumstances, literally barefoot. The symbolic "barefoot"—as well as the factual barefoot in the case of countless African descendants—straightforwardly brings attention to the reality that out of physical slavery the Afro-American started life at the level of economic destitution, and the majority of the group has been confined to poverty. With staunch and ruthless economic barriers, it has been quasi-impossible for the group to climb out of systemically maintained poverty. One must have a base economic structure in order to create more economic opportunities for oneself and one's community. Symbolically, one must first own the boots that would make it possible to pull one's self "up" and to assist in pulling one's family and community "up," to financial and overall material mobility. The first half of the 1900s marked the height of the New Negro mindset, framed by the New Negro Movement and further developed by the Garvey Movement. That era helped advance the psychological awakening of African descendants, grounded in a more comprehensive understanding of historical trajectory as well as the cultural valorization of the Black world. The restoration and valorization of the history of Africa and the African Diaspora were further established by the Pan-African Movement and the Négritude Movement. It is evident, then, that by the 1960s, Martin Luther King Jr.'s—as well as Malcolm X's—philosophies and principles for structural liberation grew out of the preceding foundational and radical Black Thought. King's observation of a continuing "disguised" form of slavery and an "emancipation" that was "a proclamation but not a fact" restated Garvey's assertion of a *camouflaged* freedom that maintained the African descendant economically, politically, and socially enslaved. It has been proven, with centuries of social and political realities, that an emancipation proclamation never meant or equated true freedom—as examined in Chapter 3 of this present work. Though there are scholarship and popular beliefs that tend to disassociate the philosophies of M.L. King Jr. from influential radical thinkers such as Marcus Garvey and, by extension, from Garvey's ideological successor, Malcolm X—El Hajj Malik El Shabazz—the writings of M.L. King Jr. evidences a continuation of foundational radical movements and the modification of contemporary philosophical and ideological thought.

On Structural Liberation: The State of the "Negro" Revolution

In the 1960s Dr. King focused his efforts on U.S. juridical institutional reform, for political and social justice. Dr. King's philosophies and efforts were built on the writings and deeds of Black activists, artists, and intellectuals of the first half of the 1900s. Their work on institutional reform, particularly education reform, for just material opportunities paved the way for Martin Luther King, Jr. King's 1963 publication, *Why We Can't Wait*, is a thorough analytical response to the impact of existing social structures on Afro-Americans in general and the future prospects of the youth in particular. King wrote and mobilized for the boy "sitting on a stoop in front of a vermin-infested apartment in Harlem. His father is one of the jobless. His mother is a sleep-in domestic."[29] King spoke on behalf of the young Negro girl "sitting on the stoop of a rickety wooden one-family house in Birmingham. Some visitors would call it a shack."[30] Economic circumstances, exacerbated by the death of her mother in a car accident, obligated the girl to stop attending the "all-Negro school." She had to function as "mother" to the "half a dozen" children left behind. The neighbors reported that the mother died because the ambulance neglected to arrive early enough to take her to the "all-Negro" hospital. King mobilized and articulated basic principles in *Why We Can't Wait* because the children could not afford another 100 years of a "mocking" empty freedom and equality, where extreme poverty would continue to rob them of their parents and their childhood, of their education, and the possibility of a successful future. While King acknowledged and built on the work of psychological and intellectual liberation of his predecessors and contemporaries, he reasoned that complete group psychological recalibration within the United States could not be achieved without concurrent restructuring of the overall national system. In 1961, in the midst of the Modern Civil Rights Movement, Saunders Redding wrote an introduction to W.E.B. Du Bois' *The Souls of Black Folk*. Redding's focus at that juncture of African American history was to advocate the reform of the systems that perpetuated the state of double consciousness African Americans have had to negotiate.[31] With the publication of *The Souls of Black Folk*, and the intellectual dialogues that followed its publication,

> Negroes of training and intelligence, who had hitherto *pretended* to regard the race problem as of strictly personal concern and who sought individual salvation in a creed of detachment and silence, found a bond in their common grievances and a language through which to express them.[32]

By the 1960s the preceding African descendant movements in the United States and across the Black Diaspora had made immeasurable progress in rehabilitating some of the minds born into a powerfully racist world. However, the process remained incomplete and was often sabotaged by members of influential institutions, particularly the education, employment, and justice systems, which continued to operate unjustly against African Americans. As a case in point, King brought forth the "Pupil Placement Law" (passed as early as 1955) and, later, the "School Placement Law." Southern states adopted both legal maneuvers—in conjunction with sheer violent intimidation—to counteract the Supreme Court's 1954 decision in the *Brown v. Board of Education*.[33] By 1963 King wrote his *Letter from Birmingham Jail*, emphasizing the reasons African Americans can no longer wait for real implementation of just laws. They "waited for more than 340 years for [their] constitutional *and* God-given rights."[34] It is easy for those who want to perpetuate race prejudice and terror to consistently ask them to wait for "equality," King further remarked.

> But when you have seen vicious mobs lynch your mothers and fathers at will and drown your sisters and brothers at whim; when you have seen hate-filled policemen curse, kick and even kill your black brothers and sisters; when you see the vast majority of your twenty million Negro brothers smothering in an airtight cage of poverty in the midst of an affluent society; when you suddenly find your tongue twisted and your speech stammering as you

> seek to explain to your six-year-old daughter why she can't go to the public amusement park that has just been advertised on television, and see *tears welling up in her eyes . . . and see ominous clouds of inferiority beginning to form in her little mental sky* . . . when you have to concoct an answer for a five-year-old son asking: "Daddy, why do white people treat colored people so mean?"[35]

Waiting was not workable. Immorally and inhumanely legalized structures, reinforced with socio-educational brainwash, systemically inculcated an injurious complex of inferiority among numerous African Americans. They had been so "skillfully brainwashed," King noted, that they "didn't know where to begin or how to resist the influences that had conditioned [them] to take the least line of resistance and go along with the white man's views."[36] As the emerging youth attempted to overcome the weight of systemic racism, their mind, heart, and soul were relentlessly imperiled by menacing forces. The extent of their inner turmoil, from daily hardship, depended on the individual's innate human threshold to witness and withstand incessant physical attacks, denigration, and systemic sabotage. Direct actions from African Americans—and from genuinely committed other allies—were necessary. King viewed the sit-ins as the decisive and constructive actions and the nonviolent *tension* that were geared "to create a situation so crisis-packed that it will inevitably open the door to negotiation."[37] Within the context of King's concept of tension, John Henrik Clarke examined that there were cross-influential impacts between the Modern Civil Rights Movement, led by Dr. M.L. King, Jr., and the work of Malcolm X, while leading the Black Muslim Movement and during his subsequent leadership of the Muslim Mosque, Inc. and the Organization of Afro-American Unity. In the edited volume *Malcolm X: The Man and His Times*, Clarke discusses the ways in which Malcolm X catapulted civil rights leaders to more definitive actions, "to the effect that [Malcolm] was a catalytic agent—offstage, sarcastically criticizing the 'civil rights leaders,' popping a whip which activated them into more radical action and programs."[38]

In his chapter "The Sword That Heals," King assessed it necessary to define and defend his approach by emphasizing that "the argument that nonviolence is a coward's refuge lost its force. . . . A nonviolent army has a magnificent universal quality."[39] His analogy to the *army* immediately called to the collective force of the participants of the sit-ins and other methods utilized. Though King privileged his approach as the most effective for his era, he acknowledged the importance of the Muslims' Black Nationalist[40] program as well as Garvey's ideological influence on Malcolm X.[41] Dr. Clarke further examines Malcolm X's influential radical activism as the force "the power holders of America had to deal with, if they didn't deal with the established 'civil rights leaders'."[42] Developed from Garveyism, Malcolm X asserted that his political, economic, and social philosophy was Black Nationalism; for Malcolm X, that meant Afro-Americans "must control the politics and the politicians in [their community]" and would no longer "take orders from outside forces . . . and [will] sweep out of office all Negro politicians who are puppets of outside forces."[43] Malcolm X's reference to "puppet" is analogous to King's remark on hand-picked African Americans being used as "token" figures in lieu of conscientiously and legally opening a space of socioeconomic equality for the masses of African Americans. The utilization of "tokenism," King discerned, was "to end the process of protest and pressure. It is a hypocritical gesture, not a constructive step."[44] While King and civil rights proponents did not demand control over the Black community—as in a separate community within the nation, a nation within a nation—they demanded that those who would be elected to work in the community were individuals of principled character and meritorious preparation, who were committed to serve constructively. M.L. King, Jr.'s recognition of the inevitable tension, if any progressive changes were to be made, was a moderate approach to Malcolm X's push for radical change, a "Black Revolution." In his April 1964 speech on the "Black Revolution," which he conceived as an international revolution, Malcolm X explained:

> Revolution is never based on begging somebody for an integrated cup of coffee. Revolutions are never based upon love-your-enemy and pray-for-those-who-spitefully-use-you. And Revolutions are never waged singing "We Shall Overcome". . . . Revolutions are never based upon that which is begging a corrupt society or a corrupt system to accept us into it. Revolutions overturn systems. And there is no system on this earth which has proven itself more corrupt, more criminal, than this system that in 1964 still colonizes 22 million African-Americans, still enslaves 22 million Afro-Americans. . . . [America's colonial system] has colonized 22 million African-Americans by depriving us of first-class citizenship, by depriving us of civil rights, actually depriving us of human rights.[45]

Beyond the brutalities of the slavery system, Malcolm X had more recent historic references that his own parents lived: the atrocities of the Red Summer of 1919, the Elaine massacre of 1919 and the Tulsa Race massacre of 1921, in addition to the habitual wanton lynchings and murders of Blacks. A year earlier, in his public "Message to the Grassroots" in 1963, Malcolm X explained that "the only revolution in which the goal is loving your enemy is the Negro revolution. It's the only revolution in which the goal is a desegregated lunch counter, a desegregated theater, a desegregated park, and a desegregated public toilet."[46] King argued against the belief that "[n]onresistance merely reinforces the myth that one race is inherently inferior to another."[47] In contradistinction, King submitted that

> the Negro's method of nonviolent direct action is not only suitable as a remedy for injustice; *its very nature is such that it challenges the myth of inferiority*. Even the most reluctant are forced to recognize that no inferior people could choose and successfully pursue a course involving such extensive sacrifice, bravery and skill.[48]

In ideological and textual dialogues between Malcolm X and King, one would note their respective attention to the definition of and commitment to the "Negro Revolution" (King) or the "Black Revolution" (Malcolm X). In King's 1963 concept of the "Negro Revolution," he explained that "just as lightning makes no sound until it strikes, the Negro Revolution generated quietly. But when it struck, the revealing flash of its power and the impact of its sincerity and fervor displayed a force of a frightening intensity."[49] Furthermore, King argued that after centuries of debasement and various modes of abuse, the voices of the revolutionaries had to be heard, unapologetically. The same year, however, Malcolm X began to critique King's ideological perspective and replaced the term "Negro" by "Black" revolution.

King's conviction that complete and foundational freedom "must be demanded by the oppressed,"[50] and the sit-ins for legislative changes as the process of such demands, deserves some scrutiny in relation to the radical revolutionary belief that freedom "must be taken." King was keenly cognizant of the fact that the African Americans could not "take" their freedom without the same intensity of violence that was executed on them. The general masses of African Americans would not exercise such level of violence for two reasons: one, for practical realities and, two, because of the importance accorded to spiritual well-being, as the African Americans conceived it. King explained that "[the Negro] knew he could not win his freedom through physical force but also because he believed that through physical force he could lose his soul."[51] In the struggle to secure equality and true freedom, nonviolence, therefore, was "a powerful and just weapon . . . proved that it could win victories without losing wars."[52] Moreover, the forces that subjugated Afro-Americans went beyond human strength—individual or group—to be lodged into far-reaching systems of oppression and exploitation. Thus, akin to Louverture in Saint-Domingue, King used social and political strategies and the mechanism of language to lead those in power to introspection or, at the very least, to help guide them to some level of reevaluation of the entrenched system of injustice as well as the hovering national chaos and affliction such structure has created. In his letter from Birmingham jail, King addressed the White clergymen on the state of the nation and its impact on African Americans. The White clergymen condemned the demonstrations of civil rights activists, who were protesting against the fiendish actions of southern Whites. Those clergymen found no faults in the vicious practices of the Whites. "My Dear Clergymen," King wrote:

> *I am sure that none of you would want to rest content* with the superficial kind of social analysis that deals merely with effects and does not grapple with underlying causes. It is unfortunate that demonstrations are taking place in Birmingham, *but it is even more unfortunate that the city's white power structure left the Negro community with no alternative.*[53]
>
> I had hoped that the white moderate would understand that law and order exist for the purpose of establishing justice and that when they fail in this purpose they become the dangerously structured dams that block the flow of social justice. . . .[54]

> You warmly commended the Birmingham police force for keeping "order" and "preventing violence." *I doubt that you would have* so warmly commended the police force if you had seen its dogs sinking their teeth in unarmed, nonviolent Negroes. *I doubt that you would* so quickly commended the policemen if you were to observe their ugly and inhumane treatment of Negroes here in the city jail.[55]

King's enumeration of the barbaric actions against Afro-Americans can be deciphered within the same technique employed by De Vastey and Césaire. In their approach, all three writers direct attention to the atrocious deeds committed against African descendants. De Vastey's description of the enslavers' actions in his *Réflexions Sur une Lettre de Mazarès, ex-colon français* and Césaire in his *Discours sur le Colonialisme* obligated—obligate in the twenty-first century—their readers and the world to face the heinous terror executed on African descendants.[56] Equally important, the descriptive occurrences unequivocally send the message that such level of physical and psychological terror, along with the structural bondage that legitimized those unimaginable horrors, could no longer be accepted. Strategically, cognizant of the material and political might of those who maintained such systemic violence, King's lucid and logical reasoning was drafted in a manner that created a dialogical space for the clergymen to respond, without disturbing their race loyalty to whiteness and without directly addressing their attachment to the resources that were *taken* from parasitically leeching the blood, sweat, and progeny of enslaved Africans. In spite of the blatant predatory and fiendish realities of his time, King punctiliously proceeds with his analysis as if the recipients of his letter (the White clergymen) had not witnessed and were not part of the violence against Blacks—directly or indirectly, vocally or silently. The very fact was that the White clergymen, along with other power holders, not only witnessed but also supported the vicious treatments of Afro-Americans; they opted to dismantle their wall of cognitive dissonance in order to align religiosity with heinousness, to reconcile religiosity with racist terror. All facts considered, King's approach gave the readers of his letter the opportunity to preserve their deceitful "honor" of men of religion, as long as he—King—could move one step closer to reestablishing Afro-Americans within their divine human rights and legal civil rights. Dialectically, King posits that the Negro "is not unmindful of or indifferent to the progress that has already been made"; if in 1963 the African American is saying "Not enough," "it is because he does not feel that he should be expected to be *grateful* for the halting and inadequate attempts of his society to catch up with *the basic rights he ought to have inherited automatically, centuries ago, by virtue of his membership in the human family and his American birthright*."[57] I am analytically compelled to draw a comparison between King's letter from jail (confined within the sea of the white power of the 1960s) and Toussaint Louverture's 1801 letter to Napoléon Bonaparte (the undeniable representative of white power of the early 1800s). During Louverture's leadership as governor general of Saint-Domingue, a

Constitutional Assembly comprised of mulatto and white representatives drafted the Saint-Domingue Constitution of 1801. The constitution declared slavery forever abolished and reasserted the human and civil rights of all Africans and their descendants as irreversible truths. Employing the European—France in particular—philosophy of Enlightenment, Louverture strategically wrote and presented such fundamentals of human liberation as a *fait accompli*, in spite of his awareness of the Europeans' attachment to human commerce, human commodity, and profit. Similar to Malcolm X's position, Dessalines closely observed the possible ineffective outcome of Louverture's diplomacy and regarded himself as the leading force with whom the French would have to contend if they were to attempt to re-enslave the Africans in Saint-Domingue. As examined in *Literary and Sociopolitical Writings of the Black Diaspora*, Louverture's rhetoric and political strategies paved the way to Black liberation, though Dessalines completed the initial phase of African liberation.[58]

In his chapter "In the Days to Come," the last chapter of *Why We Can't Wait*, King examines the assassination of John Kennedy within the context of a plagued society. Furthermore, his assertion that "we were all involved in the death of John Kennedy" resonates with Césaire's analysis on the long-standing social and global *Hitlerism*, which dates back to the day of African enslavement and genocide.[59] King examined:

> The assassination of Kennedy killed not only a man but a complex of illusions. It demolished the myth that hate and violence can be confined in an airtight chamber to be employed against but a few. Suddenly the truth was revealed that hate is a contagion; that it grows and spreads as a disease. . . . We tolerated hate; we tolerated the sick stimulation of differential application of law. . . . We mourned a man who had become the pride of the nation, but we grieved as well for ourselves because we knew we were sick.[60]

Césaire's conceptualization of *Hitlerism* as the mindset and the manifestation of violence against a group, based on color, religion, and other categories, set the framework for both King and Malcolm X to articulate the realities of the 1960s. "For too long the depth of racism in American life has been underestimated," King further examined. "The surgery to extract it is necessarily complex and detailed. As the beginning it is important to X-ray our history and reveal the full extent of the disease."[61] King's keen observation and articulation of U.S. social realities and his theological and theoretical language in *Why We Can't Wait* were—jointly—one of the strategies that led to eventual conversations, in the midst of the racial tension and violence of the 1960s. In his "Letter from Birmingham Jail," King described the Muslim movement as the organization whose members have "lost faith in America"[62] and are ready to follow the Black Nationalist agenda for community autonomy, self-protection, and self-preservation within the United States, as well as expanding an international agenda for human rights.[63] As Dr. Clarke argues in *Malcolm X: The Man and His Times*, the civil rights leaders, Dr. King in particular, presented themselves as the more pacifist alternative with which the country must contend in its inevitable necessity to address and rectify the daily wanton race violence against U.S. Blacks. Simultaneously, Malcolm incited King to be more direct and daring in his actions. In its moderate approach, King's concept of tension—for the "Negro Revolution"—was similar to Aimé Césaire's concept of confrontation. The tension caused by the sit-ins was a response to the existing racial tension/violence that was ravaging the daily existence of African Americans. The Negro tension—so to speak—was a call for dialogue, for the purpose of policy adjustment and implementation. In *Literary and Sociopolitical Writings of the Black Diaspora*, the author offers an analysis of "confrontation" which corresponds to King's notion of tension. Simply put, true transformative dialogue, for both Césaire and King, must confront existing tension in order to change damaging social realities:

> The ideological and dialogical confrontation, which occurs in forthright discussions, should lead to the recognition of each other's words and presence. Hence, it follows that there cannot be any form of dialogue between an individual and a puppet. Black leaders were convinced that before the race becomes engaged in the dialogue that must exist among humans of different races, blacks must first demand the right to be recognized and respected as thinking individuals.[64]

Puppet—similar to Malcolm X's usage—is a direct reference to African descendants who, out of complicity for self-interest or out of fear of the detrimental consequences that came with confronting injustices, unconscionably or desperately became tools of subjugation and exploitation. A "puppet" or a "token" figure is inherently fraudulent and destructive to any Black community or Black nation. While Malcolm X acknowledged King's commitment and laudable sacrifices for the uplift of Afro-Americans and the healing of the American nation, he questioned the long-term effects of the so-called Negro revolution—as King conceived it—on the full citizenship and human rights of Afro-Americans and, by extension, African descendants, globally. Given the general state of African Americans in the twenty-first century (lack of education, unemployment, underemployment, housing problems, and incarceration), Malcolm X's observations and skepticism deserve meticulous and incorruptible attention. The study of M.L. King Jr.'s principles in a balanced comparison to Malcolm X's observations and philosophies may help decipher the causes of continuing socioeconomic imbalance between African descendant communities and others, particularly Euro-American descendants. Within the United States, Malcolm X was not only King's contemporary but also his complementary voice in the cause for humanity and equality; as such, he began to expand King's approach from

U.S. geographical boundaries and preoccupations to include global Blacks. One would note that by 1964, in his last chapter, "The Days to Come," of *Why We Can't Wait*, King progressively and strategically moves from one terminology to the next: from "civil-rights struggle" to "civil-rights movement," to "civil-rights revolution," to "human rights." In time, King's modifications in terminology and thought brought him in closer ideological convergence with Malcolm X.[65] "The revolution for human rights," King wrote, "is opening up unhealthy areas in American life and permitting a new and wholesome healing to take place. *Eventually the civil-rights movement will have contributed infinitely more to the nation than the eradication of racial injustice*."[66] A profound and complex statement! "Eventually the civil-rights movement will have contributed infinitely more to the nation than the eradication of racial injustice." Pondering the manifestation of race prejudice, racism, violence and subjugation well into the twenty-first century—within the contexts of access to education and socioeconomic opportunities for African Americans and African descendants—one could question the extent to which the civil rights struggle, movement, or revolution eradicated systemic prejudice and racism. Does the color line remain a national and international problem?

One of the most significant analyses of *Why We Can't Wait* ends with a series of questions that are comparable to De Vastey's examination of the colonial system and the self-arrogated rights of enslavers/colonists on Africans and African descendants.[67] In "The Days to Come," King brings to mind the horrific situations where the Africans after working dawn-to-dark to exhaustion, for free, had to find extra time to work and save coins to eventually *attempt* to buy the freedom of a loved one, if the enslaver would agree. King links this inhumane circumstance, where one had to purchase one's own God-given rights, to the realities of the post-chattel enslavement, from 1863 to 1963. He explained:

> [There] is a terrible parallel between the outstretched and greedy hand of a slave trafficker *who sold a Negro his own person*, and the uplifted and admonishing finger of people who say today: "what more will the Negro expect if he gains such rights as integrated schools, public facilities, voting rights and progress in housing? . . . What is implied here is the amazing *assumption that society has the right to bargain with the Negro for the freedom which inherently belongs to him*."[68]

This level of arrogance and criminality, sustained with economic, judicial, and political power, confined African Americans "to traumatic ties that still bind him to slaveries other than physical."[69] As resolutions King dedicated an entire subsection of "Days to Come"—section III—on programs of reparation; for, the moral reasons and legal rational for such programs of restitution are "rooted in the robberies inherent in the institution of slavery"[70] and the de facto operations of such system after the nominal emancipation of African Americans. King reasoned that "the nation must not only radically readjust its attitude toward the Negro in the compelling present, but must incorporate in its planning some compensatory consideration for the handicaps he has inherited in the past."[71] Just as the continuous psychological awakening of African descendants must be met with structural adjustment, a superficial change of attitude of the Whites—and others—without systemic changes will perpetuate the subjugation and misjudgments of African descendants in the United States and worldwide. "It is impossible," King asserted, "to create a formula for the future which does not take into account that our society has been doing something special *against* the Negro for hundreds of years."[72] Within the framework of King's philosophical legacy—social and political—there are three crucial aspects to consider, for the possibility of more extensive and consequential systemic adjustments, both within the U.S. context and on the international landscape. One, that though King and Malcolm X are presented within the lens of *seeming* ideological opposition, I submit that there were conscious and methodic dialogues between M.L. King and Malcolm X, for the rehabilitation of Afro-Americans. Two, a thorough study of King's observations, theories, philosophies, and arguments would allow for more in-depth analyses of the structures of American society. That is, the continuous focus on sections of King's "I have a dream" speech, presented as his most defining words, is a circumscription, to some extent, of his multifaceted writings and speeches. While the speech deserves lasting merit for the overall inspiration for race and class alliance as well as its emphasis on character, it obscures—erases, for most—King's complex, profound, and detailed sociopolitical philosophies. The third and last point relates to the former but addresses the intellectuals in particular, who have accepted—or are unmindful of—the limited vista of King's articulated ideas. In *How Black Intellectuals Have Abandoned the Ideals of the Civil Rights Era*, Professor Houston A. Baker, Jr. argues that there has been a tendency, from the end of the twentieth century to the twenty-first, to disregard King's "devotion to the ideals of race people . . . his affiliation with the black majority."[73] Baker further underlines that the representation of M. L. King, Jr. glosses over

> his undeniable endorsement of race as perhaps the single most important lens and analytical category for reading (and changing for the better) the dynamics of our national history has been dishonestly buried under a mountain of universalist and neoconservative platitudes. Some of the oratory and tactics King deployed so effectively from Montgomery to Selma have been relegated to the dustbin of history.[74]

It is crucial to critically ponder the extent to which mainstream's representation of King, in opposition to the character and political assassination of Malcolm X, thwarted Black advancement in the United States. King stood against the economic, political, and social injustices of African Americans and African descendants in the United States. Yet, in spite of his acceptance into the national liberation—national harmony—narrative one should evaluate the degree to which his philosophies and sociopolitical prescriptions have been thoroughly studied and substantively applied. With the progressive impacts of the Civil Rights Movement in the 1960s, how does one reconcile the achievements of that era to the general condition of African Americans in the twenty-first century? The eventual assassination of King, three years after the assassination of Malcolm X, presaged the rate of development of the "Negro" movement. Ultimately, the onus is not on Dr. King, who died because of his efforts to establish the rights of African Americans, just as the rights of European Americans were officially established within the Constitution of 1787. King aimed to heal the nation, and he was convinced that the "Negro Revolution" was an integral part of the "American Revolution." His strategies and patience were supra-human to the extent that King transcended the average good-will, patience, capacity for love and peace of the general human being, of any color. As Wolfenstein notes in *The Victims of Democracy: Malcolm X and the Black Revolution*, the leaders of the Civil Rights Movement, King in particular, "believed that there was a world to be won within the American system, that the Negro revolution was the realization of the American revolution."[75] Beyond the geographic boundaries of the United States, African descendants need true and unfettered freedom. That is, an existence that is not chained or controlled by economic disenfranchisement and group servitude, where excess labor for minimal pay is the inescapable norm. They need the caliber of political agency that will attend to their suffering communities. As Firmin noted in 1885 in *De L'Égalité*,

> [Il] faut à la race noire la liberté, une liberté réelle, effective, civile et politique, pour qu'elle s'épanouisse et progresse. Si l'esclavage lui fait horreur, horrible aussi doit lui paraître le despotisme. *Car le despotisme n'est rien autre chose qu'un esclavage moral*: il laisse la liberté du mouvement aux pieds et aux mains; mais *il enchaîne et garrotte l'âme humaine, en étouffant la pensée*. Or, il est indispensable qu'on se rappelle que c'est l'âme, c'est-à-dire la force de l'intelligence et de l'esprit qui opère intérieurement la transformation, la rédemption et le relèvement de toutes les races, sous l'impulsion de la volonté libre, éclairée, dégagée de toute contrainte tyrannique![76]
>
> (The Black race needs liberty, true liberty, effective, civil and political, so that she may flourish and progress. If slavery horrified her, despotism should also seem horrifying. *For despotism is nothing else but mental enslavement*: it allows the liberty of movement to the feet and the hands; but *it enchains and garrotes the human soul, by throttling thinking*. But, it is indispensable that one remembers that it is the soul, that is the force of intelligence and the intellect, that operates inwardly the transformation, redemption and advancement of all races, under the impetus of free and enlightened will, free from all tyrannical constraints.)[77]

Notes

1. Carter G. Woodson, *The Mis-Education of the Negro* (Washington, DC: The Association for the Study of African American Life and History, 1933, 2005), 108.
2. Ibid., 102.
3. Ibid., 102.
4. In the 1960s Dr. Martin Luther King would use the term "creative leadership." See the chapter "The Summer of Our Discontent," of *Why We Can't Wait*, page 115 of the listed edition.
5. Woodson, *The Mis-Education*, 66.
6. Ibid., 63–64. Emphasis added.
7. Ibid., 69.
8. Ibid., 69. Emphasis added.
9. Ibid., 70.
10. Marcus Garvey, *The Philosophy and Opinions of Marcus Garvey* (Dover: The Majority Press, 1986), 6, Volume I.
11. Ibid., 17.
12. Woodson, *The Mis-Education*, 65. Emphasis added.
13. John Henrik Clarke, *A Great and Mighty Walk* (New York: Black Dot Media, 1996), @ 54:36 minutes, DVD.
14. Woodson, *The Mis-Education*, 65.
15. Ibid., 103.
16. Garvey, *The Philosophy*, 30, Volume I.
17. Ibid., 29.
18. Ibid., 29. Emphasis added.
19. Woodson, *The Mis-Education*, 70.
20. Cheikh Anta Diop, *The African Origin of Civilization: Myth or Reality*, excerpts from *Nations Nègres et Culture* (1955) and *Antériorité des Civilisations Nègres: Mythe ou Vérité Historique?* (1967), translated and edited by Mercer Cook (Chicago: Lawrence Hill & Co., 1974), 25.
21. Ibid., 25.
22. Woodson, *The Mis-Education*, 108.
23. Ibid., 108. Emphasis added.
24. Ibid., 109.
25. Ibid., 101–103.
26. Garvey, *The Philosophy*, 95, Volume I. Emphasis added.
27. Ibid., 8.
28. Martin Luther King, Jr., *Why We Can't Wait* (New York: Penguin Books, 1963), 23. Emphasis added.
29. Ibid., ix.
30. Ibid., ix.
31. W.E.B. Du Bois, *The Souls of Black Folk* (New York: Fawcett Publications, Inc., 1961), 20.
32. Du Bois, *The Souls of Black Folk*, ix. Emphasis added. Redding word choice resonates Aimé Césaire's context of *pretense* in *Discours sur le Colonialisme*. See Chapter 1 of this present work, under the subsection entitled "On Economics: The Social Complex of Inferiority and the Illusion of Superiority."
33. King, *Why We Can't Wait*, 19, 30–31.
34. Ibid., 81. Emphasis added.
35. Ibid., 81. Emphasis added.
36. Ibid., 65.
37. Ibid., 79–80.
38. John Henrik Clarke, *Malcolm X: The Man and His Times*, edited by John Henrik Clark, assisted by A. Peter Bailey, Earl Grant, and Betty Shabazz (New York: Macmillan Company, 1969), xix.

39. King, *Why We Can't Wait*, 38.
40. For a thorough examination of the nineteenth and twentieth centuries' concept of Black Nationalism, please consult Chapter 1 ("Interpreting the Concepts of Black Nationalism, Black Internationalism, Pan-Africanism, and Universal Humanism within the Diaspora") of Kersuze Simeon-Jones, *Literary and Sociopolitical Writings of the Black Diaspora in the Nineteenth and Twentieth Centuries* (Boulder: Lexington Books, 2010).
41. King, *Why We Can't Wait*, 31–35.
42. Ibid., xix.
43. Malcolm X, *Malcolm X Speaks: Selected Speeches and Statements* (New York: Pathfinder Press, 1965), 21.
44. King, *Why We Can't Wait*, 31–32.
45. Malcolm X, *Malcolm X Speaks*, 50.
46. Ibid., 9.
47. King, *Why We Can't Wait*, 120.
48. Ibid., 121.
49. Ibid., 16.
50. Ibid., 80.
51. Ibid., 35.
52. Ibid., 26.
53. Ibid., 77–78. Emphasis added.
54. Ibid., 85.
55. Ibid., 93. Emphasis added.
56. Chapter 2 of this present work, particularly the sub-section "In Defense of Humanity."
57. King, *Why We Can't Wait*, 32. Emphasis added.
58. Simeon-Jones, *Literary and Sociopolitical Writings*, 34.
59. Aimé Césaire, *Discours sur le colonialisme* (Paris: Présence Africaine, 1950), 13–14.
60. King, *Why We Can't Wait*, 144–145.
61. Ibid., 119.
62. Ibid., 87.
63. Ibid., 87.
64. Simeon-Jones, *Literary and Sociopolitical Writings*, 26.
65. King, *Why We Can't Wait*, 151–152.
66. Ibid., 151–152.
67. See Chapter 2 of this present work.
68. King, *Why We Can't Wait*, 127. Emphasis added.
69. Ibid., 127.
70. Ibid., 138.
71. Ibid., 134.
72. Ibid., 134.
73. Houston Alfred Baker, Jr., *How Black Intellectuals Have Abandoned the Ideals of The Civil Rights Era* (New York: Columbia University Press, 2008), 71.
74. Ibid., 72.
75. Eugene Victor Wolfenstein, *The Victims of Democracy: Malcolm X and the Black Revolution* (New York: Guilford Press, 1993), 11.
76. Anténor Firmin, *De L'Égalité des Races Humaines* (Paris: Librairie Cotillon, 1885), xvii. Emphasis added.
77. Author's translation. Emphasis added.

6

THE EXISTENTIAL REROUTING

The Intellectual Formation of the Youth

Diop's 1973 preface to Mercer Cook's 1974 translation of *Nations Nègres et Culture* and *Antériorité des Civilisations Nègres* offers an insightful analysis on the reevaluation of culture within a political and sociohistorical framework. He explains that only the pseudo-revolutionary can ignore the absolute need for evolving *cultural evaluations or revolutions* "which must be met if our peoples are to be reborn culturally and politically."[1] Diop's framework of "cultural revolution," which should bring about critical evaluations of cultural practices, serves in our examination of the existential rerouting of the African descendant youth—educationally and psychologically. Diop's twentieth-century advocacy for a "cultural revolution" resonates Edward Wilmot Blyden's nineteenth-century call for a "revolution of mentalities," a concept I examined in *Literary and Sociopolitical Writings of the Black Diaspora in the Nineteenth and Twentieth Centuries*.[2] In his publications, Diop prioritized historical and socio-cultural studies as methods to reconstruct the African erroneous notion of self, "distorted by colonialism." The deconstruction and reassessment of culture(s) are essential processes in the "genuine retrieval of self."[3] Throughout his intellectual career, Dr. John Henrik Clarke consistently lectured on the connection between history and the various dimensions of culture, particularly political culture, in the assessment of self. "History is a clock that people use to tell their political and *cultural time of the day*," Dr. Clarke thought.

> [I]t is a compass that people use to find themselves on the map of human geography. History tells a people where they have been, what they have been, where they are and what they are. Most important, history tells a people *where they still must go, who they still must be*. The relationship of history to the people is the same as the relationship of a mother to her child.[4]

The Implications of Unexamined Cultural Processes

In *Black Intellectuals*—the chapter titled "Beyond Incubation: A Talented but Trapped Tenth," in particular—William M. Banks references Edward Franklin Frazier's analysis on the link between economic systems and social order, to conclude that the "cultural traits of black folk, urban and rural, had been shaped by racist social and economic institutions, and the elimination of those constraints would lead to a new and improved way of life for them and all people."[5] Frazier's and Banks' examination of the function of political and economic power in the manipulation, formation, and designation of cultures and behaviors is germane to the various analyses of this chapter. Though their geographic reference is the United States, the ultimate observatory conclusion is pertinent to various regions and communities of the Black Diaspora. Understanding the complexities embedded in the concept(s) of culture(s), and the many sub-areas of the topic—race, class, nationality, ethnicity, gender, family, generations, era, etc.—the present chapter directs attention to the ability, with historical knowledge, to discern cultural behaviors that condition the mind for individual wellness and community progress *from* cultural behaviors that hinder or retard significant work of advancement for the individual, the family, and the community. In 1969, Amilcar Cabral advanced a similar focus on culture in his book *Análise de Alguns Tipos de Resistência* (The Examination of Certain Types of Resistance).[6] After addressing, in preceding chapters, political resistance and economic resistance, Cabral addressed cultural resistance (Resistência Cultural). In addition to the critique of European politics of cultural hegemony in Africa—Guinea-Bissau and Cape Verde specifically—and the denigration and dismantlement of traditional African cultures, in his chapter "La Resistência Cultural" (Cultural Resistance),[7] Cabral also urged Africans, from the urban to the rural areas, to heedfully evaluate their own cultural practices. From critical and honest evaluations, they would be able to discern which practices to maintain and which to discard; they would be able to determine which social, political, and cultural behaviors are harmful to the future of Africa and Africans, irrespective of whether such pernicious behaviors are of European colonial systems or of African provenance.

Cabral brought forth concrete behaviors and African social norms in order to point out—with concise and straightforward reasoning—the flaws and pitfalls of certain regional and community behaviors and practices. Among his topics, the analysis on education and language, in particular, as instruments to be properly used for the benefit of the people, remains an integral aspect of cultural resistance and reevaluation. To that extent, his advocacy for critical thought and examined cultural choices remain pertinent in our contemporary climate. Readers who can access "La Resistência Cultural" in its Portuguese original version or the French translation would gain significant insights for their own national and community contexts and prescriptions. Within the tradition of transnational and transgenerational dialogues, in *Concepts of Cabralism: Amilcar Cabral and Africana*

Critical Theory, Reiland Rabaka demonstrates the extent to which the Négritude Movement influenced Cabral's perspective on the connection between the socio-cultural and the political, drawing attention to the cultural processes embedded in historical trajectory/trajectories. From the late twentieth century, Frantz Fanon's and Amilcar Cabral's revolutionary activism in Africa, grounded in the intellectual activism of such predecessors as Césaire, has influenced Black political thought in relation to social theory. Presenting Fanon and Cabral as two of the "pillars of the Africana tradition of critical thought," Rabaka explains that "few contemporary Fanonists and Cabralists have been willing to acknowledge the enormous influence the Negritude Movement had, whether directly or indirectly, on the origins and evolution of Fanon and Cabral's respective critical theories and revolutionary praxes."[8] In the following text, I offer the English translation of a few of Amilcar Cabral analyses on history, on the modification of cultures and social transformation. The excerpts to follow are taken from the 1976 French version, published in the journal *Esprit.*

> Que nous soyons des hommes de la ville ou de la brousse, le colonialisme nous a inculqué beaucoup de choses dans la tête. Et il nous faut enlever ce qui ne va pas et laisser ce qui est bon. . .[9]
>
> (Whether we are from the city or the bush, colonialism has inculcated many things in the mind. And we must remove what does not work and retain what is good. . .)[10]
>
> Beaucoup de gens pensent que, pour résister culturellement, l'Afrique doit faire toujours les mêmes choses qu'elle faisait il y a déjà cinq cents ans ou mille ans. Oui, l'Afrique a sa culture en effet, c'est bien notre opinion: certains de ses éléments sont éternels, ils ne changent jamais, ils peuvent se transformer toujours en chemin, mais ils ne doivent jamais disparaître. . . . Pour préserver la culture africaine, beaucoup estiment que nous devons défendre les aspects négatifs de notre civilisation. Non, ce n'est pas notre opinion. La culture est aussi le produit du niveau économique d'un peuple. . .[11]
>
> (Many people think to culturally resist, Africa must always do the same things it has been doing for the past five hundred years or thousand years. Yes, Africa has in effect its culture, it is indeed our opinion: certain elements are eternal, they never change, they can transform in the trajectory, but they must never disappear. . . . To preserve African culture, many surmise that we must defend the negative aspects of our civilization. No, this is not our opinion. Culture is also the product of the economic position of a people.)[12]

Furthermore, Cabral's reasoning on the function of language as a cultural, political, and education tool deserves attention, mainly because numerous African descendant communities—in Africa and the Americas—have struggled with this important dimension of progress and have been divided in their perspectives. Within Cabral's national context, he referenced the Portuguese language and the African languages of Guinea and Cape Verde. For the purpose of a diasporic articulation, the overall attention in this present chapter is the relationship between the standard or official language of any particular nation and the languages of the people who emerged from enslavement and colonialism. Cabral examined:

> Nous devons combattre tout opportunisme, même dans la culture. Par exemple, il y a des camarades qui pensent que, pour enseigner sur notre terre, il est fondamental d'enseigner déjà en créole, ou alors d'autres estiment qu'il vaut mieux d'enseigner en fula, en mandingue, en balante. . . . Maintenant notre langue écrite est le portugais. C'est la raison pour laquelle il est nécessaire de parler ici aussi bien le portugais que le créole; que nous soyons mieux les fils de notre terre si nous parlons créole, ceci n'est pas la vérité. *Le fils de notre terre est celui qui exécute les lois, les ordres du parti, pour bien servir notre peuple.*[13]
>
> (We must combat all opportunism, even in culture. For example, there are comrades who think that to teach on our land, it is fundamental to already start teaching in Creole, or others believe that it is better to teach in Fulani, in Mandinka, in Balanka . . . For Now our written language is Portuguese. For that reason it is necessary for us to speak Portuguese here as fluently as we speak Creole; that we are better offspring of our land if we speak Creole, is not the truth. *The child of our land is the one who implements the laws, the regulations of the party, to better serve our people.*)[14]
>
> La langue est un instrument que l'homme a créé à travers le travail, la lutte, pour communiquer avec les autres. Et ceci lui a donné une grande force, parce que personne ne demeura fermé sur lui-même, les individus s'habituèrent à communiquer les uns avec les autres, les hommes avec les hommes, les sociétés avec les sociétés, le peuple avec le peuple, le pays avec le pays, le continent avec le continent.[15]
>
> (Language is a tool that the human being created through work, through struggle, to communicate with others. And that has given [him or her] enormous force because no one will remain enclosed in oneself; individuals became accustomed to communicating with one another, human beings with human beings, societies with societies, the people with the people, the country with the country, the continent with the continent.)[16]

Access to contents as well as the usage of such contents for the development of one's community and country is one of the fundamental functions of language. In her chapter "Living Simple: An Antidote to Hedonistic Materialism" (*Black Genius: African American Solutions to African American Problems*), bell hooks draws a similar connection between substantive contents and navigating one's environment. If we are committed to substantive contents, "we will not be talking about ebonics," bell hooks noted, "[we] will be out in the streets demanding that the public schools have enough teachers so that all kids, cross color, can read and write in standard English."[17] Furthermore, we would be more attentive to the youth's historical substance and cultural intake.

Though writing from a diasporic context, I refrain from investigating and pointing out specific cultural behaviors from the numerous nations and communities, and from the multitude of generational practices—an intricate and insurmountable task. However, it seems crystal clear that cultural practices that do not elevate the mind and that do not protect the emotional state and the physical well-being of a community, particularly that of the youth, are detrimental practices. Cultural practices that denigrate, exploit, and physically and/or psychologically brutalize Black girls and women—while concurrently rendering them invisible—are indefensibly pernicious. Abuse of alcohol and drugs cannot be tolerated as part of "cultural" practices; they are circumstantial behaviors that are injurious to the family and the community. Practices—systemic and/or individual—that do not prioritize the appropriate education and the intellectual development of the youth are deleterious. Hence, a wholesale acceptance of "cultures" or cultural performances has been detrimental to the progress of the African Diaspora for too long. A strong historical grounding—if established—would help individuals and communities unpack and deconstruct the pitfalls of undiscerning adoption of behaviors that have been designated as "cultural." Such historical foundation would provide the vital tools necessary to unmask the economic politics and the social politics that lie beneath certain behaviors; it would unveil the perpetual psychological consequences of unexamined habits and practices. For, when individuals are unaware of "the intricate connection between the patterns of their own lives and the course of world history. . . [they] cannot cope with their troubles in such ways as to control the structural transformation that usually lie behind them."[18] By the mid-1900s, African descendants became increasingly more distant from the multiethnic African socio-cultural traditions that were brought to the Americas, for the past four centuries. During the centuries of enslavement, African descendants merged and modified their multiethnic traditions in order to cope with their predicament and environment in the Americas. With each shipment and transshipment of the transatlantic slave trade, the African men and women came equipped with lessons of psychological fortitude and cultural grounding:

> In the seventeenth and eighteenth centuries, West African culture was propelled by the oral tradition. Cultural knowledge was accumulated and passed on from generation to generation through priests, respected elders and storytellers. The socialization process for young people included sessions with elders who shared the cultural material necessary for life in the tribe. Intellectual continuity flowed not through the study of great or sacred books but through recitation, lectures, and dialogue.[19]

As centuries passed, and given that enslavers violently prohibited basic literacy, the African descendants remained completely unaware of Africa's continental history and African social structures, from ancient to modern (pre-transatlantic enslavement) Africa. The Negro Act of 1740 (U.S.) made it illegal for enslaved Africans and their progeny to learn to read and write. During the enslavement era, and the lasting neo-slavery system to follow, enslavers carefully selected and cultivated Black religious leaders; by so doing, "slaveholders erected yet another *cultural mechanism* to control the minds of the slaves."[20] Thus, there have been multifarious formations and re-formations of identities, based on the historical circumstances of the colonies on the continent of America, and the Africans' and African descendants' conditions within the colonies. Given the long-standing history, this chapter focuses more on the shifts of the African descendants' cultures from the first half of the twentieth century to the second half of the century. The chapter further examines the continuous impacts of the twentieth century onto the twenty-first century, with attention on the United States, for its multiethnic and multinational African descendant communities. As African descendants continue to endure the weight of marginalization, denigration, and destitution in the last three decades of the 1900s—after the Modern Civil Rights Movement of the 1960—many coping behaviors began to set and accepted, to some extent, as habits and ways of life. In the Introduction of this book, I referenced Ruth Prescott, from the documentary *Marcus Garvey: A Giant of Black Politics*, in her analysis of economic pressures and the African descendants' needs for survival, which at times become detrimental to the individual and the community. It is worth restating here because of the acuity and relevance of her statement as it relates to the current conditions of countless African descendants:

> [There] is a lot of economic pressures . . . and the people of the capitalistic world find it to their benefit to make things so sticky for the black man and black woman that at times the black people really lose faith in themselves.[21]

The rise of harsh drugs (for profit) that destroyed the lives of men, women, and children; the prevalence of liquor stores (for profit) in Black neighborhoods; the absence of male nurturers, protectors, and providers whether due to murder, mass incarceration (for profit), or voluntary absences based on a lack of accountability for the well-being of the children and the community; and the overburdened Black females, *all* contribute to the weakening of the community; very significantly, *all* contribute to situations where the Black youth is generally not consciously cared for nor conscientiously protected. The life of Malcolm Little—before his rise as Malcolm X, El-Hajj Malik El-Shabazz—epitomized the impacts of economic pressures, social alienation, and disorientation on the youth. After the assassination of Malcolm's father (Earl Little) by the Black Legion,[22] Louise Little's mental health declined, due to the pressures of raising the children on her own in a hostile world. She was eventually confined within the Kalamazoo

Psychiatric Hospital. Without parents, the children bounced between foster homes. Malcolm ended up in the streets, and thereafter he started to lead the life of drug dealing, gambling, robbery, and so on, until his imprisonment in 1946. It was during his imprisonment that Malcolm Little started the process of self-knowledge through comprehensive race history.

Harold Cruse's *The Crisis of The Negro Intellectual*, published in 1967, offers detailed and cogent analyses on the politics of culture(s) as well as the interconnection between capitalism and the processes of cultural fabrication, alteration, adaptation, representation, and misrepresentation, from the 1920s (with the Harlem Renaissance vogue) to the 1960s. In the 1984 preface to *The Crisis of the Negro Intellectual*, Bazel E. Allen and Ernest J. Wilson submitted a conclusion that is increasingly pertinent in the twenty-first century. They observed that "many of the old problems of economy and culture are still with us, and new ones have come to the surface that are, in many ways, even more perplexing and difficult to resolve."[23] As *The Crisis* investigates the tasks, successes, and failures of different factions of the Black intelligentsia, it examines the social challenges of Black communities. Cruse scrutinizes the African descendants' cultural adoptions and adaptations, from taking in cultural constructs and performing cultural misrepresentations for either material survival or opportunistic ends, as dangerously degenerative. Cruse demonstrates the extent to which the Harlem Renaissance vogue is a time in African American cultural history where White patrons dictated what should be presented as the Negro essence, as Negro culture. However, "[a] cultural renaissance that engenders barriers to the emergence of the creative writer is a contradiction in terms, an emasculated movement," Cruse reasons. Furthermore, "the creative edge of the movement has been dulled, the ability of the movement to foment revolutionary ideas about culture and society has been smothered."[24] The New Negro Renaissance philosophy of the 1920s, then, with its political, intellectual, and socio-cultural objectives, grounded in the historical trajectory of African descendants, sought to counter the economic influences of White patrons who arrogated the right to define Black culture and to dictate Black cultural representation. After the momentum of the civil rights and human rights movements of the 1960s (with the assassination of Malcolm X and Dr. King), the late 1970s ushered another period of unchallenged cultural intakes and performances; with that era also came a decreasing commitment to the well-being of the community, along with the dwindling commitment to the children. Referencing Charles Wright Mills' examination of the impact of the *cultural apparatus*—with its all-encompassing spheres of influence—Cruse discerns that nineteenth-century capitalism was not bolstered with the level of cultural capitalism of the twentieth century. Moreover, "nineteenth-century capitalists might have controlled the press, but they did not have radio, television, film industries, advertising combines, electronic recording and computer industries, highly developed telecommunications networks, and so forth."[25] It suffices to note that Mills is speaking from the 1950s and Cruse from the 1960s, decades—light-years from, so to speak—before the more rapid technological and social media advances of the twenty-first century.

In "Simple Living: An Antidote to Hedonistic Materialism," bell hooks underlines "the ideologies of imperialist, white supremacist, capitalist patriarchy [as] the basic founding principle of culture in the United States."[26] A culture of domination and insatiable profit must and will keep individuals in "constant states of yearning."[27] The ever-present desires to acquire whatever is available, to continuously dispose of and replace, preoccupy quotidian life. Similar to many clear-sighted observers, bell hooks examines that too many individuals are so intensely gripped by selfishness "that they do not have time to think about a world larger than self. Everything in our culture is telling us that anything we do for money is ok."[28] This general culture that bell hooks refers to as "hedonistic materialism" has been part of other racial cultures—in various forms—but is more particularly detrimental to African descendant communities, given the necessity to rebuild from centuries of imposed socioeconomic havoc. The Black youth will have access to wealth for mindless or compromising entertainment productions before they are given access to well-resourced schools and comprehensive education; the latter are foundations that should lead to lasting and progressive outcomes, not only for the individual but also for his or her community and succeeding generations. In the biographical movie on the late acclaimed rapper Tupac Shakur, disseminated in 2017, the character conveying the late Afeni Shakur's message—the rapper's mother—warns her son and, by extension, contemporary Blacks about the pitfalls of destructive behaviors revolving around exaggerated materialism, substance abuse, gangster culture, the disrespect of self, and the disrespect of others. "They are going to give you the tools that you need to destroy yourself," Afeni Shakur admonished.[29] Such infamous tools include the guns, the drugs, the alcohol, and the grim path to a violent death or imprisonment. While incarcerated, the rapper admits "they gave me everything . . . and I fell for it."[30]

If there is a purveying socioeconomic culture that creates and exaggerates illusions of "needs" and "wants," the individual and the community must accept and perform those fallacies as truths for them to hold any influential and sustained power. As mentioned in the Introduction of this present work, V.P. Franklin's 2005 observation on the impact of social media, expressed in the foreword of *The Mis-Education of the Negro*, is, unfortunately, increasingly relevant with time. This analysis is not to negate the important positive aspects of social media but to underline its undeniably perverse impacts.[31] In addition to existing negative stereotypes of Blackness repeatedly displayed on television and the internet during the past decades, the culture of ostentatious overconsumption, instant gratification, and unscrupulous money-making is further eroding the esteem and substantive focus of the youth. The concoction of stories and affectatious collages on social media, the senseless attacks and conflicts for fatuous entertainment and misconceived ego satisfaction, are all part of the new way of life where truths, realities, and illusions are indistinguishably blurred. Confusion reigns. Given that entertainment is no longer a healthy part of life but the crux of daily life for too many, the toxic entertainment that pervades is poisoning the mind of the youth, who are overly exposed and/or are actively participating. For the global African descendant community, but particularly within the geographical context of the United States, such level of absurd and/or toxic diversion is yet another barrier to the full development of the youth's intelligence and consciousness; it is yet another impediment to her or his advancement in addition to systemic challenges. The increasing screen time distractions weaken thorough and attentive thought not only for the adult but more so for the young mind in formative development.

Ultimately, African descendant communities must reevaluate respective national and community concepts of culture, and reassess the extent to which current cultural performances will negatively impact or positively serve future generations. Equally important, it is crucial to understand the political and economic forces behind the emergence of what is assigned and accepted as cultural norms, from one generation to the next. Stated differently, one must grasp the weight of sociopolitical and economic structures on generational cultural performances. Dr. Joy DeGruy's observatory expression "there's poison in the cookies"[32] is relevant to the examination of behaviors, deemed cultural. What seems appealing or savory is in effect poisonous to the individual and the community. Thus, the study, the reconsideration, and the manifestation of a "New Negro" mentality, within the twenty-first-century context and realities, are indispensable in order to gauge and mitigate the perils of unexamined cultural practices. The greater masses along with the intellectuals and activists of the late 1800s and early 1900s revitalized the mindset of African descendants in the United States and abroad, with the New Negro Renaissance philosophies, publications, and practices. "Each generation, however, will have its creed," Alain Locke asserted in "New Negro" essay, "and that of the present is the belief in the efficacy of collective effort, in race co-operation."[33] The various generations to be formed in the twenty-first century will undoubtedly have many creeds based on the degrees of social progress and/or social regression. Given that it has been, unjustifiably, too many centuries of economic enslavement and destitution as well as social and psychological oppression, for the purpose of faster, efficient, and sustainable progress, the two leading social creeds for African descendants must be: one, collective historical consciousness; two, informed and shrewd examinations of contemporary cultural practices, in relation to the overarching institutional structures of their respective nation and global systems. The New Negro Renaissance of the early twentieth century emerged during an era when African Americans of the United States and African descendants in Harlem were redefining and recalibrating themselves culturally, politically, and economically. Contemporarily, the adults who have the task of preparing the next generations of the twenty-first century must also devise a new collective psychology that understands and progressively attenuates—if impossible to extirpate—the toxic socio-cultural impacts from the late twentieth century onward. "With this renewed self-respect and self-dependence, the life of the Negro community is bound to enter a new dynamic phase, the buoyancy from within compensating for whatever pressure there may be of conditions from without."[34] Preparing the youth to navigate, in spite of outside forces and conditions, is a lesson that transcends generations and national barriers. As the sociopolitical movements of the early twentieth century—such as Pan-Africanism, Garveyism, and Négritude, in their Black Internationalist cooperation approach—aimed to foster in the mind and nurture in the heart of African descendants sober and uplifting cultural exchanges, in the twenty-first century, it is vital that the youth is formed from a comprehensive historical grounding that will aid to discern cultural practices *of elevation* from practices of degradation. Through social media the African descendants in the United States hold significant cultural influences abroad, thus the conscious examination and manifestation of their cultural performances is weighty. A transformed and transforming psychology of U.S. African descendants has, and will have, profound international reverberations for African descendants abroad. The concept and practices of Black Internationalism within the twenty-first-century context must hold the psychological restoration and intellectual preparation of the youth as one of its core principles. Jane and Paulette Nardal emphasized the lessons of history and cultures—particularly through literary works and various works of art—that inspired introspection and excellence.[35] Building on the legacy of the thinkers of the early twentieth century what must remain embedded in the African descendants' ever-changing cultures are consciousness and conscientiousness—that is, the conscious and conscientious elevation of race, of the youth. The term "elevation," here, is significant for its conceptual development in Martin R. Delany's *The Condition, Elevation, Emigration and Destiny of the Colored People of the United States*. In his conclusion, titled "A Glance at Ourselves," Delany addresses debasing practices that had become part of the African American unexamined cultural behaviors; such cultural practices further hinder the social and psychological elevation of the race. Delany expresses the following criticism, among a number of important social observations of his era[36]:

> young men and women among us, many of whom have good trades and homes, adequate to their support, voluntarily leave them, and seek positions, such as servants, waiting maids, coachmen, nurses, cooks in gentlemens' kitchen, or such like occupations when they can gain a livelihood at something more respectable, or *elevating in character*.[37]

For Delany, the aspect that deserves most attention is the perception of such pursuits as "fashionable," to the extent that such limited aspirations "have become second nature, and they [those who accept those limitations] really become offended, when it is spoken against."[38] Delany's example of that specific unexamined behavior was aimed to underline that Blacks who were taught or have chosen to view everything associated to whiteness—regardless of its true value—as worth pursuing sought out positions that would place them in closer proximity to whiteness, in whatever menial capacity. In 1933 Woodson noted that if African descendants are taught to devalue their African origins, they will either seek to imitate whiteness or adopt American-born cultural behaviors they have been conditioned to believe are inherent to Blackness. If they are aware of the achievements of their ancestors, they would expect and forge a life from uplifting practices. If they know the truth about the past of other races, they will know that African descendants have nothing disgraceful in their past, at least not more disgraceful than others. Their knowledge would unveil the need for greater commitment to self-education and a greater commitment to protecting the youth from negative influences and pressures.

Contemporarily, conscionable adults have the responsibility to nurture and safeguard the intellectual and true artistic aptitudes of the youth, so they do not succumb under the quotidian pressures of popular materialism, mediocrity, or vagabondage—to use C.G. Woodson's choice of word.[39] The youth must be taught that certain behaviors that are presented as part of their so-called inherent race "culture" are simply *not*; in fact, they are resigned acceptance of a life of survival at all costs, even if that means the immediate or the slow process of destruction of self, of one's brother and/or sister, and/or of one's community. Simply put, they are behavioral responses to environmental factors. The void of fundamental knowledge of self, and the unawareness of the works of the forefathers and foremothers, continuously exacerbate the problem of low confidence in self and the community. In the final analysis, "[there] can be no real black revolution in the United States without a cultural revolution as a corollary to the scheme of 'agencies for social change'."[40] Only a transformed or transforming psychology can lead to fundamental cultural reevaluation and social changes within Black communities, internationally. Every insightful and influential intellectual of the past two centuries grasped and keenly transmitted the importance of the indispensable processes of cultural evaluation and reevaluation, for the preservation of the practices that serve the continuous progress of the race. The Awakened African descendants of today will not eschew critical observation of cultural practices, and they will not discount the lessons of social responsibilities; that is, they will not avoid the responsibility of being reflective and sober examples for succeeding generations.

The Effects of Intellectual History in the Formation of a Collective Youth Consciousness

In 1954 George G.M. James summarized the primary focus and purpose of his historiographical work, as a scholar and an intellectual activist. I submit, unhesitatingly, that the fundamentals below are that of every conscious and conscientious intellectual. He wrote:

> From the outset my readers and co-workers in the solution of a common problem, must be reminded that our philosophy of redemption is a psychological process, involving a change in belief and mentality to be followed by a *corresponding change in behavior. It really signifies a mental emancipation, in which the Black people will be liberated from the chain of traditional falsehood*, which for centuries has incarcerated them in the prison of inferiority complex and world humiliation and insult. This mental emancipation or redemption, it must be remembered, has two functions . . . a general emancipation of both races in order to effect a solution. . . . On the other hand, emancipation or redemption is specific, when we refer to the effects of the phenomenon of unwholesome race relations upon Black people.[41]

The psychological process that leads to consonant comportment is paramount. The youth must grasp not only the political and philosophical significance of history, and the process of epistemological frameworks, but also the weight of certain cultural adoptions and adaptations, which are inextricably embedded in the political, that is, in political agendas. In "I Can," particularly written for the benefit of the youth, Nasir Jones reminds society and especially the youth itself that "[if] the truth is told, the youth can grow . . . they [can] learn to survive until they gain control . . . Read more. Learn more. Change the globe. Ghetto children do your thing."[42] The youth must understand the ways in which certain cultural practices are molded from established sociopolitical systems then sold as inherent behaviors. Without such knowledge, there cannot be *a corresponding change in behavior*. As African descendants become aware of erroneous or illusory "traditions," they will refrain from performing learned destructive behaviors that have been passed on over time, from systems of oppression, destitution, abandonment, and despair.

The "color line" of the twentieth century[43] remains the problem of the twenty-first century. Color is still the major obstruction for African descendants worldwide, though the problem has been hazed out, to some extent, with underdeveloped arguments on the class divide. Hubert H. Harrison is esteemed as one of the first critical thinkers—along with Garvey—to unreservedly dismantle the conceptual separation of race and class; early in the 1900s, he published and lectured on the intricate interconnection between race and class for the majority of African descendants within the world. Harrison joined the activist scholars of his time to advocate education—in the humanities and the social sciences as well as in the natural sciences and engineering—as one of the most effective paths to socioeconomic progress and self-awareness. As long as African descendants, as a race, do not have access to quality and appropriate education (in contents), and ensuing employment opportunities, they will remain in lower economic status. In the September 1919 article "Education and Race," Harrison particularly examined the discipline of history to assert that "[courses] in Negro history and the culture of West African peoples, at least, should be given in every college that claims to be an institution of learning for Negroes."[44] Furthermore, as an internationalist, he reasoned that the African descendants "need above all a knowledge of the wider world and of the long past. But that past is history, modern and ancient."[45] African descendants must also know, he continued,

> [our] place in the human processus, to strengthen our minds by contact with the best and most useful thought-products evolved during the long rise of man from anthropoid to scientist; to inspire our souls and to lift our race industrially, commercially, intellectually to the level of the best that there is in the world about us. For *never until the Negro's knowledge of nitrates and engineering, of chemistry and agriculture, of history, science and business is on a level, at least, with that of the whites, will the Negro be able to measure arms successfully with them.*[46]

In addition, Harrison sought to awaken the attention of his readers—and listeners—to the generational and multidimensional effects of identity distortions and cultural toxins. "What seem to escape attention," he wrote,

> is the fact that the Negro boy and girl, getting the same (though worse) instruction, also get from it the same notion of the Negro's place and part in life which the white children get. Is it any wonder, then, that they so readily accept the status of inferiors; that they tend to disparage themselves, and think of themselves worthwhile only to the extent to which they look and act and think like the whites?[47]

The schools, then, are not only educational institutions but concurrently cultural institutions. "In spite of logic, educational ideas and ideals spread from above downwards."[48] As part of the process for considerable transformation, in 1973 Cheikh Anta Diop observed and pointed out to his contemporaries that

> [only] a loyal, determined struggle to destroy cultural aggression and bring out the truth, whatever it may be, is revolutionary and consonant with real progress; it is the only approach which opens on to the universal. Humanitarian *declarations* are not called for and add nothing to real progress.[49]

Declarations without de facto implementation are null and worthless.

While all nations are fixated on further developing manufactured resources for profit, while some nations are dedicated to preserving natural resources for better life quality—necessarily so and understandably—the world's greatest resources have been abandoned and neglected to waste: that is, the intelligence, the intellect, the industrial and professional abilities of the youth of African descent. The intellectual and industrial potential of millions of African descendants' youth—in developed and so-called developing nations alike—are neglected or completely lost within increasingly chaotic global atmospheres, compounded to the existing realities of racism and prejudice. In the long run, such degree of lost brain power is unconscionable and of benefit to no one—directly or indirectly. The earlier publications from thinkers such as Garvey, Woodson, and Diop speak to the educational contents for the world, and the Black youth in particular, as part of the problems. One of Garvey's main messages is that the Creator never intended the imprisonment of the human's mind and energy. In spite of the efforts to imprison or neglect the mind of some, the truth is eternal (as Firmin noted in *De L'Égalité*); it will eventually manifest itself. The youth can be routed to its true potential and abilities.

Playing up crimes and shortcomings, while concealing the truth about the race's intellectual achievements and scrupulous leadership abilities—from antiquity to present times—have only led to the real-life re-creation and continuation of such shortcomings. Moreover, systemic exclusion from quality education and/or professional opportunities only generates more poverty and degenerate behaviors of survival. It is indeed a vicious cycle. The limited space in the world of entertainment for profit, particularly in the age of social media, has led to questionable behaviors in the quest for relative stardom. Excepting the military and the exclusive access to professional sports, the Black youth still experiences—in the twenty-first century—blockade from the world of socioeconomic mobility. Yet, this unfortunate reality in advanced industrialized countries is the best-case scenario. In impoverished countries of Africa, the Caribbean, Central and South America, the African descendants—those phenotypically recognized as such—face more dire conditions, where access to basic food subsistence and basic literacy is impossible. It follows that the African descendants who do not have access to basic literacy programs cannot possibly have access to the comprehensive history of the race; therefore, they cannot access true knowledge of self and, by extension, true awareness of their aptitudes and capabilities. Self-assertion grows from in-depth understanding of one's community, of one's national, racial, and global histories, and one's position within such interconnections. With opportunities to literacy and the contents of history—that unveil the economic, social, and philosophical formations of societies—the youth can "imbibe" the spirit of the ancestors, and "answer the present call of duty with equal nobleness of soul."[50] The global preoccupations with excessive material profit, the global atmosphere of individualist quest for socioeconomic advancement for one's own interests, have rendered the dire plight of the masses of African descendants more complex to solve. From the nineteenth century—post chattel slavery in the Americas—to the twenty-first century, the needs of the generations have indeed changed along with the individuals and the communities; thus, for the success of African descendants, in the present and onward, "the only hope to function efficiently in society is to know themselves and the generation which they are to serve. *The chief value in studying the records of others* is to become better acquainted with oneself and with one's possibilities to live and to do in the present."[51]

The Course to Rehabilitation

The students who have been adversely affected from childhood (elementary school) onward become reactionary and hypersensitive, to a level that further harms their already-scant possibility of success. They have been traumatized and continue to be traumatized into adulthood, as they watch—and relive—their children undergo the same educational and economic impasse, with no prospect of meaningful change for the generations to follow. Others have disengaged, and their children have detached from the educational system and resigned to the lifestyle that has been imposed for generations: low-pay jobs or the street life. The street life, and all that it entails, is viewed as the only alternative to the labor that does not offer adequate pay for decent living. Some would reason that they can only play the proverbial cards they were dealt, and the street life is part of the game. There is a level of resignation or despair in having to survive by playing the cards that were dealt—so to speak. It is precisely against this life of despair and distress that our societies have the responsibility to prepare the youth—boys and girls. If the youth is taught to expect more of herself or himself, and is giving more as preparation, he or she will accomplish more. The nurturing process of high esteem for self goes back to the process of psychological formation studied throughout this present book, particularly in Chapter 1, "Philosophies of Existence, Freedom, and Humanity," in the subsection titled, "On Economics: The Social Complex of Inferiority and The Illusion of Superiority." The preparation must be supported by systemic measures. If one has been conditioned to believe that he or she is only fit for the "street life," he or she will most likely live the "street life." If he or she has been conditioned, prepared for, and accepted into a respectable professional life, he or she will, in most probability, opt for such life of economic security and contribution to one's community and one's nation. Regrettably, as it relates to the youth of African descent, most have witnessed and lived normalized educational prejudices that ought to be illegal. On June 28, 1964, Malcolm X delivered a speech to publicly announce the founding of the Organization of Afro-American Unity. Malcolm spoke extensively on a number of important aspects for the liberation of African Americans, and African descendants in general. On his program he included topics such as education and politics, economics, and culture. Malcolm X was keenly aware of the interconnection between comprehensive education and the critical evaluation of cultural practices, for viable psychological and social redemption as well as for fundamental economic and political reforms. That "[our] children are being criminally shortchanged in the public school system of America" was the crux of his observation on the education system. "The Afro-American schools are the poorest-run schools in the city of New York. Principals and teachers fail to understand the nature of the problem with which they work and as a result they cannot do the job of teaching our children." Equally important, he called attention to the process of identity sabotage through the erasure or degradation of valuable historical and cultural frames of reference.

> The textbooks tell our children nothing about the great contributions of Afro-Americans to the growth and development of this country. When we send our children to school in this country they learn nothing about us other than that we used to be cotton pickers. Every little child going to school thinks his grandfather was a cotton picker. Why, your grandfather was *Nat Turner*; your grandfather was *Toussaint L'Ouverture*; your grandfather was *Hannibal*. Your grandfather was some of the greatest black people who walked on this earth. It was your grandfather's hands who forged civilization and it was your grandmother's hands who rocked the cradle of civilization. But the textbooks tell our children nothing about the great contributions of Afro-Americans to the growth and development of this country.[52]

Well into the twenty-first century, while the schools that are marked as predominantly Black schools have blatant below-standard resources, African descendants who attend schools recognized as predominantly White schools face different set of challenges—the extent may vary based on regions or the uniqueness of a particular school. Among such challenges is the questioning of his or her identity and the worth of his or her race. Their anxious inquiries are formed from the disciplines of history and social studies contents of the curriculum, and the overall atmosphere of the school. A sense of alienation sets in, as they become victims of unfair academic grading, based on particular teachers' conscious or subconscious prejudices and illusory perceptions of Blacks' aptitude (inaptitude). Let us briefly add to the pernicious equation the twenty-first-century practice of frivolous and non-stop social media distractions, of which some of the K–12 teachers are also active participants. The result seems evident. In 1933 Woodson questioned (his query is pertinent today): "But can you expect teachers to revolutionize the social order for the good of the community? Indeed we must expect this very thing. The educational system of a country is worthless unless it accomplishes this task."[53]

While the tasks Dr. Woodson posed are crucial, parents of the African descendant youth should not completely entrust the transference of all historical and social knowledge in the hands of the teachers—for a number of reasons. In the late nineteenth century, Alexander Crummell impressed on parents the responsibility to train and prepare their children. For, "you are accountable to God for the soul, the life, the character, and the conduct of your child," he entreated. "Hence duty and responsibility are the two paramount considerations which are to be allied with the entire training of your children."[54] Dr. John Henrik Clarke's principle "do your best" work should be heeded by parents and children. For the youth, it is to maintain academic persistence and intellectual stamina against all odds and sabotages, from within the system and the classrooms. For the parents, it is the responsibility to help ground the youth academically and psychologically; it is also the responsibility to help them navigate both the virtual world of social media and the physical world—so they do not fall prey or victims. Both worlds are fraught with myriad distractions and pitfalls. As for the African descendant youth living in regions and circumstances without access to the internet and social media, but thereby also do not have direct connections to toxic representation and misrepresentation of "Blackness," they too face life challenges, among which are dire destitution and no means to literacy and basic education. The long-standing normativity of the *unjustifiable* has reached the point of irreparable social and economic damages for countless African descendants across the globe. The deep-seated obstacles to rehabilitation have remained exceedingly difficult to extirpate, even with the most willing and well-intentioned minds. Contemporaneously, the correlations between the socioeconomic position, the political voice, and the educational structures, for the majority of African descendants, are evident across the globe. Africans and African descendants have greatly contributed to world advancement, from antiquity to their achievements even under the yoke of enslavement and neo-enslavement. In the twenty-first century, Africans and African descendants should be further excelling; yet, in spite of some success the majority is stagnant or regressing, from a joint force of political and economic oppression. The overall present conditions of the masses of the African descendant youth, in different national circumstances, unveil the perennial significance of the collective objectives the conscious Black leaders set forth centuries ago but remain unaddressed: one, the means for substantive reparation and, two, the opportunities to excel.

Notes

1. Cheikh Anta Diop, *The African Origin of Civilization: Myth or Reality*, translated and edited by Mercer Cook (Chicago: Lawrence Hill & Co., 1974), xiv.
2. Kersuze Simeon-Jones, *Literary and Sociopolitical Writings of the Black Diaspora in the Nineteenth and Twentieth Centuries* (Boulder: Lexington Books, 2010), 49.
3. Diop, *The African Origin of Civilization*, xv.
4. John Henrik Clarke, *A Great and Mighty Walk*, distributed by Cinema Guild (New York: Black Dot Media, 1996), DVD. Emphasis added.
5. William M. Banks, *Black Intellectuals: Race and Responsibility in American Life* (New York: W. W. Norton & Company, 1996), 101.
6. Author's translation.
7. Amilcar Cabral, "La Résistance Culturelle," *Esprit*, translated by Manuelle Gacha, Nouvelle Série, No. 457 (Mai, 1976), 872–891.
8. Reiland Rabaka, *Concepts of Cabralism: Amilcar Cabral and Africana Critical Theory* (Boulder: Lexington Books, 2014), 31.
9. Cabral, "La Résistance Culturelle," 875.

10. Author's translation.
11. Cabral, "La Résistance Culturelle," 876.
12. Author's translation.
13. Cabral, "La Résistance Culturelle," 889. Emphasis added.
14. Author's translation. Emphasis added.
15. Cabral, "La Résistance Culturelle," 889.
16. Author's translation.
17. Bell hooks, "Living Simple: An Antidote to Hedonistic Materialism," *Black Genius: African American Solutions to African American Problems*, edited by Walter Mosley, Manthia Diawara, and Clyde Taylor (New York: W.W. Norton & Company Inc., 1999), 141–142.
18. Charles Wright Mills, *The Sociological Imagination* (New York: Oxford University Press, 2000), 4.
19. Banks, *Black Intellectuals*, 6.
20. Ibid., 5. Emphasis added.
21. Howard Johnson, *Marcus Garvey: A Giant of Black Politics* (New York, N.Y.: Films Media Group, 2008, 2013), @ 44:44 minutes, DVD.
22. An offshoot of the Ku Klux Klan.
23. Harold Cruse, *The Crisis of the Negro Intellectual* (New York: Quill, 1984), iii.
24. Ibid., 37.
25. Ibid., 474.
26. hooks, "Living Simple," 129.
27. Ibid., 139.
28. Ibid., 139.
29. Tupac Shakur, *All Eyez on Me* (Movie), produced by L.T. Hutton, David C. Robinson, and James G. Robinson (Santa Monica: Summit Entertainment, 2017).
30. Ibid.
31. I am completing this manuscript in the midst of the 2020 global pandemic—the Coronavirus or COVID-19. I cannot fathom life without access to the internet and social media. Perhaps, after the devastating pandemic our relation to or use of the internet will remain valuable and beneficial, that is, the possibility to stay connected to family, friends, colleagues, and students in constructive intentions and uplifting ways.
32. Joy DeGruy, *Post Traumatic Slave Disorder* (London: Artikal Films Production, 2008), @14:30–14:40.
33. Alain Locke, "The New Negro," *The New Negro* (New York: Touchstone Book, 1997), 11.
34. Ibid., 4.
35. Simeon-Jones, *Literary and Sociopolitical Writings*, 88.
36. Martin R. Delany, *The Condition, Elevation, Emigration, and Destiny of the Colored People of the United States* (Baltimore: Black Classic Press, 1993), 38, 46–48.
37. Ibid., 198.
38. Ibid., 198.
39. Carter G. Woodson, *The Mis-Education of the Negro* (Washington, DC: The Association for the Study of African American Life and History, 1933, 2005), 4.
40. Cruse, *The Crisis of the Negro Intellectual*, 475.
41. George Granville Monah James, *The Stolen Legacy* (Trenton, NJ: Africa World Press, Inc., 1992), 158–159. Emphasis added.
42. Nasir bin Olu Dara Jones, "I Can," *God's Son* (New York: Ill Will and Columbia Records, 2002).
43. W.E.B. Du Bois, *The Souls of Black Folk* (New York: Fawcett Publications, Inc., 1961), 23.
44. Hubert Harrison, *When Africa Awakes: The "Inside Story" of the Stirrings and Strivings of the New Negro in the Western World* (New York: The Porro Press, 1920), 131.

45. Ibid., 133.
46. Ibid., 134.
47. Ibid., 130.
48. Ibid., 130.
49. Diop, *The African Origin of Civilization*, xvi. Emphasis added.
50. Woodson, *The Mis-Education*, 77.
51. Ibid., 77.
52. Malcolm X, *By Any Means Necessary: Speeches, Interviews, and a Letter by Malcolm X*, edited by George Breitman (New York: Pathfinder Press, 1970), 43–44. Emphasis added.
53. Woodson, *The Mis-Education*, 81.
54. Alexander Crummell, *Africa and America: Addresses and Discourses* (Miami: Mnemosyne Publishing, Inc., 1969), 339.

EPILOGUE IN LIEU OF CONCLUSION

Toward the Twenty-First-Century Renaissance of the Black World

An integral part of the viable socio-cultural and politico-cultural transformation of African descendants is rooted in the position of African descendant women. This aspect was recognized, very early on, in the programs of development articulated by foundational activists-leaders and educators-intellectuals of the nineteenth century and early twentieth century. The sage grasped that "the education and respect of the woman . . . signify the respect of her progeny; the elevation and advancement of the race depended on the education of black women."[1] In "Womanhood: A Vital Element in the Regeneration and Progress of a Race," Anna Julia Cooper posits that "the fundamental agency under God in the regeneration, the retraining of the race, as well as the ground work and starting point of its progress upward, must be the black woman."[2]

> No people are elevated above the condition of their females; hence, the condition of the mother determines the condition of the child. To know the position of a people, it is only necessary to know the condition of their females; and despite themselves, they cannot rise above their level. . .[3]
>
> I think that the progress of the country will be more rapid and permanent when the girls receive the same general training as the boys; and our women, besides being able to appreciate the intellectual labours of their husbands and brothers, will be able also to share in the pleasures of intellectual pursuits. We need not fear that they will be less graceful, less natural, or less womanly; but we may be sure that they will make wiser mothers, more appreciative wives, and more affectionate sisters.[4]

Those were the principles that the critical thinkers and activists of the nineteenth century hoped would permeate the mindset of Black communities. However, the disregard, denigration, exploitation, and abuse of African descendant women—from childhood to adulthood—are what have taken place throughout the centuries. During the enslavement era, her direct perpetrators were White enslavers. After the enslavement era, her direct perpetrators became both White and Black males. By the late twentieth century, while the White capitalist system remains her economic exploiter—unequal pay, unequal access to jobs and professions—Black males remain her physical, sexual, and psychological abusers; one could submit to her economic abuser to some extent, if she is left as the only parent responsible for the children. In *How Capitalism Underdeveloped Black America: Problems in Race, Political Economy, and Society*, Manning Marable explains:

> Women have been the foundation of Black culture and society, yet their contributions have been generally ignored, or relegated to second class status by most Black male activists, historians and social scientists. They felt the sting of the lash upon their backs in Georgia's cotton fields; they knew the pain of losing children from lack of decent medical care; they felt the hot sun beating down upon their foreheads as they walked to work as maids in whites' homes; *they fought to preserve their humanity from white and/or Black men's sexual abuse. The underdevelopment of Black America will end only* when Black men begin to seriously challenge and uproot the patriarchal assumptions and institutions which still dominate Black civil and political society.[5]

To justify the disregard, abuses, and exploitations against Black women, the stereotype of the "Angry Black Woman" was forged. One is compelled, then, to inquire what came first: the wanton abuses and exploitations (physical, sexual, psychological, emotional, and economic) with impunity or the Black woman's human response to her circumstances, defined as "angry." Marable examines the ways in which the stereotypes attributed to her have been used as politics of aggression and silencing against her being. He explains the following points:

> Well before the Civil Rights Movements, a not-so-subtle reaction began to form within Black civil society which reinforced patriarchal relations between men and women. The Depression and *war years produced within the popular culture the figure of Sapphire*: a Black woman who was "evil, treacherous, bitchy, stubborn, and hateful." The Sapphire stereotype was utilized by white males who "could justify their dehumanization and sexual exploitation of black women," and Black males, who could reasonably "claim that they could not get along with black women because they were so evil." Black patriarchal society employed *Sapphire to explain away any Black woman who exhibited tendencies of strength that were designated for males only.*[6]

The Sapphire caricature, synonymous to the "Angry Black Woman," holds greater de facto significance than the mere stereotypical and derogatory name-calling; it is, above all, a "social control mechanism that is employed to punish black women who violate the societal norms that encourage them to be passive, servile, non-threatening, and unseen."[7] Thus, "[the] Sapphire portrayal has been around for as long as black women have dared to critique their lives and treatment. . . . The Sapphire name is . . . a label designed to silence dissent and critique."[8]

In 1994, in the documentary *Aimé Césaire: A Voice for History*, the then president of the République de Bénin, Nicéphore Dieudonné Soglo, acknowledged the abysmal reality of the majority of Black women in Africa. Significantly, he connected the future of Africa to the development of African women, to the positions that African institutions accord to its women. Soglo asserted that "there will not be a renaissance in Africa without the renaissance of the woman . . . without the respect that we owe our mothers, our sisters and our daughters . . . that is fundamental."[9] ("Il n'y aura pas de renaissance en Afrique sans la renaissance de la femme . . . sans le respect que nous devons à nos mères, nos sœurs et à nos filles . . . c'est capital.")[10] The deplorable reality of the social neglect and institutional exploitation of women of African descent inescapably plague the future of the Black youth. If it is accurate that there cannot be a renaissance in Africa without the renaissance of the woman, without the support and "without the respect we owe our mothers, our sisters and our daughters," it follows that the stagnation (in some cases) or further deterioration (in other cases) of predominantly Black nations and communities will persist without the preparation of Black girls and the elevation of Black women. Equally significant, without the upliftment of the woman, there cannot be the elevation of the children—boys and girls. The perception, recognition, and position of African descendant women are consequential dimensions for the collective psychological progress of the race. Such recognition, respect, and support can only take place in constructive socio-cultural grounding. In 1964 Malcolm X offered his thought on the significance of women in African descendants' efforts toward social progress. Malcolm X's consideration came as an evolution of his philosophies of liberation. He explained:

> One thing that I became aware of in my traveling recently through Africa and the Middle East, in every country you go to, usually the degree of progress can never be separated from the woman. . . . So one of the things I became thoroughly convinced of in my recent travels is the importance of giving freedom to the woman, giving her education, and giving her the incentive to get out there and put that same spirit and understanding in her children. And *I frankly am proud of the contributions that our women have made in the struggle for freedom* and I'm one person who's for giving them all the leeway possible because *they've made a greater contribution than many of us men.*[11]

In the final analysis, *The Intellectual Roots of Contemporary Black Thought: Nascent Political Philosophies* seeks to examine and demonstrate the extent to which the political, social, and cultural philosophies of pioneer Black thinkers and activists are pertinent to the progress of African descendants of the twenty-first century. Historical grounding through comprehensive education, for the purposes of knowledge of self, and confidence in one's aptitudes and capabilities are the foundational lessons. Concurrently, the particular recognition of the position of Black women within societies and the support and respect that should have been accorded and should be accorded to them *ought* to remain fundamental objectives. Early in the twentieth century, Hubert Harrison spoke to the need for developed consciousness—in all aspects of Black life—for sustained and sustainable advancement. In *Africa Awakes: The "Inside Story" of the Stirrings and Strivings of the New Negro in the Western World*, Harrison wrote: "the chains snap from the limbs of the young giant as he rises, stretches himself, and sits up to take notice. But let him, for his future's sake, insist on taking notice."[12] After the chains of enslavement snapped, there remained momentous systemic challenges. Miseducation or extremely limited education, as it regards the history and achievements of African descendants, circularly continues to afflict communities and families, from one generation to the next, irrespective of region. In the United States, university-level students increasingly have access to transformative historical contents. However, the major problem is that the majority of African descendants do not have the opportunity to make it to higher education; too many are existentially derailed—early on—into servitude, menial jobs, low-pay jobs, the street life, or imprisonment. Moreover, the pressures of and decisions for material survival, in addition to constant trivial distractions, render the psychological grounding of African descendants increasingly more complex. The global context of exceedingly toxic capitalism disregards the outstanding economic reparation and necessary systemic adjustments due to Black nations and communities. For their "future's sake," however, African descendant parents and youth must be awakened; they must "insist on taking notice"[13] to their unique cumulative predicament.

Notes

1. Kersuze Simeon-Jones, *Literary and Sociopolitical Writings of the Black Diaspora in the Nineteenth and Twentieth Centuries* (Boulder: Lexington Books, 2010), 63.
2. Anna Julia Cooper, "Womanhood: A Vital Element in the Regeneration and Progress of a Race," *The Voice of Anna Julia Cooper*, edited by Charles Lemert and Esme Bhan (New York: Rowman & Littlefield Publishers, Inc., 1988), 62.
3. Martin Delany, *The Condition, Elevation, Emigration, and Destiny of the Colored People of the United States* (Baltimore: Black Classic Press, 1852, 1993), 199.
4. Edward W. Blyden, *Christianity, Islam, and the Negro Race* (Edinburg: University Press, 1967), 89.
5. Manning Marable, *How Capitalism Underdeveloped Black America: Problems in Race, Political Economy, and Society* (Chicago: Pluto Press, 2000), 103.
6. Ibid. 85. Emphasis added.
7. David Pilgrim, *The Sapphire Caricature* (MI: Ferris State University), Website: ferris.edu/jimcrow.

8. Ibid., Website: ferris.edu/jimcrow.
9. Author's translation.
10. Nicéphore Soglo, *Aimé Césaire: A Vocie for History* (San Francisco: Newsreel, 1994).
11. Malcolm X, *By Any Means Necessary*, edited by George Breitman (New York: Pathfinder Press, 1970), 179. Emphasis added.
12. Hubert H. Harrison, *When Africa Awakes: The "Inside Story" of the Stirrings and Strivings of the New Negro in the Western World* (New York: The Porro Press, 1920), 127.
13. Ibid., 127.

BIBLIOGRAPHY

Adler, Alfred. *Connaissance de l'Homme: Étude de Caractérologie Individuelle.* Translated by Jacques Marty. Paris: Editions Payot, 1927, 1949.

Anderson, Claud and Rue L. Cromwell. " 'Black Is Beautiful' and the Color Preferences of Afro-American Youth." *The Journal of Negro Education* 46, no. 1 (Winter 1977): 76–88.

Asante, Molefi Kete. *Cheikh Anta Diop: An Intellectual Portrait.* Los Angeles: University of Sankore Press, 2007.

———. *Maulana Karenga: An Intellectual Portrait.* Cambridge: Polity, 2009.

Baker, Houston Alfred Jr. *How Black Intellectuals Have Abandoned the Ideals of the Civil Rights Era.* New York: Columbia University Press, 2008.

Banks, William M. *Black Intellectuals: Race and Responsibility in American Life.* New York: W.W. Norton & Company, 1996.

Benjamin, George J. *Histoire Diplomatique: la diplomatie d'Anténor Firmin, ses péripéties, ses aspects.* Paris: A. Pedone, 1960.

Blaise, Pascal. *Pensées.* Paris: Garnier-Flammarion, 1670, 1976.

Blyden, Edward Wilmot. *Christianity, Islam, and the Negro Race.* Edinburg: Edinburg University Press, 1967.

Boisrond-Tonnerre, Louis. *Mémoires Pour Servir à l'Histoire d'Haïti, Précédés de Différents Actes Politiques Dus à sa Plume, et D'une étude Historique et Critique Par Saint-Remy.* Paris: France Libraire, 1851.

Bonaparte, Napoléon, Premier Consul. *Loi du 30 Floréal An X: Relative à la traite des Noirs et au régime des colonies.* Paris, 1802.

Bouvet de Cressé, Auguste Jean Baptiste. *Histoire de la Catastrophe de Saint-Domingue.* Paris: Librairie Peytieux, 1824.

Brown, William Wells. *Clotel; or, the President's Daughter.* London: Partridge & Oakey, Paternoster Row, 1853.

———. *The Black Man: His Antecedents, His Genius, and His Achievements.* Boston: James Redpath Publisher, 1863.

Cabral, Amilcar. *Análise de Alguns Tipos de Resistência.* Cabo Verde: Seara Nova, 1974.

———. "La Résistance Culturelle." *Esprit*, Translated by Manuelle Gacha. Nouvelle Série, No. 457, 5 (Mai 1976): 872–891.

Cary, Hector. *L'Actualité d'Anténor Firmin: hier, aujourd'hui et demain; actes du colloque International Anténor Firmin*. Port-au-Prince: Éditions de l'Université d'État d'Haïti, 2014.

Césaire, Aimé. *La Tragédie du Roi Christophe*. Paris: Présence Africaine, 1963.

———. *Aimé Césaire: A Voice for History*. San Francisco: Newsreel, 1994.

———. *Discours Sur Le Colonialisme*. Paris: Présence Africaine, 1950, 2004.

Champollion, Jean-François. *Grammaire Égyptienne ou Principes Généraux de l'Écriture Sacrée Égyptienne*. Paris: Typographie de Firmin Didot Frères, Imprimeurs de L'Institut de France, 1836.

Chanlatte, Juste. *Hayti Reconnaissante*. Cap-Henry: Imprimerie Royale, 1819.

———. *Histoire de la Catastrophe de Saint-Domingue*. Paris: Librairie de Peytieux, 1824.

Christophe, Henry (King Henry Christophe, Roi Henry 1er). *Manifeste du Roi*. Cap-Henry: Chez P. Roux, Imprimeur du Roi, 1814.

Clarke, John Henrik. *The Second Crucifixion of Nat Turner*. Baltimore: Black Classic Press, 1968.

———. *Malcolm X: The Man and His Times*. Edited by John Henrik Clark, Assisted by Peter Bailey, Early Grant, and Betty Shabazz. New York: Macmillan Company, 1969.

———. "The Impact of the African on the 'New World': A Reappraisal." *Présence Africaine Éditions*, Nouvelle Série, no. 79 (3e Trimestre 1971): 3–16.

———. "The Influence of Arthur A. Schomburg on My Concept of Africana Studies." *Phylon* 49, no. 1–2 (1992): 4–9.

———. *A Great and Mighty Walk*. Distributed by Cinema Guild. New York: Black Dot Media, 1996.

Cone, James H. *A Black Theology of Liberation*. Philadelphia and New York: J.B. Lippincott Company, 1970.

Cook, Mercer. *An Introduction to Haiti: Selections and Commentaries*. Washington, DC: Department of Cultural Affairs, Pan American Union, 1951.

Cooper, Anna Julia. "Womanhood: A Vital Element in the Regeneration and Progress of a Race." *The Voice of Anna Julia Cooper: Including a Voice from the South, and Other Important Essays, Papers, and Letters*. Edited by Charles Lemert and Esme Bhan. New York: Rowman & Littlefield Publishers, Inc., 1988.

Crummell, Alexander. *Africa and America, Addresses and Discourses*. Miami: Mnemosyne Publishing, Inc. 1891, 1969.

Cruse, Harold. *The Crisis of the Negro Intellectual*. New York: Quill, 1967, 1984.

DeGruy, Joy. *Post Traumatic Slave Disorder*. London: Artikal Films Production, 2008.

———. *Post Traumatic Slave Syndrome: America's Legacy of Enduring Injury and Healing*. Portland, OR: Uptone Press, 2005.

Delany, Martin R. *The Condition, Elevation, Emigration, and Destiny of the Colored People of the United States*. Baltimore: Black Classic Press, 1852, 1993.

———. *Official Report of The Niger Valley Exploring Party, by M.R. Delany, Chief Commissioner to Africa*. New York: Thomas Hamilton, 1861.

———. *Principia of Ethnology: The Origin of the Races and Color, With an Archeological Compendium of Ethiopian and Egyptian Civilization, from Years of Careful Examination and Enquiry, by Martin Delany*. Philadelphia: Harper & Brother Publishers, 1880.

Dessalines, Jean-Jacques. *Liberté ou La Mort. Proclamation. Jean-Jacques Dessalines, Gouverneur Général Aux Habitans D'Haïti*. Le Cap: Chez P. Roux, Imprimeur du Gouvernement, 1804.

———. *"Procès-Verbal de la Proclamation De l'Indépendance D'Haïti," and "Acte d'Acceptation par le Gouverneur-Général de sa Nomination à La Dignité Impériale."* Le Cap: Chez P. Roux, Imprimeur du Gouvernement, 1804.

Diop, Cheikh Anta. *Nations Nègres et Culture*. Paris: Éditions Africaines, 1955.

———. *Antériorité des Civilisations Nègres: Mythe ou Vérité Historique?* Paris: Présence Africaine, 1967.

———. *The African Origin of Civilization: Myth or Reality*. Translated by Mercer Cook. Chicago: Lawrence Hill & Co., 1974.

Du Bois, William Edward Burghardt. *The Souls of Black Folk*. Chicago: A.C. McClurg & Co., 1903.

———. *Against Racism: Unpublished Essays, Papers, Addresses, 1887–1961*. Amherst: The University of Massachusetts Press, 1985.

Fanon, Frantz. *Peau noire masques blancs*. Paris: Éditions du Seuil, 1952.

Firmin, Anténor. *De L'Égalité des Races Humaines; Anthropologie Positive*. Paris: Librairie Cotillon, 1885.

———. *L'Effort Dans Le Mal*. Port-au-Prince: Éditions Panorama, 1962.

Franklin, John Hope and August Meier. *Black Leaders of the Twentieth Century*. Chicago: University of Illinois Press, 1982.

Frazier, Edward Franklin. "The Status of the Negro in the American Social Order." *The Journal of Negro Education* 4, no. 3 (July 1935): 293–307.

Garvey, Marcus. *Philosophy and Opinions of Marcus Garvey*. Compiled by Amy Jacques Garvey. Dover: The Majority Press, 1923, 1986.

———. *The Poetical Works of Marcus Garvey*. Edited by Tony Martin. Dover: The Majority Press, 1983.

Glissant, Edouard. *Monsieur Toussaint*. Boulder: Lynne Rienner Publishers, Inc., 1961, 2005.

Gordon, Lewis. *Existentia Africana: Understanding Africana Existential Thought*. New York: Routledge, 2000.

———. "African-American Existential Philosophy." *A Companion to African-American Philosophy*. Edited by Tommy L. Lott and John P. Pittman. Oxford: Blackwell Publishing Ltd., 2003.

———. *An Introduction to Africana Philosophy*. Cambridge: Cambridge University Press, 2008.

Harris, Leonard. *The Philosophy of Alain Locke: Harlem Renaissance and Beyond*. Philadelphia: Temple University Press, 1989.

Harrison, Hubert Henry. *The Negro and the Nation*. New York: Cosmo-Advocate Publishing Co., 1917.

———. *When Africa Awakes: The "Inside Story" of the Stirrings and Strivings of the New Negro in the Western World*. New York: The Porro Press, 1920.

Hebrews. *The Holy Bible*. Grand Rapids, Michigan: Zondervan Corporation, 1996.

hooks, bell. "Simple Living: An Antidote to Hedonistic Materialism." *Black Genius: African American Solutions to African American Problems*. Edited by Walter Mosley, Manthia Diawara, and Clyde Taylor. New York: W.W. Norton & Company Inc., 1999.

James, Cyril Lionel Robert. *The Black Jacobins*. New York: Vintage Books Edition, 1963, 1989.

———. *State Capitalism and World Revolution*. Chicago: Charles H. Kerr Publishing Company, 1969, 1986.

———. *A History of Pan-African Revolt*. Oakland: Merlin Press Ltd., 1969, 2012.

James, George Granville Monah. *Stolen Legacy*. Trenton, NJ: Africa World Press, Inc., 1954, 1992.

Janvier, Louis Joseph. *Les Constitutions d'Haïti (1801–1885)*. Paris: C. Marpon et E. Flammarion, 1886.

Johnson, Howard. *Marcus Garvey: A Giant of Black Politics*. New York, N.Y.: Films Media Group, 2008, 2013.

Jones, Nasir bin Olu Dara. "I Can." *God's Son*. New York: Ill Will and Columbia Records, 2002.

King, Martin Luther. *Why We Can't Wait*. New York: Mentor, 1964.

Laurent, Gérard Mentor. *Coup D'œil sur la Politique de Toussaint-Louverture*. Port-au-Prince: Henri Deschamps, 1949.

———. *Six Études sur J.J. Dessalines*. Port-au-Prince: Les Presses Libres, 1950.

Lawrence, Harold G. *African Explorers of the New World*. Los Angeles: John Henry and Mary Louisa Dunn Bryant Foundation, 1962.

Lhérisson, Justin and Nicolas Geffrad. *La Dessalinienne*. Haïti: Quartier-général des Gonaïves, 1903.

Locke, Alain. "The New Negro." *The New Negro*. Edited by Alain Locke. New York: Simon & Schuster Inc., 1997.

Louverture, Toussaint. *Toussaint Louverture à Travers sa Correspondance, 1794–1798*. Madrid: Industrias Gráfica España, 1953.

Marable, Manning. *How Capitalism Underdeveloped Black America: Problems in Race, Political Economy, and Society*. Chicago: Pluto Press, 2000.

Maran, René. *Batouala, Véritable Roman Nègre*. Paris: Albin Michel, 1921.

———. *Batouala*. Translated by Barbara Beck and Alexandre Mboukou. London: Heinemann, 1987.

Marley, Robert Nesta. "Redemption Song." *Uprising*. Jamaica: Island Records, 1980.

Martin, Tony. *Literary Garveyism: Garvey, Black Arts and the Harlem Renaissance*. Dover: The Majority Press, 1983.

Mills, Charles Wright. *The Power Elite*. New York: Oxford Press, 1956, 2000.

———. *The Sociological Imagination*. New York: Oxford Press, 1959, 2000.

Neal, Larry. "The Black Arts Movement." *The Drama Review*, Black Theatre 12, no. 4 (Summer 1968): 28–39.

Nesbitt, Nick. "The Idea of 1804." *Yale French Studies*, The Haiti Issue: 1804 and Nineteenth-Century French Studies, no. 107 (2005): 6–38.

———. *Universal Emancipation: The Haitian Revolution and the Radical Enlightenment*. Charlottesville: University of Virginia Press, 2008.

Nicholls, David. *From Dessalines to Duvalier: Race, Colour and National Independence in Haiti*. New Brunswick: Rutgers University Press, 1979, 1996.

Obenga, Théophile. *Cheikh Anta Diop, Volney et le Sphinx: Contribution de Cheikh Anta Diop à l'historiographie mondiale*. Paris: Présence Africaine, 1996.

———. "Hommage à Anténor Firmin (1850–1911), égyptologue haïtien." *ANKH Égyptologie, Histoire de l'Afrique, Sciences* (2008), www.ankhonline.com

Pathé, Diagne. *Cheikh Anta Diop et l'Afrique dans l'Histoire du Monde*. Paris: Harmattan, 1997.

Peck, Raoul. *Profit & Nothing But!: Or, Impolite Thoughts on the Class Struggle*. Brooklyn, NY: First Run, Icarus Films, 2001.

Pilgrim, David. *The Sapphire Caricature*. Big Rapids, MI: Ferris State University, ferris.edu/jimcrow

Price-Mars, Jean. *Joseph Anténor Firmin l'indomptable lutteur, mal aimé et martyr: une grande partie de l'histoire d'Haïti à travers la formation et le destin d'un homme.* Port-au-Prince: Price-Mars, 1964.

Rabaka, Reiland. *Africana Critical Theory: Reconstructing the Black Radical Tradition, from W.E.B. Du Bois and C.L.R. James to Frantz Fanon and Amilcar Cabral.* Lanham: Lexington Books, 2009.

———. *Concepts of Cabralism: Amilcar Cabral and Africana Critical Theory.* Boulder: Lexington Books, 2014.

Saint-Rémy, Joseph. *Mémoires du général Toussaint Louverture, écrits par lui-même, suivis d'une étude historique et critique.* Paris: Pagnerie, 1853.

Sauray, Éric, Guy Cétoute and Jean-Jacques Dessalines. *Lettres ouvertes à Jean-Jacques Dessalines; suivies du Discours du 1er janvier 1804.* Paris: Dauphin Noir Édition, 2004.

Schomburg, Arthur A. "The Negro Digs Up His Past." *The New Negro.* Edited by Alain Locke. New York: Touchstone Book, 1925, 1997.

Shakur, Tupac. *All Eyez on Me* (Movie). Produced by L.T. Hutton, David C. Robinson and James G. Robinson. Santa Monica: Summit Entertainment, 2017.

Simeon-Jones, Kersuze. "Haiti's Politico-Cultural Transcript: Moving Toward National Rehabilitation." *Negritúd: Revista de Estudios Afro-Latinoamericanos* III, no. 1 (Summer 2009): 64–75.

———. *Literary and Sociopolitical Writings of the Black Diaspora in the Nineteenth and Twentieth Centuries.* Boulder: Lexington Books, 2010.

Sonthonax, Léger-Félicité. *Proclamation.* Cap-Français: Imprimerie de P. Gatineau, 1793.

Trouillot, Hénock. *Dessalines ou la Tragédie Post-Coloniale.* Port-au-Prince: Éditions Panorama, 1966.

———. *Dessalines ou le sang du Pont-Rouge.* Port-au-Prince: Imprimerie des Antilles, 1967.

Trouillot, Michel-Rolph. *Haiti: State Against Nation, The Origins and Legacy of Duvalierism.* New York: Monthly Review Press, 1990.

———. *Silencing the Past, Power and the Production of History.* Boston: Beacon Press, 1995.

Van Sertima, Ivan. *They Came Before Columbus: The African Presence in Ancient America.* New York: Random House, c.1976.

Vastey, Pompée Valentin (Baron de Vastey). *Le Système Colonial Dévoilé.* Cap-Henry: Chez P. Roux, Imprimeur du Roi, 1814.

———. *Le cri de La Patrie.* Cap-Henry: Chez P. Roux, Imprimeur du Roi, 1815.

———. *Réflexions sur une lettre de Mazères, ex-colon français, adressé à M.J.C.L. Sismonde De Sismondi, sur les Noirs et les Blancs, la Civilisation de l'Afrique, le Royaume d'Hayti, etc.* Cap-Henry: Chez P. Roux, imprimeur du Roi, 1816.

Volney, Constantin-François. *Voyage en Syrie et en Égypte, Pendant Les Années 1783, 1784 et 1785* (Tome Premier). Paris: Volland, Libraire, Quai des Augustins, 1787.

Walker, David. *Appeal to the Coloured Citizens of the World, but in Particular, and Very Expressly, to Those of the United States of America.* Boston: Revised and Published by David Walker, 1830.

Walter, Mosley, Manthia Diawara, et al. *Black Genius: African American Solutions to African American Problems.* New York: W.W. Norton & Company, 1999.

Walter, Rodney. *How Europe Underdeveloped Africa.* Washington, DC: Howard University Press, 1972.

West, Cornel. *Race Matters.* Boston: Beacon Press, 1993.

Wolfenstein, Eugene Victor. *The Victims of Democracy: Malcolm X and the Black Revolution.* New York: Guildford Press, 1993.

Woodson, Carter Godwin. *The Mis-Education of the Negro*. Washington, DC: The Association for the Study of African American Life and History, 1933, 2005.

X, Malcolm. *The Autobiography of Malcolm X*. New York: The Ballantine Publishing Group, 1964.

———. *Malcolm X Speaks: Selected Speeches and Statements*. Edited by George Breitman. New York: Pathfinder Press, 1965.

———. *On Afro-American History*. New York: International Socialist Review Publishing Association, 1967.

————. *By Any Means Necessary: Speeches, Interviews, and a Letter by Malcolm X*. Edited by George Breitman. New York: Pathfinder Press, 1970.

INDEX